Living Christ's Passionate Life

I John 1:4-6 NIV "The man who says, 'I know him,' but does not do what he commands is a liar, and the truth is not in him.

5) But if anyone obeys his word, God's love is truly made complete in him:

6) Whoever claims to live in him must walk as Jesus did."

by

Jim and Merry Corbett

Published by
Covenant Support Network

From Our Father's Heart

Jesus lived a passionate life.
He involved His entire being in every task presented to Him.
Equipped from Our time together
and empowered by Our Holy Spirit,
His presentation of truth caused some remarkable changes
in those who came near to Him.
Ordinary people went on to do extraordinary representations
of My desires because they followed His pattern of living.
That same presence is available to you.
The same Holy Spirit that lived in everyone
totally committed to Our way
is available to you if you will only surrender fully to Him.
Choose this day who you will passionately serve.
Choose each moment to submit fully to the Lordship of Jesus
over every aspect of your life.
Determine to live the kind of life that is your heritage.
Become zealous about presenting the Truth
to a world that lives in lies.
Live as Jesus did.

Psalm 111:2 NIV "Great are the works of the Lord; they are pondered by all who delight in them."

Isaiah 2:22 Amp "Cease to trust in [weak, frail, and dying] man, whose breath is in his nostrils [for so short a time]; in what sense can he be counted as having intrinsic worth?"

Matthew 11:12 NIV "From the days of John the Baptist until now, the kingdom of heaven has been forcefully advancing, and forceful men lay hold of it."

When was the last time you became passionate about the Lord's plans? For that matter, when was the last time the Lord's plans for your life took priority over the other demands you face each day?

God is clearly requiring each of us to make Him our priority. Still, most of us agonize over the demands of simply living out each day - paying the rent, providing for food, etc. To stop, even for a day, and spend it entirely with the Lord should He ask us to do so would be beyond comprehension for some of us. We are convinced that the answer is heart commitment.

Merry and I believe that each and every one of us, who call ourselves Christians, must make a choice to live Christ's life passionately throughout our very ordinary days. We are to approach the tasks and the people placed before us with His kind of zeal and unquestioning love, presenting every one of them as an offering to the Lord for His glory. We are convinced that this life is not so much about what we do as it is about the One for whom we are doing it.

If everything that we become involved in is truly offered to the Lord and placed under His Lordship, the fluff will fall away and the eternal purposes of God will become priorities to us. Living Christ's passionate life unto the Lord will change us and those around us who are looking for answers.

Take our stuff and replace it with Your stuff, Lord

Jim and Merry Corbett

1 Kings 8 The Message Bible "May he keep us centered and devoted to him, following the life path he has cleared, watching the signposts, walking at the pace and rhythms he laid down…"

Welcome to Step Two in the Christ's Passionate Life Series!

Now that you have completed Step One, the novel, A White Stone, this Living Christ's Passionate Life guidebook is designed to walk you through the heart positions needed as you personally address and move toward an exciting and thrilling life in Christ that is full of freedom and power.

To live out Christ's life in the world around us with the same passion and heart commitment that Jesus lived when He walked among His creation is:

1) the only fitting response to the life, death, and resurrection of Jesus Christ.

2) the proper and honorable representation of Jesus to a world that is dying and out of answers.

3) the highest form of praise that can be given to the Lord as you emulate Him.

4) the proper response to the call of the Holy Spirit to prepare your heart as a waiting bride for the return of Jesus.

5) the only way to overcome the perilous times and seasons in which we are living, so that you can fulfill your purpose in life.

These publications - plus continual interaction with the teachings, audio recordings and other pertinent information on our Web site, www.christspassionatelife.com, and our personal e-mail encouragements - are a "beginning to end" opportunity to seek the Lord in depth for those who embrace fires of refinement in their lives, choose to buy gold and proper clothing from their God, and take proper nourishment only from their Master's table. All are designed to direct your attention to the Lord's covenant with you, break your heart; and allow you to understand your desperate need of a renewed relationship with Jesus.

A White Stone provides fertile soil to stimulate taste buds for a deeper walk with the Lord. This life-changing novel confirms to the searching heart that there really is more to walking with the Lord than attending church and praying cold prayers. It is often referred to as a book that gave readers clear direction for their lives.

This verse is pivotal to your life and this study.

Read it intently and refer to it often to keep yourself focused on what you are doing with God and why you are doing it.

Journal your comments, thoughts, and points of interest in these columns.

This is a great place for your stuff!

This <u>Living Christ's Passionate Life</u> guidebook provides guidelines and insights on how to recognize, embrace, and live out the crucified life. It is a dynamic, interactive work, which is continually updated on our Web site as new teachings are available; and it's designed to help prepare you to live a Christian life that is honorable to the Lord and lead you to an intimacy with your Father God in which you will be introduced to His heart - a bridal heart - as you await the coming of your Lord.

This guidebook is written for those who choose to properly respond to what Jesus has done for us, no matter what the cost, and go deeper with God. We call this work a guidebook rather than a workbook, because it is intended that you use it continually as a lifetime roadmap on your way to bridal love.

The <u>Living Out Christ's Love</u> portion of this guidebook study with its prayer journaling system, (described in detail later,) will be a "hands on" opportunity to really live out the tenets and insights you encounter as you apply what the Holy Spirit teaches you while covering these pages.

Because we are always in the process of learning, and because we could never provide an all-inclusive volume of every lesson the Lord would like us to share, we have designed this book to be a continual dynamic work. We suggest that you acquire a three ring binder to contain the future pages from our Web site, <u>www.christspassionatelife.com</u>, as they become available.

As you involve yourself in this work and God uses the enclosed materials to expose your heart, accept them as a means to drive you to prayer and to His lap. Keep them available for reference in the future. Refer to them as directed by the Lord, make notes, listen to the recommended tapes on our Web site; and add your own materials as needed.

There is purposely little structure in this study. We trust that the Lord will have a unique route tailor-made just for you as you head in the direction of bridal heart preparation. None of us is at exactly the same point in our walk with the Lord, so why would we take a fact-finding, textbook approach where we're all expected to come up with the same answers?

Our materials are designed to stimulate questions about your own Christian life in light of what is presented. Go to the Lord for His wisdom, knowledge, and insight on how to pray, how to allow the Lord Jesus to live through you; and most of all, how to repent of any foolish ways that you have inaccurately labeled Christianity.

This is not a workbook - it is a guidebook that shows you signposts in your life that will lead you to Jesus.

Tuck away quietly with this work as you would with your favorite book.

Make notes on what the Lord teaches you as you read.

Talk to the Lord out loud.

Ask Him your heart questions and write His answers anywhere you please.

We want to encourage you to springboard from what you find in these pages and spend intimate time with the Lord to see what He specifically wants to reveal to you and make real to you through His presence and His Word.

It is vital to remember that no course can change your heart. No amount of reading, answering questions, or memorizing can give you what is needed to be like Jesus. Self-will and determination will possibly make you appear more like a representative of Jesus, but any fleshly work will never form the character of Christ in anyone. Only intimacy with Father God, a waiting on Him to impart Himself to you, will bring forth the life of Jesus in you.

Any attempt to use this or any study, physical abilities, or personal knowledge in place of intimate, heart-searching, prayerful times with God and His Word will bring death, not life. That is why this course is designed as it is. Most studies leave little room for God's intimate direction to your heart. They give step-by-step instructions on where to read, what to study, and what to memorize, which leaves little time for changes to occur by waiting on God – a vital aspect of your relationship with Him – and searching His Word as He directs you.

Plan to have your flesh offended. Plan to have your doctrines challenged. We don't claim to have all truth, but what is truth will stand the test of scrutiny. The doctrines or traditions of man need to make way for what the Holy Spirit desires to work in you, which will always line up with Scripture in its correct context.

If you disagree with some of the statements, opinions, or doctrinal slants presented here, that is fine. However, do not allow the enemy of your soul to hinder your growth because of small differences. Small issues have divided the church far too long. Dig in. Keep going, and find a place where the Lord can minister to you. What you disagree with may be the tool that the Lord will use to expose some area of your life that is hindering you from going deeper with God. Only as you are truly broken, and turn from what you have been shown to be out of line in your life, can the fragrant oil of the Holy Spirit escape from you to draw others to their Lord and Savior, Jesus Christ.

We have provided ample room in the margins for your notes and thoughts, so don't be afraid to mark up, underline, highlight, and personalize these pages. Well-wrinkled and disfigured pages signify a devoted follower of Jesus on his/her way to knowing the heart of God. (Tearstains are optional, but quite effective in showing others how spiritual you really are. That's a joke!) You may also want to initiate a personal journal that will be part of your continued study.

In most workbooks, 1+1=2, so you simply fill in the blanks and forget about it in a few weeks.

With this guidebook, 1+1=whatever the Holy Spirit teaches you that a "2" really is, while you spend time with your Father for lifetime lessons.

Sometimes it hurts when the Lord changes us, but pleasing the Lord is far more important than any hurt we encounter.

Nobody but you will ever read your notes unless you let them.

These are your "heart words" to your ABBA.

Don't try to keep up with others as they do this work.

God has a pace for you to follow, so allow each line to minister to you as you are led by the Holy Spirit.

The Holy Spirit led one woman to ponder a paragraph such as this for over a week, revealing Himself over and over during that time, changing her life.

As you journal your thoughts and answer the questions in this series, it would be good to remember that no one but you needs to ever read what you write down. This is not a test, and you cannot fail in any way if you choose to surrender to what you are shown with a submissive heart. Take your time. This is also not a race, and you are not in a hurry to finish this adventure of love.

Remember: You, the seeker of the passionate life of Jesus and His bridal heart, must learn to discern and put aside the "alligator fights" of worldly life - those issues that appear to be in need of godly intervention on your part, but actually distract you from focusing on God's desire that none should perish. Is it more important to focus on a cause or on the souls involved on both sides of the issue?

These pages will guide you to be the honest representation of Jesus Christ to your immediate world. You are to allow Christ's passionate life to be lived through you for His good and for the glory of Father God.

Remember: This guidebook is designed for continual use, a foundation for other information that comes your way as you grow. Any true work of the Lord must continually modify the hearts and lives of those involved, or it's simply a futile exercise and of no lasting value. When God uses the materials to expose you, accept them as a means to drive you to prayer. Keep them available for reference for any future need. Refer to them often, and add your own materials and notes as needed, especially when you start reaching out to others when you begin living out Christ's passionate life.

As you meditate on these pages, give God the freedom to show you your specific needs through the Word, examples, stories, text, and associated materials, which you will find on our Web site free-of-charge. These materials are not written to give you answers - although you will receive many - but to direct you to the One who is the answer, Jesus Christ.

As you grow in Christ, you must learn to joyfully embrace a life of repentance before Him. Delight in what He is doing in you as you are shown who you are not. Understand that you are still very welcome in His presence. You are a deeply loved work in progress. Submission to the changes the Lord is making in you develops your ability to present Jesus to the world, which is your heritage and God's original plan for your life. He knows who you are and everything you are not. Real heart changes are needed in all of us and can only take place when spending quality time with Him to know His heart, and looking to Him alone for all things.

Above all, remember that your relationship with Jesus Christ is the most astounding privilege that anyone could possibly have. You are cherished.

Keep the following in mind. The sole purpose and singular motive for everything you, as a remnant believer, are to do is to glorify and please God through spending time with Him, finding His will, and living it - in His love - for Him and for others.

That posture for living is translated into two simple heart actions:

1.)   Submission and preparation for the return of the Lord Jesus Christ by seeking God's face to become like Him; and

2.)   the urgency to bring as many souls into the kingdom as possible before the Lord calls us all home.

Take your time to cultivate a working intimacy with your Lord during this experience. Talk to Him, sit quietly and open-heartedly before Him, listen to Him; and then keep your ears open to His heart's desire throughout each day as these materials challenge you. You will be surprised at how much His life in you will increase.

Thoughts and prayers

Go over what you have already read to see what you might have missed for your life. Wait on God to show you what He has planned for you to learn. Read each sentence carefully and determine in your heart to wait on God from now on.
Fight the urge to "get on with this" as one more project. You are not in a race. You may be nourished in ways that will surprise you if you take your time and look for the Lord's "private manna" in the simplest of sentences.
Include God in your reading and your thinking process. Begin to find a new understanding of waiting on God during this introduction and throughout this work. Allow the Lord to teach you from His hand, rather than simply following instructions.

Now write down what you have learned or indicate how you need His help.

Everything else is only a platform for God's purpose for our lives!

Don't rush through these beginning pages.

The Lord is setting the stage for deep lessons further into this work, but many heart decisions must be made now before that can happen.

There is much "hidden manna" in these beginning pages. Enjoy the hunt.

Embrace what you learn.

You will need it as a foundation for your other lessons.

Living Christ's Passionate Life

Galatians 2:20 Amp "I have been crucified with Christ [in Him I have shared His crucifixion]: it is no longer I who live, but Christ (the Messiah) lives in me; and the life I now live in the body I live by faith in (by adherence to and reliance on and complete trust in) the Son of God, Who loved me and gave Himself up for me."

An Overview

Very simply stated: Jesus lived an exuberant, passionate life because He loved deeply and knew the truth. Everything that He did had love as its foundation, its continual motivation, and its ultimate goal. Nothing, not even death, could move Him from expressing that love to and for those around Him.

Because He was One with and knew His Father intimately, He understood the truth about the fate of mankind as a result of the fall. Because He lived with His Father in all of eternity past, He knew what separation from His Father for all eternity future really meant for those He loved and created. He felt His Father's heartbreak because some would perish.

Jesus was brought into a world so perilous that children were killed at the whimsical edict of an evil king, crucifixions were as commonplace as morning walks, and people were held in slavery to ignorant teachers and foolish guides, yet He was absolutely fearless. His passionate love, His intimacy with His Father, and His zeal for imparting truth made Him "Teflon" in a world seething with infectious evil and eternal danger. His presence in any society was a gift of love from His Father God. We are in training to be the same kind of gift to those around us wherever our Father sends us.

Jesus could be fearless because He loved perfectly. He cared only for others and desired nothing for Himself. Even though He had all power, He was under full submission to the will of His Father. In His heart, He had given away everything, so He had no fear of someone robbing Him, even of His life. He held Himself in lower esteem than everyone, even the lowly leper, so no one could destroy His reputation. Jesus' love was so pure that He was absolutely free from any peril that the world would attempt to place on Him.

I John 4:18 Amp "There is no fear in love [dread does not exist], but full-grown (complete, perfect) love turns fear out of doors and expels every trace of terror! For fear brings with it the

Jesus was a gift of love to those around Him.

Are you?

You're supposed to be!

He was fearless!

Are you?

You are supposed to be if you really are in Christ!

17

thought of punishment, and [so] he who is afraid has not reached the full maturity of love [is not yet grown into love's complete perfection."

We really don't know what love is.

Why is that?

Ask your friends.

Ask God!

Most of us, in contrast, love only ourselves. Few of us really know what it is to love God, each other, and those around us. We mouth the words, sing the songs, and build the right-sounding programs; but we have little effect on our world because few people see the kind of love that Jesus expressed when He was with us. We live in fear of the loss of the things that we own - that own us - every moment of our days to the point that our lives are consumed, weak, fruitless, and absent of any of the characteristics of Jesus' kind of love in the eyes of the One that we say we serve.

Throughout most of our lives, the enticements that the world offers us, not the passions of the Lord, have proven to be the focus of our attention. They are the basis for our selfish pleadings to our Father and really are the gods that we serve.

Begin to prepare your heart for the deep, searching lessons ahead.

Because of our lack of desire to focus on our life in Christ as the only reason that we breathe, when the world grows darker as predicted by the Bible, most of us will be so consumed with fear that we will be unable to represent Jesus to those who desperately need Him. We will walk around the same as those in the world, wide-eyed and drooling rather than being able to rise above all of the clamor as Jesus did.

God is calling those who will listen.

The Holy Spirit is wooing the church of Jesus Christ to prepare as a bride would prepare for a coming wedding of hearts. Through trials, tribulations, and extreme challenges, He is posturing each of us to get our priorities straight. By leading us to the end of ourselves, and placing a new hope in those who will listen, He is calling us to set aside all of the ways of the world and embrace the ways of Jesus as our only reason for living. In doing so, we will be prepared for His coming and able to overcome the hazards that are soon to come our way.

Holiness is attainable for those who submit fully to the Lord's work in them and should be pursued by each of us.

This call is a call to holiness - a pursuit oftentimes not considered attainable or even a necessary part of every Christian's heart - which will initiate a bridal heart desire that will allow the Lord to live His passionate life through devoted, surrendered vessels. It can be one of the most exciting adventures of your life if your heart's desire is to increasingly make room for more of the most priceless treasure ever given to anyone – Jesus Christ. As you respond to the heart of God and increasingly develop a posture of waiting for Jesus' timely return, you will then guide others to His heart as more hear the same call.

The Holy Spirit is asking each of us to reevaluate all of our reasons for doing what we do and reexamine some of the life-changing wonders that are included in our incredible relationship with our God through the death, resurrection, and continued life of Jesus. He is asking us to study them, embrace wholeheartedly what is truth, and discard what does not represent the heart and character of Jesus. We must then allow Him to incorporate whatever is absolute truth into our lives, through the power of His Holy Spirit, as we wait on our God to change us.

Few of us even know how to wait on God for Him to reveal Himself and His desires, and for our true nature to be revealed to us so that we can repent and turn fully to Him. That is why there is very little memory of what has been studied when we read the Word, and little continued life change soon after most organized studies have been completed.

Only as we examine our ways in the light of the Holy Spirit, compare them to the ways of our Lord, and realize our own bankruptcy, do we have any hope for change. We need the Holy Spirit to direct us to guideposts in our lives that God is using to break us, remove our flesh, and bring us closer to Jesus.

Prayers and thoughts

Your awareness of who you are not is the beginning step toward living Christ's life passionately!

Why don't you begin to thank the Lord for showing you that now is the perfect time for change in your life?

Why don't you determine in your heart to join Him in the destruction of everything that will stop you from becoming who you are really supposed to be.

From Our Father's Heart

As I challenge each of you to become like Jesus,
you must remember one very important fact.
I am the only One
who can make the changes that are needed in you.
You can never change yourself.
Any attempt to do so enters into the realm of religion
and destroys My concept of relationship.
Religion is man's vain attempt to become good before Me.
It causes striving,
a system of good works in an attempt to impress Me,
and much condemnation
when you realize that you will never achieve the goal of holiness.
A person who has an honest relationship with Me, however,
understands his complete and total bankruptcy.
In his deepest inner parts, there is no hint of the possibility
of achieving anything in his own strength.
Anything that might be accomplished in him
or through him is understood to come from Me.
That is the kind of relationship for which Jesus died.
He died so that you could cease
from any striving to better yourself.
I promise to do all of the work of perfecting you
and making you holy.
All I ask you to do is come and spend time with Me.
As you do that, I will impart Myself to you.
Each time We visit, a little more of you is perfected.
While We enjoy each other, My Word is accomplishing its task.
The call that I have on your life
is impossible for you to accomplish,
especially in the coming times and seasons
when I will require the out-flowing of Jesus in your daily walk.
It will require total death to your flesh, a painful process.
Although there will be times of agony,
when all you can do is hang on to My promises,
I will be hanging on to you, holding you close to Me.
In the easier times, let's have fun together
while I am accomplishing My work in you and for you.

The realization of your total inability to achieve anything in your own strength is total freedom and the beginning step on the road to the Lordship of Jesus.

Jer.2:13 Amp "For My people have committed two evils: they have forsaken Me, the Fountain of living waters, and they have hewn for themselves cisterns, broken cisterns which cannot hold water."

Gal.2:20 Amp "I have been crucified with Christ [in Him I have shared His crucifixion]; it is no longer I who live, but Christ (the Messiah) lives in me; and the life I now live in the body I live by faith in (by adherence to and reliance on and complete trust in) the Son of God, Who loved me and gave Himself up for me."

Phil.2:12b-13 Amp "...work out (cultivate, carry out to the goal, and fully complete) your own salvation with reverence and awe and trembling (self-distrust, with serious caution, tenderness of conscience, watchfulness against temptation, timidly shrinking from whatever might offend God and discredit the name of Christ).

13) [Not in your own strength] for it is God Who is all the while effectually at work in you [energizing and creating in you the power and desire], both to will and to work for His good pleasure and satisfaction and delight."

Hebrews 10:14 NIV "because by one sacrifice He has made perfect forever those who <u>are being made holy.</u>"

We are perfect in His eyes now; we are being made holy!

Do you really know that you are accepted by God as perfect if you have surrendered your life to the Lordship of Jesus?

Talk to your Father about how you feel.

Are your feelings in line with His Word?

Those who desire to draw closer to the Lord and become all that they are intended to be know that religion, good works, and striving have no part in their lives. Sometimes, however, every one of us has a tendency to fall into the trap of each one of those elements, especially when we hear the call to holiness and preparation for the coming of our Lord.

As the Father reveals all aspects of His heart, sometimes I reel with the overwhelming challenge that I am called to face. I begin to condemn myself for who I am not, cower at the prospects ahead of me as a Christian in the coming times, stagger at the weight of my responsibility to represent Jesus properly; and become discouraged as I attempt to prepare for His return. It is then that I remember that none of this was my idea in the first place. My Father has ordained my life and has promised to fulfill His plan for it and in it. My job is simply to need Him desperately.

In the above verse in Hebrews 10, I am so encouraged by the statement "those who are being made holy." The wonderful part of "have [already] been made perfect" [in God's eyes] is pretty incredible and difficult for me to understand fully, but "being made holy" soothes my heart.

The Lord is in the process of allowing us to lovingly say "ABBA," not grudgingly say "uncle."

At this very moment - and every moment until we are with our Father in Heaven - the process of making us holy is being accomplished, because we have surrendered our lives to Jesus and His completed work on the cross. When God is in the process of breaking us, He's not trying so much to get us to say "uncle" as He is trying to get us to say "Abba."

Isa.30:18 The Living Bible "Yet the Lord still waits for you to come to him, so he can show you his love; he will conquer you to bless you, just as he said. For the Lord is faithful to his promises. Blessed are all those who wait for him to help them."

It is time for each of us who are responding to the call to holiness, desiring to please Jesus above all else with our lives, and choosing to live His passionate life for all the world to see to jump on the lap of our Father and whisper "ABBA."

How comfortable do you feel with allowing the Lord to change you rather than you attempting to change yourself?

Prayers and thoughts

From Our Father's Heart

Most of you, My children,
have become thin-skinned and easily offended.
You can receive nothing, because you run from correction.
You immediately take offense
when you are challenged to rise to a higher standard in Me.
You separate yourself from those
who call you to places to which you need to go,
so that you can mature.
What will you do when those who hate you enough to kill you
are in your face?
What will you do when those who thrive on hatred
are in your world?
Will you hate them back?
Will you despise who they are
and harbor unforgiveness and murder in your own heart?
You are missing the very essence of My Word
and what I am doing in those who are My remnant.
I am moving those who love Me
to be able to love even their enemies.
It is the way Jesus loved.
I call you to love as He does.

Jeremiah 12:5 Amp "[But the Lord rebukes Jeremiah's impatience, saying] If you have raced with men on foot and they have tired you out, then how can you compete with horses? And if [you take to flight] in a land of peace where you feel secure, then what will you do [when you tread the tangled maze of jungle haunted by lions] in the swelling and flooding of the Jordan?"

Amos 3:3 KJV "Can two walk together except they be agreed?"

Luke 23:34, NIV "Jesus said, 'Father, forgive them, for they do not know what they are doing.'"

Rev. 3:19 Amp "Those whom I [dearly and tenderly] love, I tell their faults and convict and convince and reprove and chasten [I discipline and instruct them]. So be enthusiastic and in earnest and burning with zeal and repent [changing your mind and attitude]."

Father God is developing a bridal heart and the same character that Jesus has in those who will respond. We must be like Him in our hearts if we are to intimately walk with Him and live passionately for Him. Can you imagine Jesus coming for a church that is selfish, self-centered, and harbors murder in her heart?

Can you imagine Him enjoining Himself to one who looks to the delicacies around her that please her more than He pleases her? Does it seem possible that Jesus would function in a relationship where His bride would not have the same desires, the same motives, and the same purposes in all that they do together? To think so is ludicrous!

How then is Jesus going to form us, who need His character developed in us during these end days, before He comes? He is going to allow us to see who we really are. He will allow us to face ourselves, so that we can come to repentance. He will do what it takes to expose our sin. Each time we repent, He will change us to be more like Him. It is an act of astounding love on His part. It is also our choice to respond or reject His efforts.

Are you hearing the call to holiness and bridal heart preparation?

It's not about getting better or doing more things.

Jer.17:9 Amp "The heart is deceitful above all things, and it is exceedingly perverse and corrupt and severely, mortally sick! Who can know it [perceive, understand, be acquainted with his own heart and mind]?"

Here's a thought! Let's all declare personal bankruptcy, so that we can function as that new creature in Christ, which we became when we put Jesus in charge of our lives. Confusion and difficulty arise when we continually try to become better Christians.

God never asked us to do that. His desire is that we become *empty*, so that the life of Jesus is free to function in us. We seem determined to add our own efforts to God's plan for us, and then we never reach the fullness that total dependence on God brings. Selah! (Pause, and calmly think of that!)

John15:5 Amp "I am the Vine; you are the branches. Whoever lives in Me and I in him bears much (abundant) fruit. However, apart from Me [cut off from vital union with Me] you can do nothing."

Take Time to Reflect with the Holy Spirit's Assistance

What has the Lord been trying to get through to you over the last years? Months? Days? (Pray about it before you answer.)

What is the most recent thing God has been trying to work in you? Do you see the trials in your life connected to it?

What have your trials taught you? Do you see them as an act of love on God's part?

What has been your response to your trials? Is your main focus to get out of them? Why or why not?

You know this book is designed to be marked up, scribbled on, highlighted, and written in.

Are you using it to express your heart, and write down your opinions?

Are you asking God to reveal His heart to you?

Romans 2 The Message Bible "God is kind, but he's not soft. In kindness he takes us firmly by the hand and leads us into a radical life change."

2 Cor. 1:8-10 NIV "We do not want you to be uninformed, brothers, about the hardships we suffered in the province of Asia. We were under great pressure, far beyond our ability to endure, so that we despaired even of life.

9) Indeed, in our hearts we felt the sentence of death. But this happened that we might not rely on ourselves but on God, who raises the dead.

10) He has delivered us from such a deadly peril, and he will deliver us. On him we have set our hope that he will continue to deliver us…"

2 Cor. 7 The Message Bible "…but that you were jarred into turning things around. You let distress bring you to God, not drive you from Him. The result was all gain, no loss.

Distress that drives us to God does that. It turns us around. It gets us back in the way of salvation. We never regret that kind of pain. But those who let distress drive them away from God are full of regrets, end up on a deathbed of regrets.

And now, isn't it wonderful all the ways in which this distress has goaded you closer to God?"

What do you desire most when you think about your association with the Lord? Is it His desire, too? (If so, He wants it infinitely more for you than you want it for yourself.)

Additional prayers and thoughts

Let's Start to Become Like Jesus
(So That His Reputation Is Not Tarnished)

In the eyes of the world, most of the church of today is little more than a carnival act. It is a sideshow that is discredited and laughed at by those who boast of their sin openly. Unbelievers see it as powerless to hinder them or help them in any way. They have no fear of strong words that are meant to challenge them and little or no respect for the ones who speak those words, and rightfully so.

Many of the visible actions, traditions, and expressions purported to be God's Word or as having God's hand upon them are nothing more than well-rehearsed slight-of-hand and practiced deception. Fools have taken His Word out of context and out of line with its original intent for their own purposes, which has confused the distracted, the needy, and the spiritually hungry. What is heralded across the land as having the presence of God associated with it is often nothing more than emotional manipulation coupled with Biblical text to supposedly give it authenticity.

You, the real church of Jesus Christ, have quietly been in training and are being prepared to represent Jesus properly. Although it may not appear to be so during the trials you are being taken through, you have been learning discernment directly from the heart of God. You are being exposed to absolute truth at the feet of Jesus, driven there by the pressures put on you by your own attachment to sin, the sin-embracing world, and some parts of the church.

You are now being invited to receive the heart of God in the presence of God during your intimate moments with Him. We believe that you will soon be brought forth in power to affect this closing generation with the truth and presence of the Word of God.

In the near future, we believe that the real church of Jesus Christ will rise from the ashes of the lives of those who have willingly submitted to the refiner's fire. The true church will consist of those who have craved holiness, truth, and only the presence of God in their lives. She will be adorned with the wonder of the heart of Jesus, equipped with the mighty sword of the Word, and dressed in the spotless garments of the glory of God. She will not have a hint of flesh, nor the slightest taste for anything that the world has to offer.

The remnant bridal heart is now in training and will soon be a sold-out, holy people who are looking only for the coming Bridegroom and moving only for His desires. She will be a holy people in their world, making proper choices when others

Do you know that the world considers the things of God laughable?

Could it be in part because they have never seen the power of a person under the complete Lordship of Jesus exhibiting the power that took Him to the cross?

Would you like that to be you?

Why?

You have been in training

How do you feel about the statements in these paragraphs and your part in what they are saying?

flounder, always serving everyone as Jesus did; but completely set apart from those who have chosen to remain in their empty religion.

Take your time to answer this.

This is not to be a whimsical decision.

Do you choose to submit fully to God's hand of training? Why?

Prayers and thoughts

From Our Father's Heart

If Jesus would return today, where would you stand?
Do you think that you would go with Him,
or would you be left behind?
Let me ask you some questions.
Is the priority of every moment of your life
to submit to Him in every way,
so that He comes back for an unblemished bride,
without spot or wrinkle?
Is looking for His return
the most important thing in your life?
Are you preparing for Him so that He is pleased,
or so that you can go?
Unfortunately, many in My church are filling their days
by padding their comfort areas,
instead of preparing for His return.
You need to make sure that whatever you have in your hand
is worth the price that you have placed on it.
It may be far more expensive
than you could possibly have imagined.

We pay a high price for things that have little eternal value.

Matthew 25:1-13 NIV "At that time the kingdom of heaven will be like ten virgins who took their lamps and went out to meet the bridegroom.

(2) Five of them were foolish and five were wise.

(3) The foolish ones took their lamps but did not take any oil with them.

(4) The wise, however, took oil in jars along with their lamps.

(5) The bridegroom was a long time in coming, and they all became drowsy and fell asleep.

(6) At midnight the cry rang out: 'Here's the bridegroom! Come out to meet him!'

(7) Then all the virgins woke up and trimmed their lamps.

(8) The foolish ones said to the wise, 'Give us some of your oil; our lamps are going out.'

(9) 'No,' they replied, 'there may not be enough for both us and you. Instead, go to those who sell oil and buy some for yourselves.'

(10) But while they were on their way to buy the oil, the bridegroom arrived. The virgins who were ready went in with him to the wedding banquet. And the door was shut.

(11) Later the others also came. 'Sir! Sir!' they said. 'Open the door for us!'

(12) But he replied, 'I tell you the truth, I don't know you.'

(13) Therefore keep watch, because you do not know the day or the hour."

God is
always
concerned
with heart
position.

Whether you equate the above verses with the return of Jesus for His bride or not is not the point of the use of these verses. The point for this discussion is the heart position of the virgins in the story.

First off, all of the characters mentioned are called "virgins" in contrast to the other people in the world, most of whom are probably not even aware of the pending wedding banquet. The others not mentioned were probably tending to the priorities of their lives, happily unaware that something wonderful was about to take place in their midst, a wedding banquet of all things!

They either had no idea that there even was a banquet, or they ignored all of the invitations that probably came their way over the years. Could it be that this "unaware" group was the vast majority of those living at that time and that the two factions of the "virgin" group are a very small percentage of the total number who could have come if they had chosen to prepare themselves?

Matt.7:13-14 NIV "Enter through the narrow gate. For wide is the gate and broad is the road that leads to destruction, and many enter through it.
14 But small is the gate and narrow the road that leads to life, and only a few find it."

This small "virgin" group was narrowed down even more. They were divided into those who were called "wise" and those who were called "foolish," a label significant enough to keep the "foolish" from entering the banquet, even though they were aware of it and had taken the time to consider it important enough to wait quite a long while for the bridegroom to appear.

Wherever you choose to place the "trimming of lamps" upon the heralding of the bridegroom vs. "lamps going out," we can all agree that the idea of having enough provision to be able to wait for a tarrying bridegroom is vitally important. The time it took to go and buy more oil was just too much time, regardless of what the oil is.

For our study, I would like to suggest that the "oil" that is needed refers to heart position. (I realize that most, if not all, interpretations believe that the "oil" is the Holy Spirit. In a very prominent way, that is true because the Holy Spirit woos, encourages, teaches, and directs - among other things - everyone to intimacy with Jesus. As one draws close to Him, a proper bridal heart - one that is identical to His heart - is available to those who hear the call and respond.) It seems that the "foolish" virgins arrived on the scene because they heard of the banquet and knew it would be very good for them to be a part of what would be taking place. The problem was they were not ready to enter in, and what they lacked could not be given to them by the "wise" virgins. They had to get it themselves. Unfortunately, they missed the deadline.

On the other hand, the "wise" virgins had come prepared. Taking the invitations seriously over time, they more than likely investigated what they would need for acceptance into the chamber. They probed all of the possibilities, and prepared themselves to please the bridegroom. They had "enough" to wait out any delay or any situation. Their time was His time. Their purpose for being there was to please Him, not because it was good for them.

In these end times, we are convinced that many invitations to prepare for our Lord have been given out, whether it be for His coming, or simply for His proper representation on this earth. Our experience has been that the vast majority of those who call themselves followers of Jesus Christ are not responding. Business as usual is the order of the day.

Do you feel uncomfortable with most of what is called "Christianity" today? If so, why do you think that is?

Those who are aware of the times and seasons in which we live are divided into two groups. One group is preparing with moderate zeal because they understand how wonderful it would be to be part of what might soon take place. They are flowing in their usual "this is gonna be good for me" attitude and believe that it will be adequate for whatever happens, whenever it happens.

You could start now!

Ask Jesus to change your heart.

The other group, those of you who have chosen to live as Jesus lived, have heard the same call, only you have learned from intimate times with the Father that compromise is not part of the character of Jesus. You know that the kind of heart that finds satisfaction in anything other than the Father's will is in no way similar to Jesus' heart.

You have learned that it is important to the Father that Jesus recognize Himself in those who are waiting and/or working for Him. You know that responding to the present call to intimacy is important to God and are willing to do so for no other reason than to glorify the Father and please Jesus. You know that falling in love with Jesus, a vital and often missing part in the fulfillment of God's plan, is necessary and you desire to do what it takes to go there.

Allow the Holy Spirit to give you His insight into the above scenario. Write down what He brings to your mind. (Share it with someone doing this study if you're led.)

Here's a Thought

There is a fair amount of controversy over what most call the rapture of the church. If we would allow the Lord to develop the heart of the bride in us now, then it would no longer matter at what point the rapture does or does not occur. The reason is that we would be prepared and ready no matter what the Lord's timeframe is; and if we are prepared as a waiting bride, our hearts will have the proper motives for who we are and what we do.

Our passion will be to continually be on the lookout for our Bridegroom for His reasons, whether that be to function another day on this earth or to go and be with Him for eternity. Our motives would be founded upon our love for Jesus our Bridegroom, the One with whom we are enamored, the One we long to please for His sake.

It would be really good for you to set aside quiet time to listen to the tapes suggested.

Pray and write down what you need to remember.

A free, in-depth audio discussion of this topic entitled,

"Are You Part of the Waiting Bride?"
is #43
in the audio section on our Web site,
www.christspassionatelife.com

Prayers and thoughts

Getting to Know Father God is Really Important

Jesus could love His Father passionately because He knew His Father intimately. He could love others because He had His Father's love in Him to do so. They were one in every way. His death and subsequent resurrection provided a way for each of us to have that same relationship and shared intimacy, if we choose to embrace all of the provisions we need in order to do so.

Our relationship with God through Jesus is, above and beyond anything else, a wondrous love story between an omnipotent Father God and His precious children. It is the foundation of all of history, the focal point of all past and future generations; and the promise that we have for eternal well-being. No other biography in all of time is packed with more adventure, intrigue, danger, excitement, and moment-by-moment thrills.

If you were to take all of the imaginations of mankind, all of the wealth, knowledge, and power of all of the men and women that have ever lived and combine them, multiplied by one million to the millionth power, it would not compare to the wonder of one moment of God in His ordinary (for Him) daily activities and interactions with us. With all that our Father God is and has and has done, His heart has favor toward the opportunity He created for those He formed from the ground of the earth to be in association with Him.

This love association is an unparalleled drama that has overwhelmed the mind of the scholar, disgusted the heart of the bigot, softened the heart of the needy, and filled to overflowing the heart of the child. In all of the wonder that is our God, the most amazing aspect, which has baffled mankind throughout his time in existence, is the well-put phrase in the Book of Psalms, "Who is man that you are mindful of him?"

To grasp the concept that our Father God is the originator of all life is more than enough for most scholars; but to understand that He loves us deeper than we could ever know and that His focus is on our existence for this time in creation is the most difficult truth to understand. It is beyond our scope of thinking. It must be received by the faith in your heart that He really means what He says, if you are ever to grow closer to Him.

"But without faith it is impossible to please and be satisfactory to Him. For whoever would come near to God must [necessarily] believe that God exists and that He is the rewarder of those who earnestly and diligently seek Him [out]." Heb. 11:6 Amp

To go any further in this study, and for that matter in your walk in Christ, you must cease viewing your relationship with God

It's wonderful to know that we are loved and fully accepted by our Father in Heaven.

God has created an opportunity for each of us to have wealth and freedom beyond our wildest imaginations, no matter what is going on around us.

35

We need to change our approach to this life in Christ from one of acquiring knowledge about our Lord to one of really becoming intimate with Him as our primary goal.

as a series of religious dogmas and right-looking actions. You must begin this very moment to embrace the truth that all of what has been accomplished through Jesus was done because your Father in Heaven craves to be intimate with you. He desires to know you as a husband and wife who are deeply in love know intimacies with each other. If you do not choose to embark on that kind of relationship, you might as well close these pages, and remain in the state in which you are. Hopefully, there is a stirring in your heart, which won't even allow you to consider that.

To understand the depth of what has transpired to allow mankind to have the privilege of associating with such a magnificent God and Father, we have to put aside all of the typical character traits that make us "normal," and have wounded us in the world. There is no place for us to hold on to the idea of rejection in our association with God, especially when we feel that we have been "bad." We cannot accept the typical concept that we are separated from Him when things are going "badly," and fully accepted when we see that things are going "well."

He does stuff to make us come to Him!

2 Samuel 14:14 NIV "God does not take away life; instead, he devises ways so that a banished person may not remain estranged from him."

Do you believe that Father God pursues you rather than rejects you when you sin? Why or why not?

Is your belief in perfect alignment with the Word and heart of God? How?

Very important!

To go deeper with your Lord, you must be willing to accept the concept that a loving Father has gone about the business of purposely designing everything that He has done – no matter what it looks like – so that you and He can enjoy a vibrant, fulfilling relationship on this earth and for eternity. Remember, He initiated the salvation process with Jesus.

Once you grasp the concept of the kind of love that the Father has for you, and you understand that when you go to Him He will impart Himself and His desires to you, you will see that one of His desires is that none of us should miss the kind of life He offers. If you approach Him in this way, you will begin to take on His heart and its passions. Seeking Him this way will convince you that everyone needs to come to Him through Jesus; and that after they do, they should be directed to His kind of love relationship. As Jesus was a passionate advocate for His Father and is now our advocate, we are to be advocates for both of Them, one another, and for those who need to see who He is.

How have you approached Father God in your prayers?

Is your time with Him delightful and restful, or full of cautions? How would you describe it?

Do you sometimes go to Him because your time together is so wonderful and pleasing to Him? Why or why not?

You may need to stop and think right here.

Maybe it's time to reevaluate your association with your Father God! Since you know Jesus, the Father really is your "ABBA," you know!

Prayers and thoughts

We Must Learn to be Advocates for Father God, for Jesus, and for Each Other if We Are to Live Christ's Passionate Life

The dictionary definition of "advocate" is "one that pleads the cause of another." Our mission is to be advocates for one another, maintaining a cause for each other in prayer at a minimum, and with our very lives as Jesus did, if necessary, through the power of the Holy Spirit.

The New International Dictionary of the Bible defines "advocate" as "counselor, comforter, supporter, backer, helper." It says, "The Holy Spirit is the advocate of the Father with us, therefore our Comforter (KJV, John 14:16,26; 15:26; 16:7; RSV, NIV translate, "Counselor"). As applied to the Holy Spirit, the Greek word is so rich in meaning that adequate translation by any one English word is impossible. The KJV "Comforter" is as satisfactory as any, if it is taken in the fullest sense of one who not only consoles but also strengthens, helps, and counsels, with such authority as a legal advocate has for his client."

Allowing the Holy Spirit to comfort us in the full sense of that word and then extending that comfort in the Name of Jesus is what is commonly referred to as Christianity. It is seen in action as we study the passionate life of Jesus as He walked on this earth. It should be seen in our everyday actions as we follow Him. To do less is a modified form of following Christ, which causes a partial presentation of the Gospel to the world and a cold, fruitless life.

Even though we are at the very center of the heart of God, we must never place ourselves and our needs at the center of our attention. We must allow the Holy Spirit free reign to move us to desire the very heart that Jesus had for His Father and for others, and allow our own needs to fall by the wayside, so to speak, knowing that our Father knows them well and will take care of them as we go about His business. What a concept!

Be Encouraged

As you grow toward Jesus and His passionate life, chart your progress. Don't give up or get discouraged as God reveals your deepest sins and the true motives for all that you do and you realize that you are light years away from the life that is intended for you because of Jesus. Your sins must be exposed, so that you can know of the desperate need that you, along with all of us, have of His mercy. Once you realize the extent of your bankruptcy, you will be able to truly repent and allow His wonderful changes to take place.

When was the last time you defended your best friend, Jesus, as He was belittled or lied about?

When have you stood with someone who was standing alone in his/her passion for Jesus?

What really is Christianity in action?

It's a good thing to see what needs to be changed.

True submission is a life-long heart attitude and process. Keep pressing in, possibly referring to parts of this study during your prayer time on a continual basis as you live this adventure day by day, year by year. Make these pages your personal notes to God. Use them as you would use a diary, expressing your most intimate needs to Him.

Prayers and thoughts

Who do you love more than yourself?

There is a Difference Between Knowing God and Just Serving Him

Oftentimes we choose to serve God rather than get to know Him, because it is easier to focus on and control what we do than it is to focus on becoming who God desires us to be. The Lord's main concern centers on us reflecting the character of Christ, and the only way that occurs is by spending time in His presence. Interestingly enough, it's also the only way to truly serve Him, because how do we really know what He desires us to do if we do not wait in His presence to find out?

Remember, even Satan would be pleased to have you busy with good things if it stops you from becoming intimately acquainted with the Lord, and walking in the real power that comes through surrender and obedience.

Study the chart below and note the differences between serving God and truly knowing Him.

It's all about who we are becoming, not what we are doing!

Serving God (What We Do)	Knowing God (Who We Are)
1. Tends to focus on self and how we see things	1. Tends to focus on Him and how He sees things
2. Easier, more controllable by us, flesh tends to intrude	2. Costly, God's in charge, crucifies the flesh
3. Performance-based (man's criteria,) formulas, position of strength	3. Becoming (God's criteria,) intimacy, position of vulnerability
4. External, issues regarding man's approval or disapproval	4. Internal, produces confidence in God
5. Can produce pride	5. Produces humility (we see who He is/ who we are not
6. Can feed the flesh, it's about us	6. Feeds the spirit, it's about Him
7. Gifts emphasized (false sense of power)	7. Fruits developed (true power)
8. Can become ritual, formulas, and worshiping worship	8. Presence of God, relationship, worshiping in spirit and in truth

What areas are out of line with the above chart at present?

Do you agree that there is need for change if you are to fall deeply in love with Jesus and, for that matter, with others who are sent to you?

Loving deeply is sometimes scary. It makes us vulnerable.

Author's note

Merry and I are convinced that perilous times are on the horizon. Biblical times and seasons that parallel the kinds of seasons that are labeled as the "Biblical end times" are unfolding right before our eyes. Soon, the world and most of the unresponsive church will be walking around in a fearful stupor because of the unprecedented anguish that will start to consume them. Only those who heed the call of God that is being heralded now will be prepared for what is ahead.

To live victoriously during these next years, you must renew your relationship with Jesus. You must shake off all of the traditions, dogma, and habits that hinder you from living the full, exuberant life of Jesus in your ordained sphere of influence. Do not be afraid to be different from those who also call themselves Christians. If they are not moving closer to Jesus with a passion as their only reason for breathing, find new friends who are.

It's not scary to love Jesus deeply.

He will always love us back and teach us to love others.

Can you determine if there is anything that is stopping you from selling out completely to the Lord at this present time? What is it? Is it more than one thing?

When peril comes, most of those who call themselves Christians will "hunker down" in an attempt to be safe; but they'll be powerless to protect themselves. In a time when the Jesus they have said that they serve is needed most, they will not know how to call on Him or even know who He really is. Therefore, they will hide in fear, thinking that they will find a place of safety. Wherever they go, it will be a tomb for them spiritually speaking.

The only place of safety is to be solely and completely locked up in Jesus Christ, living His passionate life. In times of peril, His overcoming presence will not be with the cowering masses. He will be displayed in all of His radiant glory through those who take the time this very day, perhaps this very moment, to surrender fully to Him and His ways. He will be with those who use their every breath of life for His benefit and the benefit of those who need to see Jesus.

As the Holy Spirit changes you, you will be acquiring the tools you need to not only overcome perilous times, but to prosper during them through the power of the Holy Spirit. You will move in anointed power to represent the Lord.

What was just said? Please use your own words and detail what was said above. Add your own comments and modifications. Make it a statement of belief for yourself. Use a separate sheet of paper if necessary.

Note: As said before, later in these pages, you will be introduced to our "Living Out Christ's Love" section, which addresses Jesus' heart of caring for others. It is a fact that our relationship with others is the day-to-day working out of insights we receive from God.

Somebody really needs you!

Learning about Jesus and not living like Jesus is incomplete Christianity. It leads to cold, dead people, who sit in the frozen pews of useless churches that are doing little to further the work of God, even though they are engaged in many programs. (If that last sentence seems too strong, wait on the Lord quietly to see how He really feels about it.)

At first, this kind of active loving may be foreign to you, but soon you will be surprised at how much your spiritual life will increase. Begin to see that your relationship with others is as important to God as your relationship with Him when you are in Jesus Christ. Jesus never sat on the sidelines, stuffing Himself on the Father's "goodies." He took what the Father gave Him and gave it to others. He was alive with His passionate life to share.

43

Remember: You are not necessarily to start doing more things for God or becoming more active. The passionate life of Christ was birthed in fellowship with His Father and implemented only when and where His Father said it should be done.

When Jesus walked this earth, I'm convinced that He was a joy to be with, even through the most intense expressions of His Father's will. He had fun and freedom in doing His Father's desires because His heart was in the posture to do only that.

No one, in either the church or the world, is attracted to a religious prune face. The best part of your adventure with God is the covenant fact of your security in Him and His great love for you. Learn difficult lessons with joyous enthusiasm, astounding acceptance, and open arms.

Rev. 3:19 Amp   "Those whom I [dearly and tenderly love, I tell their faults and convict and convince and reprove and chasten [I discipline and instruct them]. So be enthusiastic and in earnest and burning with zeal and repent [changing your mind and attitude]."

Navigate hard times with loving, humble aggressiveness, knowing that you are being drawn closer to the Lord and that a valuable lesson is being learned as you choose to hear what it is. Reach to others during these times, so that the enemy doesn't nullify your testimony.

You're going to do great!

As you are shown areas that need to be changed by His loving hand, respond graciously. Your exhibition of a dedication to responding joyfully will be a magnet to those who follow in your footsteps in developing an intimate relationship with Jesus. Be encouraged. You are valuable!

The Next Steps

"Whoever says he abides in Him ought [as a personal debt] to walk and conduct himself in the same way in which He walked and conducted Himself." I John 2:6 Amp

By continuing this far, you have answered the call of the Lord and been shown how to move away from a formal, cold, religious lifestyle, joining those who have discerned the times and seasons and have chosen to prepare themselves for the return of the Lord Jesus Christ for His bride. We commend you for choosing to break from the ranks of the business as usual and pursue the freedom of a crucified life that was always intended for those who call themselves Christians. Realizing that many have gone before you, and many will come after you because of your responses, let's proceed with diligence.

Remember, it's the Holy Spirit's power that is working in you and allowing you to come this far.

10) The Levites who went far from me when Israel went astray and who wandered from me after their idols must bear the consequences of their sin.

11) They shall serve in my sanctuary, having charge of the gates of the temple and serving in it; they may slaughter the burnt offerings and sacrifices for the people and stand before the people and serve them.

12) But because they served them in the presence of their idols and made the house of Israel fall into sin, therefore I have sworn with uplifted hand, that they must bear the consequences of their sin, declares the Sovereign Lord.

13) They are not to come near to serve me as priests or come near any of my holy things or my most holy offerings; they must bear the shame of their detestable practices.

14) Yet I will put them in charge of the duties of the temple and all the work that is to be done in it.

15) But the priests, who are Levites and descendents of Zadok and who faithfully carried out the duties of my sanctuary when the Israelites went astray from me, are to come near to minister before me; they are to stand before me to offer sacrifices of fat and blood, declares the Sovereign Lord.

16) They alone are to enter my sanctuary; they alone are to come near my table to minister before me and perform my service.

Ezekiel 44:10-16 NIV

In the above verses, the Levite tribe – the only tribe that was ever allowed to minister to the Lord in His inner chamber, the Holy of Holies – was separated into two categories by the Lord: those who had wandered away from Him, pursuing their idols; and those who remained faithful during times of waiting for His plans to develop. We believe that these verses are similar in heart to the wise and foolish virgins and also describe the formal "church" in these last days.

Those who went after their idols were allowed to remain in service to the Lord, doing good works in the temple; but they were not allowed into the inner chambers. The sons of Zadok, who remained faithful to the Lord, were now the only members of the tribe allowed into the presence of the Lord to minister to Him.

At one time, all of the tribe had the privilege of ministering to Him. Now, even though all of them still were allowed to serve as priests and to the uninitiated eye appeared to be in service to the Lord, only the faithful had access to an intimacy with God in His inner chamber. So it will soon be again.

In these end times, there are two "churches" being raised up. It is a separation of those who choose to remain as they have always been – in compromise, doing all kinds of good-looking, religious activity – and those who will be faithful to the Lord and His overall plans with enthusiastic abandon, regardless of the cost. A look at the book of Revelation and God's opinion of the churches He mentions give us a pretty good indication of the heart of God toward religious activity.

Note: It might be informative to study the characteristics of the churches mentioned in Revelation at this time. Notice that everything that the Lord mentions has to do with the heart position of those mentioned.

It's really about heart position.

Become equipped and then go get others.

Jesus' passionate life is a heart position of pursuing selfless love, which means a purposeful death to everything that is fleshly vs. choosing to hold onto some of the things that "can't be so bad because they are widely accepted." Religious people will always appear spiritually prosperous in most ways as they work hard for the Lord. In almost every case, however, they will not have the presence of the Lord with them in all of their "good" activities, even in their activity of winning souls; because they have decided to take the easy route of compromise and self-service.

Note: It is the Holy Spirit who actually brings people to Jesus. He will use anyone and any means in line with the heart of the Father to do so.

It seems evident that all of these "hearts" will function side by side within any given body of believers. The one that will be most distinguishable, however, will have the heart of a waiting bride being raised up; the others will function with a business-as-usual attitude of religious service, unaware of the absence of the Lord's presence.

Your choice to respond to the call that draws you closer to the Lord is a good indication of your desire to be at the center of what God is doing at this time and a positive response to the heralding by the Lord - that is at hand all across the land - to sell out. It's time to delight in your Lord. Those who choose to press in with the Lord will acquire a heart to minister to Him in His inner chamber, seeking only His face, and prepared for the true service of unending love to others and living the passionate life of Jesus in the coming end times.

Your Lord is enjoying your heart of responsiveness to His call, why shouldn't you?

"God is kind, but he's not soft. In kindness he takes us firmly by the hand and leads us into a radical life-change."
Romans 2 The Message Bible

Prayers and thoughts

This is a delightful, purposeful opportunity to flow in the answer to all of life's questions.

From Our Father's Heart

As I promised,
I am going to make you into the likeness of My Son, Jesus.
The challenges before you will be death to your flesh.
Sometimes they will cause you to despair,
if you don't understand that I am truly rebuilding you.
While we are working together and you are being prepared,
I have some suggestions to help you along the way.
As you go, I will convict your heart
and help you with other thoughts for your journey.
Start here.
Let's delight in the journey together.

2 Cor. 2 The Message Bible "In the Messiah, in Christ, God leads us from place to place in one perpetual victory parade. Through us, he brings knowledge of Christ. Everywhere we go, people breathe in the exquisite fragrance. Because of Christ, we give off a sweet scent rising to God, which is recognized by those on the way of salvation - an aroma redolent with life. But those on the way to destruction treat us more like the stench from a rotting corpse."

2 Cor. 6 The Message Bible "Dear, dear Corinthians, I can't tell you how much I long for you to enter this wide-open, spacious life. We didn't fence you in. The smallness you feel comes from within you. Your lives aren't small, but you're living them in a small way. I'm speaking as plainly as I can and with great affection. Open up your lives. Live openly and expansively!"

What a joy to honor Jesus with our lives!

Jesus endured the cross because of the joy of what it was accomplishing. In contrast, so many of us walk around prune-faced because God is doing some carving of our flesh. Because of how we function during times of trial, most people would not desire to serve the Lord, no matter what we say. Our countenance would drive them away.

Why wouldn't we approach this incredible walk with God not only from a spiritual aspect, but from the physical also, so that we can be a proper witness all of the time? We prepare for everything else we do. Why wouldn't we take some logical steps to insure that things that hinder us from accomplishing our journey are eliminated? Why wouldn't we add anything to our lives that would help us be a better witness?

List your reasons why!

Things that have no bearing on a proper relationship with our Lord get in the way. They are like rocks in our backpack. Why would we give notice to them, much less carry them?

49

Begin Now!

Love passionately.
Have more fun, knowing that you are in the Lord's hands.
Sell or give away at least one third of all that you own.
Eliminate everything in your life that "owns" you.
(Get rid of or limit the use of your TV
and video games; they own you.)
Do not walk closely with fools
who talk of foolish ideas that are not in the Word.
Eat right.
Take long walks alone or with a friend.
Decide to love people through Jesus.
Determine to see others as Jesus sees them.
Smile a lot.
Smile some more.
Become a study of your mate's needs.
Love your mate passionately.
Go on dates with your mate.
Pray with your mate.
(If you don't have a mate, focus your love on Jesus.)
Be satisfied with your present state.
Stop striving to achieve something in the future,
even good ministry goals.
Physically bless your mate and your children.
Study your children as the gifts that they are.
Love your children passionately with holy love.
Spend time with your children or help someone with theirs.
Find some way to honestly compliment everyone.
Take more time to do everything; slow down.
Be at peace with your relationship with Jesus,
especially when He is challenging you.
Sing more.
Rest more.
Sit and talk with God anytime you can.
Go to God more often, simply to be together.
Cultivate Biblical reasons to be hopeful.
Get your eyes off of yourself and your own needs.
Learn to devote yourselves to the needs of others.
Tell others that they are valuable.
Forgive.
Forgive.
Forgive some more.
Seek to make new friends.
Remember that this life is not a trial run;
it is the real thing.
Remember why you are living this life.
Do not be afraid to live it as passionately as Jesus would live it.
Jesus desires to live His life through you.
Be blessed in your comings and goings.
God loves you!

Make sure that you are led by the Lord with all of this.

This could be fun!

This relationship with God that we have entered into because of Jesus is the most astounding life that anyone could live. Our future is bright. We need to do what it takes to eliminate anything that clouds our perspective of the inner joy we should be having in the journey, even in rough times.

Romans 9:16 Amp says: "So then [God's gift] is not a question of human will and human effort, but of God's mercy. [It depends not on one's own willingness nor on his strenuous exertion as in running a race, but on God's having mercy on him.]"

"We have as little power to increase or strengthen our spiritual life as we had to originate it. We "were born not of the will of the flesh, nor of the will of man, but of the will of God." Even so, our willing and running, our desire and effort, avail nothing; all is "of God that showeth mercy."

"All the exercises of spiritual life, our reading and praying, our willing and doing, have their value. But, they can go no farther than this, that they point the way and prepare us in humility to look to and depend upon God Himself, and in patience to wait His good time and mercy. The waiting is to teach us our absolute dependence upon God's mighty working, and to make us, in perfect patience, place ourselves at His disposal. They that wait on the Lord will inherit the land; the promised land and its blessing. The heirs must wait; they can afford to wait."

from Waiting on God by Andrew Murray

From Our Father's Heart

Ignorance of Me is a liberty in which
you cannot afford to indulge.
It is now time to bring those who will hear
to a renewed knowledge of who I am
and what I desire to accomplish
in these end times.
I sent My Son to show you how to act before the world,
so that many would come to salvation.
Few see His likeness in you, so they will not turn to Me.
That is about to be over.
Soon My power will change the heart
of anyone who desires to hear My call.
I will develop His character in surrendered individuals
and then corporately change My church.
I am raising up a holy people, a true bride who is looking
only to be formed into His image.
If you surrender to My heart,
the world will see Jesus in you and come to Me.
Understand that I am not wanting you to do more to be like My
Son.
I am going to do more in you, so that you will be like Him.
You must surrender all of you;
I will do the rest.

Jesus never intended His followers to be fearful, stodgy, or religious. He never wanted anyone who didn't love Him to tell others about His reasons for dying on the cross, attempting to do so because of obligation. Before the cross, He sent His friends two by two into the cities. He said, and I paraphrase, "You guys tell that city that the kingdom of God is about to exist in their midst."

He was saying that their world was about to change. Life as they had known it was over and would never be the same again because He had come. Those who received His message became His friends. He allowed those who didn't to go on their way. He loved them, but did not choose to deal with them at that time, nor allow them to be part of what God was doing in their midst. There were too many with an open heart who needed Him and would respond to what was being done.

After the cross, He sent all of those who believed that He was God to tell others of His "death-to-self" kind of life. He created exact reproductions of Himself by supernaturally imparting His very Spirit to those who believed. His disciples showed others who Jesus was because they lived like Jesus would live in front of them. In the time that He was with them, He showed them how to live.

He's saying it again.

Your world is about to change.

Will you be ready - for the proper reasons?

After He went to heaven, He imparted His nature to them. All of His characteristics, loves, desires, and available communion with His Father through the Holy Spirit was theirs. He was originally one, who became twelve, who became thousands.

If you have given your life to Jesus, you are one of the millions upon millions of reproductions almost 2000 years later who have inherited His marvelous heart and exuberant, wonderful life. We have the freedom to become passionate about the things that He is passionate about, because we have inherited His character as part of our new birth.

Do you believe that you can live and walk just as Jesus did when He was on this earth?

Why have you answered as you did?

Is your answer in perfect alignment with the Word and the heart of Father God? Why or why not?

When Jesus walked on this earth, He was showing us all how to live. He had the ardent desire and the God-inherited freedom to be deeply in love with His Father and with everyday, ordinary people. Most of those whom He loved freely, and therefore touched the deepest, didn't have a clue as to who He really was at first. They only knew deep down in their hearts that this special man who lived in their midst somehow loved them in a way that they had never been loved before. It was a love that contained a mysterious kind of power and they wanted to find out what that power was.

Seeing His bright-eyed, mouth-open kind of happiness when they were healed or delivered, people knew He had something special to give them and that He was probably worth following, at least long enough to learn more about Him. When He put His hands on and embraced the outcast, or when He intimately

This must have been fun to watch!

54

contacted the lonely, chastised leper - something that just wasn't done in His society - He was viewed as being noticeably different. When He laughed and bear hugged in the wonder of the healing moment with that same lower element of society, He broke their stony hearts and planted a new kind of hope in their souls.

Would you like to be this free?

What is really stopping you from displaying this kind of passionate life?

Are your reasons valid biblically? Why or why not?

The life of Jesus was a stark contrast to the stagnant religion of the self-important, pompous, segregated, and aloof religious leaders of that day. Ordinary people were free to love Him because He loved them first, something never equated with things that were called "godly" up until that time.

Honest, longing people enthusiastically chased Him everywhere He went to hear more about and experience His kind of love. They chased Him until they themselves were caught up in the wonder of eternal life.

Have you ever wondered about the situations and conversations that Jesus had with His chosen twelve that were never chronicled? Have you ever thought about the jokes they played on each other, and the fun they must have had together? Remember, the guys that Jesus chose to be with were "from the street." They were all very worldly and full of typical "guy stuff."

I think Peter would have been interesting to watch.

It's easy for you and me to forget that He was on a "God-designed" mission of love, His Father's deep kind of love. He was fellowshipping first hand for the first time in the wonder of those He had actually created.

When Jesus walked on the earth, God was physically present with His creation for the first time since the Garden of

Eden. His "adventure" allowed Him to experience the joy of those He loved first hand, while expressing His love to them, and at the same time birthing His Father's kind of love in their hearts.

When Jesus was around, the people He was close to fell crazy in love with Him.

He may not have spoken a black '57 Chevy convertible with fender skirts and a continental kit into existence for their entertainment or anything like that; but when He left their immediate presence, He sure had a bunch of devoted people to carry on His work. They were crazy in love with Him - crazy enough to enthusiastically set a passionate enough life course that would probably lead to their deaths.

After they understood the full impact of what they were called to do and were empowered by God to do it, they embraced their mission heartily. They chose an all-out, fully committed, enthusiastic denial of self, and embraced the life of the One who showed them what love really was. Their passion set the world on a course of change, just as yours could in this day. In fact, that is exactly what you have the privilege of doing.

The kind of adventure that the first century church embarked upon didn't begin in them because the Lord simply preached good stuff, exhibited a sour countenance to hearty fishermen, or compromised His teachings while in private. They followed the example of a life worth following, a life worth dying for.

What kind of life course are you ready to set for yourself?

Comment about your perspective of Jesus and the way He might have lived.

Is it a little different than the way you are living?

Would you like to have been able to watch Him? Why?

We've Missed Jesus
(Because We Don't Know Jesus)

I believe we have dropped the ball of exhibiting Jesus' kind of wonderful love to others. Because we don't show His kind of love to them, few people see enough of Him in us to leave their dead-end existence so that they can embrace His future-filled eternity.

We really don't know how to do this.

Our Generation Also Misses Jesus

Almost two thousand years after His resurrection, Jesus is still joyously reproducing every fiber of His being in anyone who embraces Him as Lord and chooses to sell out to His kind of life. That is the Father's chosen way of bringing lost people to Himself.

The life of Jesus is imparted to us through the Holy Spirit and we are supposed to simply carry Him to others by allowing Jesus to live His life through us. It is a wonderfully ordained concept of one living God's way in front of another, who does the same in the midst of others, and so on.

How can it be then that we, as exact reproductions of the Lord because of His Holy Spirit living within each of us, can live daily among the inhabitants of this land and go unnoticed as resembling Him?

Today, most of us tell the story about a man named Jesus and expect people to embrace it unto salvation. Because of our lackluster Christianity, we talk of miracles of the past to show the power of God, name the heroes of the faith as the only testimony of God's kind of life being lived through people; and rely on "preachers" to evangelize those to whom we should be showing Jesus. It never dawns on us that we are the message as well as the messenger. That's too big a price to pay for most "Christians."

Possessing the full character of Jesus is the perfect goal for our lives.

We Need to Give Christ to Others

No one can give away what he does not possess. We can only give away what we actually own. If we do not "own" the life and character of our Lord, it is impossible to exhibit that character to anyone.

Your talk may resemble the talk of someone who owns the character of Jesus, but your walk will not back up His kind of life unless His life is actually allowed to flow through you. If His life does not flow through you, people will see your powerless life and never be drawn to Jesus no matter how much you preach at them, do good works in front of them, or even show them about Him through the testimony of others. They want to see Him in you.

One day the full life of Jesus should be your only desire. That desire can only come from being with Him all day, every day, as your only reason for living. When it is impossible to be with Him because of everyday circumstances, your only desire should be to get back into His presence. You must be ardent in your desire to have anything that stops you from getting to be like Him eliminated from your life.

It's Not Who We Are in Christ, It's How Much of Christ We Allow to be Lived Through Us

We get confused, just like the early disciples did. We think Jesus has come so that we can finally be somebody special. He fooled our carnal thinking. He gave us the example of dying to self, so that we could do the same regarding our own lives and allow Him to live His life through us.

In God's economy, if you want to truly be somebody, you have to become nobody – not something the flesh wants to embrace. Greatness in the Kingdom of God centers on servant-hood, not on being seen and served.

How does that differ from what you've been taught?

How do you feel about the concept of serving everybody else?

Note!!!

You need to note and be careful of this: If we spend our time pursuing the concept of who we are in Christ, there is a tendency to become self-focused and even self-exalting, which sets us up to allow for the patterns we followed when we functioned in our old nature, that nature that always wanted its

58

own way. If we become too self-absorbed, we even get to the point where "dying to self" becomes self-centered and all about us!

What do you think is the solution?

The solution to your dilemma is to find out who Christ really is and then make it your life's work to fall in love with Him! If that becomes your goal, your focus will be on the wonder of His Person, and everything else will begin to fall in place.

Note: Initially, as you begin to see who Jesus is, you will also see who you are not. Please do not let that deter you from pursuing Him. It should actually drive you to Him, because you cannot be truly free until you realize your total bankruptcy, inabilities, and desperate need of Him. That realization alone can cause you to cling to the Lord and is a great step in the direction of being able to depend solely upon Him and who He is, not upon yourself and who you are (or aren't.)

Believe it or not, that recognition of personal bankruptcy can become a very peaceful place to be because it will constantly remind you of your need for God in all areas, and the fact that He is always looking for you to depend on Him in all things. As we all pursue Jesus, we will eventually become so taken up with who He is, that we will no longer come out of need, but out of love – the highest form of relationship. Then watch what happens!

Being bankrupt is the perfect heart position.

Are you comfortable with being totally bankrupt before God? Why or why not?

Before we go any further, what is in your heart at this moment? Take the time to really pray through your thoughts before you answer.

Once Upon a Time
(A Short Story)

Once upon a time in a far off land there lived a gracious, benevolent, all-powerful Father King. The castle home of the King was arrayed in the most precious trappings available – gold, silver, jewels, the finest appointments. With its spacious rooms, magnificent architecture, and palatial integrity, it was almost more than one could comprehend or fully appreciate. The sprawling gardens, rivers of purest water, and finest orchards on vast landscapes that blanketed the magnificent terrain – unlimited resources farther than the eye could see - provided a totally fulfilled life of joy for its residents.

This kingdom, aside from its splendor, had one quality that made it unique in comparison with all the kingdoms that surrounded it. Far more beautiful, far more valuable - actually priceless – was the ability to have true intimacy between the Father King and all those who chose to live in His Kingdom home.

This intimacy, the unashamed sharing of oneself, allowed the Kingdom home to radiate with a beauty that left all other kingdoms in darkness by comparison. The King's heart wanted only what was best for those who lived in His home. They, in turn, served the King and each other with the same intimate heart that He had. Life in the home of the King was joy beyond measure, for people cared more for each other and their King than they did for themselves because the heart of the King was firmly engrafted in each of them. Being of one heart, there was no reason or need to function in any other way. This allowed the King's love to continuously radiate to everyone. This way of life burst forth and was visible to all the kingdoms of darkness that surrounded the King's home.

It was the greatest joy of the King's Son to make this heart of His Father available to anyone who desired one. Although He was the Son of the richest King in the land and heir to the throne, He would dress Himself in His well-worn servant's garb, and move from town to town in each kingdom, sharing the need and wonder of receiving the King's heart while loving His people. He knew there could be no real life without His Father's heart. No one could enter His Father's home unless this unique heart was accepted and engrafted into his or her own life. The desire and love for those in need of the heart encouraged Him onward. After all, He Himself had His Father King's heart: They were one. He also knew that one day, without warning, the heart would no longer be available; and those without it would never be able to live in the Kingdom home of His Father. They would never share the intimacy that set this Kingdom apart from every other kingdom. Without this new heart, the desire for intimacy was absent, and the Father could not impart Himself to them.

Others, who simply didn't understand, were buying, selling, or giving away other hearts from other kingdoms that made them feel needed; but the Father King's heart was unique in that once imparted, it created a desire for intimacy with Him and Him alone. As all who fully accepted that heart turned in one accord to the Father, His Kingdom grew strong, for all desired only what the Father and Son knew to be best for everyone.

These other counterfeit hearts would be tainted, containing pieces that appeared to come from the Father King's heart, but actually did not. In their kingdoms, good deeds, moral restraint, folklore, and religious traditions were evident. As the people were caught up in these pursuits, they had no desire for intimacy with the Father King, nor any desire to live in His Kingdom home or follow His ways. Oh, how important it was to receive the heart of the Father King and no other!

As the inconspicuous Servant Son traveled from kingdom to kingdom telling of His Father's home and the need for a new heart as a requisite to living there and partaking of its everlasting love, some joyously received the new heart. Having tired of other hearts from other kingdoms, they could easily see the value of this one. They fully received it, allowed it to change them, and even shared the Servant Son's good news with those around them.

Some felt no need for a new heart or a need to live in a better place, if that place really even existed! Others laughed at the foolishness of the Son, very willing to stay in the dark kingdoms. Still others tried to stop the Servant Son from telling others about the new heart. If someone accepted the heart of the Father King from the Son, it was one less customer for the seller of the counterfeit heart.

The majority of the residents of all of the surrounding kingdoms, however, saw great value in only selected parts of the Father's heart. Feeling that a totally new heart was unnecessary, they modified the Father King's heart to suit their own understanding. Most removed the part that required intimacy, for it took too much time away from the things that seemed much more important. The heart still looked very much like the Father's, but the light of the Father's life could not radiate from it because He was not an integral part of it. The people with the modified hearts would visit the Father King's home and enjoy the visit very much, but they never got close enough to the Father to make it a permanent stay. In many cases, they looked and acted very much like the residents of the Father's home, but it was only a cover for deeply disturbing selfish interests that were hidden inside of their lives.

Some even came back to the Servant Son and other residents of the surrounding kingdoms to convince them that their modified hearts were as good, or even better, than the Father King's heart. They insisted that their hearts made the kingdoms of darkness that pervaded the other kingdoms a brighter and better place to live. Oh, how they sacrificed much for the Father King's home (or so they said;) and they pointed out how they even made those who accepted other hearts from other kingdoms do the Father's will because of their sacrificial efforts. The majority of residents of most of the surrounding kingdoms embraced these modified hearts, believing that they were as good and powerful as the Father King's heart. This grieved both the Father and the Son.

Wonderful times were available to those who lived in the Father King's home. The Father was always available to His people. As they spent time with Him, He would reveal the wonders of His Kingdom home in greater and greater detail and the plans that He had for all of the residents. He always imparted Himself to those who desired this intimacy. Each encounter revealed who the Father really was, and the plans and reasons behind all He did. Hearts joined in intimacy with the Father exploded with love. There was no room for fear or self or need in the hearts of those enjoined to the Father King.

All was in order at the home of the Father King, which was a great contrast to the homes of the other kingdoms. The modified heart kingdoms and their residents could not understand why there was so much peace and brightness there and why the Father King would not help clean out all of their kingdoms. Some even cursed those who lived with and for the Father King. How could those in the Father's Kingdom not help with all of the needs when there was still so much darkness? The modified heart could not see that the darkness could not be changed; it would always be there. It could only be given a new heart from the Son to make it bright, and it had long ago rejected that as its only option.

It came to pass that a great banquet was being prepared in the Father King's home to honor His Servant Son. In anticipation of this glorious event, all the residents of the land ceased from any activity that interfered with their preparations. Each examined his banquet garment to make sure it had no spots or wrinkles or anything that was not bright, for no form of darkness would be allowed at this event.

Much joy was evident as preparations were made. The whole Kingdom began to ring with a wondrous sound as intimacy with the Father King increased, knowing of the upcoming, wondrous event. This harmony brought strength and power to the Father King's land, which could be felt in all the surrounding kingdoms. Those who were steadfast in their belief that their modified heart was as good as the Father King's heart were disgusted at the sound of the preparations because there was so much other work to be done. Their distaste for the Father King grew deeper and deeper as the joyous sound of the preparations got louder and clearer.

Increasing numbers of the residents of the kingdoms of darkness heard the sound and accepted the Father King's heart, so that they could live in His land and help with the preparations. Others, however, hated the sound and did all they could to block it from their hearing and from the hearing of others. A great effort was put forth in the kingdoms of darkness to cover the sound with a noise of their own. This created much strife in these kingdoms as the battles needed to change the land, which were being fought by the modified hearts, increased with intensity.

With more and more warriors from these kingdoms accepting the Father's pure heart and leaving the battle lines to live in intimacy with the Father King in His Kingdom home, less and less progress was being made to bring brightness to these kingdoms even though the efforts increased. Weariness, fatigue, and frustration were the daily fare of the modified hearts. Violent anger would manifest itself toward the Servant Son who was busy giving the Father's Heart away, seemingly oblivious to all of their battles.

The leaders of the modified hearts agreed that something had to be done. "We must present our needs to the Father King. The few battles that we win are more than nullified by new battle fronts, and we need help to fight."

It was decided that the modified heart leaders of all the battles in the surrounding kingdoms would join together to seek an audience with the Father King to tell Him of their dire circumstances. He surely would side with their causes and help them, for they were right and just.

The day arrived when all the leaders of the surrounding kingdoms met to begin their pilgrimage to the land of the Father King to share their woe. They traveled for many days and overcame many perils to get to the home of the Father King. Weary and battle worn, the peace and serenity that overwhelmed them as they entered the land of wonder when they arrived only kindled their anger. As they traveled toward the residence of the Father King, the stark contrast between the preparations for the banquet honoring the Servant Son and their own battle preparations only served to intensify their disdain. Their minds seethed with the thought of the many warriors they had lost to this seemingly unnecessary effort. Did the Father King not care at all? Didn't He see the need to help them? By the time they reached the castle home of the Father King, the leaders were convinced that their missions were a necessity, their causes were just, and their anger was righteous. They were ready for an all out war, if necessary, to win their right to be helped in their plight.

The splendor, majesty, and peace of the Father King's home and the radiance of the Father King Himself did not dampen the zeal of the leaders of the surrounding kingdoms. They had come to plead their causes and were determined to stay as long as it took to achieve their goals.

"Unfair!" the modified heart leader from the Kingdom of Perversion declared. "I have a heart that sees what is wrong, but You won't help me fight the battles. The Kingdom of Perversion grows darker no matter how hard or how often we fight!"

"That's right!" chimed in the modified heart leader from the Kingdom of Murder. "No matter how convincingly we show them how wrong it is to murder, they still kill. In fact, as it grows darker, they even believe that we are the ones who do that which is wrong and they have determined to kill every one of us."

"The same thing is happening where I live!" declared the modified heart leader from the Kingdom of Covetousness. "All of our properties and rights are being taken away. No matter how hard we fight, they just change the rules to suit their own needs. They don't care if things are fair or honest anymore. They're only concerned with rules that allow them to function unhindered. We lose more of our rights the more we fight."

"The same with us," added the leader of the Kingdom of Woundedness. "We have asked you for help to get close enough to our enemies to be able to reason with them; but when we try, they only hurt us more."

Each leader was impassioned in expressing his battlefront to the Father King, who listened attentively. Finally, after each leader had his say, the modified heart leader of the battle in the Kingdom of Religious Fervor asked, "Why would You direct us to fight these battles and then not provide the means for us to win? In fact, you even took most of our warriors away with the announcement and sounds of the preparation for the banquet for Your Servant Son. And He doesn't seem to care either! Why would You be so cruel as to leave us alone in the battles You have created?"

With that, the Father King held up His hand for silence. A great hush fell over the assembly of the surrounding kingdom leaders with their modified hearts as the Father King rose to speak.

The Father King began, "I have great sorrow for all of you and all of your concerns. However, I have allowed the kingdoms of darkness to exist for many years to be a catalyst so that you can make proper choices. It has grieved My Son and Me to see how many of you choose to live in darkness when all this is available to you." He gestured toward the vast expanse of His wondrous Kingdom as He spoke. "Every opportunity to receive My heart has been presented to each resident of every kingdom. The choice has been yours as to where and how you wanted to live – either in pain and darkness forever or with Me in abundance and joy. I wish that none of you would choose darkness, but such is not the case; and it saddens Me more than you could ever know."

The compassion in His voice deepened as He stood to move closer to the modified heart leaders. "But," the Father King stated, "it must be so. Freedom to choose must be extended to each resident. It is then that I know who truly desires to be with Me and be a part of future works and future kingdoms I will build or who desires to do everything independent of My will and pay the consequences.

"The simplicity of accepting My pure heart is the means I have chosen so that all residents, regardless of their past, would have access to the joy of My Kingdom home. No one can ever say that he or she could not achieve the right to live with Me, for citizenship in My Kingdom is freely given and available simply by asking for the new heart from My Servant Son."

The modified heart leaders became restless because it seemed that the Father King was avoiding their petitions. They knew battles were raging in their home kingdoms even as they were listening. Accustomed as they were to warfare, they had difficulty quieting themselves to hear the Father King.

"What about us?!" cried a voice from the rear of the assembly. "What about our needs? While all of the turmoil is going on, our homes are threatened, our freedoms are being destroyed, and the darkness gets worse. What are You going to do about that?!"

"I have already done all that I am going to do," the Father King said to the astonishment of everyone present. "My plans have been laid out for everyone to see from the beginning, and all is proceeding according to schedule. It is in proper order," He said calmly.

Then, raising His hand again to quell the rising tide of hostility that sprang up among the wide-eyed leaders, He continued: "You have come here today to tell Me of My need to help you in your quest to change the kingdoms in which you live. I would like to ask you these two questions: Who has asked you to fight the battles in which you have engaged? And from whom have you received your orders and battle plans?"

"Why, You did!" came the unanimous response. "You showed us the difference between right and wrong, and we have spent our lives showing others what we know and what they need to do. We have worked only for You – to bring Your desires to those in our kingdom homes. Our only purpose was to please You, for we know how much it grieved You to see the darkness. Our only intent was to make our fellow residents see the light of Your Kingdom home and to try to make their darkness light, too."

"Friends!" the Father King exclaimed, as He walked among the assembly and placed His hand on their shoulders to calm them. "Please listen carefully. I have appreciated your zeal and desire to please Me. I have noticed your efforts with great concern, but you have been mistaken as to My ultimate purpose for what you see happening. My purpose for you has never been to change the kingdoms in which you now live. My purpose has been for you and those who you reach with My heart to come out of them and live here with Me, for they are destined to grow darker and are doomed to failure.

"Nothing can live apart from the light of My pure heart. You've seen that anyone who receives My pure heart leaves the battle to live with Me and then returns only to assist My Servant Son in giving away more of My pure heart. You've seen My Son Himself focus only on those who would receive My heart from Him; others He allows to go their own way.

"Don't you see that as My pure heart is received, the accompanying desire for intimacy with Me eliminates all strife and fears and empowers you to discern the wonder and joy of doing things My way? As I share My plans and desires with those who come to Me, they see that there is no more need to engage in the kind of battles determined by the kingdom of darkness. Our warfare is different. I only ask My people to bring others to Me, so that they too can receive all of Me and understand their part in My plans. When all is in order, and the timing is perfect, nothing will hinder My brightness from overcoming all of the darkness that seems so strong to all of you and your kingdom residents.

"Those who choose to live in the darkness will perish. My only desire for you is to accept My heart. I would rather have all of you with Me than have you win all of your battles for Me. The most important gift you can give Me is yourself. I desire to be with you above all else. Out of the intimacy we share, you will desire to tell others about My heart; and they, too, will share My love. The rest is already planned, and I will accomplish it very soon. Have no fear, for I choose to protect those who accept My heart from any eternal harm or strife."

Then the Father King paused and looked at those assembled with eyes that held a love they had never seen before. He stepped closer, and with words that were given as gifts to be unwrapped by each of them, He said, "Don't you see? If you give yourself completely to Me, I take you as My own. And as you come to Me in intimacy, I impart Myself to you and We become one." His voice grew quiet and impassioned with love. Almost whispering, He continued, "All battles are already won through My Servant Son and His ways, which are My ways. All I want is all of you, for I love you."

A great calm came over the assembly as the Father continued to reveal more of Himself to those gathered there. He walked close to the crowd, touching some of them as He spoke. Many times as He had a specific word of encouragement for certain individuals, He would take their hands or hold their shoulders and look them directly in the eyes as He spoke intimately to them. As the wealth and wisdom of the Father King's heart and His plans for those who chose it were unveiled, antiquated weapons were quietly laid on the floor throughout the great room. Tears of repentance flowed freely from the battle-hardened warriors. Now that they were experiencing the Father's love first-hand, an urgency to tell of that love - available only by accepting a true heart - replaced anger and hatred in their hearts, even toward the enemies of the Father King. Worn, bloody battle raiment was exchanged for clean white garments of submission and praise in honor of the Father King.

The wisdom of accepting the pure heart of the Father King overshadowed all other desires of all the leaders, as one by one they received the pure heart and all that it contained. The thoughts of distant battles seemed like forgotten memories as the Father King's wisdom and love unfolded before the eyes of the awestruck assembly.

Clenched fists of fury became open hands of service to the Father King. Striving zeal gave way to peace and freedom, as the desire for intimacy replaced the cold urgency of warfare. A knowledge of the true mission of bringing residents out of the kingdoms of darkness, rather than changing those kingdoms, soon became the only mission of the gathered warriors. All those who came to see the Father King that day came to a place of rest, knowing that the battle was already won by Him and that their "battlefronts" were only distractions that obscured the Father King's true purpose.

The return trip home was filled with much wonder for the newly impassioned followers of the Father King. The sounds of preparation for the great banquet now brought overwhelming joy to the changed travelers, as they peacefully journeyed toward their former homes. The bountiful landscapes of their new home welcomed them at every turn, increasing their desire to return as soon as they made the Father King's heart available to those who were left on the raging battlefronts.

The now pure hearts were at peace as they returned to the kingdoms of darkness, which they knew were about to perish. The commitment of every heart included the realization that the same zeal with which they had fought against darkness would now be implemented for the brightness of the Father King and His Servant Son. There was much rejoicing in the Father King's heart as He bid a temporary farewell to His new Kingdom home residents.

Soon afterward, the time for the great banquet arrived. A call was issued throughout the land to all who had received the Father King's heart. All was now ready for the Father King to reveal the wonder of all that was available to those seated at the banquet table.

The weariness of preparation and the warfare that occurred during the distribution of the Father King's heart became only faded memories as His servants received their reward of eternal splendor. While the kingdoms of darkness spiraled to depths of decadence never observed before, the Father King presided in all of His glory, rejoicing at the joy of His servants as He unveiled His provision to those who chose to live with Him.

His greatest joy, however, was the presentation of His Servant Son – now the glorious King – to the pure-hearted. All power, honor, and majesty to destroy the kingdoms of darkness and reign throughout the Father King's land were given to the once inconspicuous Servant Son. The Father King rejoiced as the pure-hearted received His now radiant Son with love. All was at peace and in order in the Kingdom home of the Father King.

From Our Father's Heart

The following message # 7
is explored in detail on our Web site:
www.christspassionatelife.com

"There is No You Without Me!"

I wish to make something very clear to you.
"There is no you without Me."
So many of My people have brought Me down to their level.
I have become something they have added
to their lives, instead of their only source of life.
Do not make that same mistake.
Ponder what I've said until it becomes truth to your heart.
It will change your life, increase your faith,
and renew the proper sense of awe
needed to trust Me fully once again.
I gave the first breath to Adam.
If I should turn My attention from you for a single moment,
you would cease to exist.
However, you need to fear nothing.
Your days are planned by My desire and are numbered by Me.
No one and nothing will rob you of a single moment.
Fear nothing!
Love everyone!
Begin to see a larger picture of things.
I spoke the universe into being.
I formed you and I keep you.
You will live by My will.
It would be wise for you to live for My will.

Psalm 46:10 NIV   "Be still and know that I am God..."

Psalm 150:1-6 Amp   "Praise the Lord! Praise God in His sanctuary; praise Him in the heavens of His power!
2) Praise Him for His mighty acts; praise Him according to the abundance of His greatness!
3) Praise Him with trumpet sound; praise Him with lute and harp!
4) Praise Him with tambourine and [single or group] dance; praise Him with stringed and wind instruments or flutes!
5) Praise Him with resounding cymbals; praise Him with loud clashing cymbals!
6) Let everything that has breath and every breath of life praise the Lord! Praise the Lord! (Hallelujah!)"

Proverbs 20:24 Amp   "Man's steps are ordered by the Lord...."

Jeremiah 15:19 Amp *"Therefore thus says the Lord [to Jeremiah]: If you return [and give up this mistaken tone of distrust and despair], then I will give you again a settled place of quiet and safety, and you will be My minister; and if you separate the precious from the vile [cleansing your own heart from unworthy and unwarranted suspicions concerning God's faithfulness], you shall be My mouthpiece.*

Romans 3 The Message Bible *"What we've learned is this: God does not respond to what we do; we respond to what God does. We've finally figured it out. Our lives get in step with God and all others by letting him set the pace, not by proudly or anxiously trying to run the parade."*

Prayers and thoughts

The Very Basics

As stated previously, you and I have been given an invitation to be intimate with our heavenly Father. There is no question that the blood of Jesus has given us the right and the favor to call Him "ABBA," but it never gave us the right to diminish who He really is because of our pride. Most of our words about our sovereign Almighty God have lost their impact because of familiarity and loose usage.

Because of His abounding mercy and grace, some of us have lost perspective and minimized Him as God in our eyes. Some have brought Him to the level of being made in our image, demanding that He serve our needs, rather than understanding that we are made in His image and are formed to serve Him.

In this present time, there is an onslaught to destroy the faith of weak or ignorant Christians. The best way that the enemy can destroy who we are, or what has been done for us through Jesus and the corresponding wonder of our relationship with Him, is to diminish who God really is in our eyes. We must never forget that this is the very same God Moses could not look upon because of His glory.

The "smaller" our God and Lord can be made to appear to us, the weaker He will seem and our faith will become. The weaker He seems, the less we will be in awe of Him. That is hazardous to our walk with Him; and consequently, to our wonder *of* Him and trust *in* Him as God.

Fact is, there is only One God. He is El Shaddai. He is more powerful than any need, greater than any foe; and worthy of all honor and glory. His will brought everything into being by simply speaking it into existence. He is God and there is no other. He held our first breath and owns our last. It is right to serve Him and live only for Him.

It is vital that every one of us understands where we are placed within the eternal plans of God. This life we live is about His plans and not ours. The extent to which we grasp that truth, right or wrong, will color every one of our actions as we go on this journey called Christianity; and in this case, living Christ's passionate life.

Father God is ABBA, but He is Sovereign.

He is El Shaddai!

Very important to remember!

Does the idea that your life, ideas, needs, and wishes fall a far second to anything God desires and plans shake you up at all? Do you have to modify your thinking somewhat to operate fully in this truth? Explain!

How does the phrase, "There is no you without Me (God,)" affect you? Explain!

Start writing down some of the things you believe that might be in question.

Go to the Word and to your Father God.

What we deeply believe will determine who we are, why we pray, how we pray, why we attempt to bring others to see who Jesus is; and cause us to form a perception of why He did all that He did. This perception will be a foundation for how we interpret the Word of God; and consequently, how we carry out what we have learned, also showing others that same perception.

Where we place God in our plans will determine how we perceive the nature and purpose of our salvation. Wrong perception in this area will cause us to flounder blindly in a fog of religious activity, striving to find purpose for our life at best, and actually working against the real desires of God at worst.

Before you go any further, write down your honest perception of God as you have seen Him up until this point. Then write down how you view your relationship with Him and your view of what He thinks and feels toward you.

Note: You may not have enough room for all that the Lord shows you as you wait on Him, and you should really start a special notebook for your thoughts and journaling.

OK. Let's Get Into It!

Let's begin to allow Father God to destroy our flesh and allow the "inner man" to come forth. (It's gonna be ok, really!)

After many years of full time ministry, Merry and I have come to the conclusion that most of us, as members of the most wonderful association ever created - the covenant association between our Father in Heaven and us through Jesus Christ - have little clue as to how to function in it properly. We believe that all of our weaknesses, tangent doctrines, and downright foolishness as God's family have these two common traits:

1) We simply do not know our God.

2) We do not really know what His intentions are for our association with Him. Most of us have been so busy listening to self-serving teachings, that we have missed the astounding wealth of submitting ourselves to the Lord to keep our old man crucified and allowing the resurrected life of Jesus that resides in us to burst forth in the fullness and power of the Holy Spirit.

To find this treasure chest of "God-ordained life" means a purposeful death to our own lordship in every area of our lives and a full abandonment of doing anything in our own strength. It means a conscious submission of all that we have been, are, and desire to be to the cross and leaving it there.

The following three Father's Heart messages represent the cross, the tomb, and the resurrection. We have accompanying audio programs on our Web site, www.christspassionatelife.com. It would be wise for you to listen to them as you spend time with the Lord, so that you can gain His perspective on the bridal heart and what is needed to attain it.

When it is time for you to go to the cross, lay yourself at the feet of Jesus, willing to die to your specific ways, and allow Him to nail them to the cross. Read the following to help you get started in that direction.

If you really get this, your world will never be the same.

If you haven't already done so, write down the exact day, hour and moment that you chose to sell out to the Lord in every area of your life.

Determine once and for all that you will never, never turn back

From Our Father's Heart
Audio Tape #2
"Stay Dead"

The Cross

You, My people, have missed some steps in your walk with Me.
You have avoided the cross, fled the grave,
and attempted to live a resurrection life
without My life-giving hand upon you.
When Jesus returned from My presence,
He was flesh and bone.
There was no blood or humanness in Him.
(The life of the flesh is in the blood.)
That blood was shed,
so that you don't have to shed yours to be like Him.
Your inner being has been renewed into the likeness of Jesus.
It has been born alive to the Spirit and responds only to the Spirit.
Pray that your inner man is endued
with power and might
by the power of My Holy Spirit to be free
to respond to My ways.
Pray for the determination to no longer walk
in the futile life of your flesh.
Pray for the power to become dead
to all that resembles the world and its ways,
so that you will be aligned with My ways and in My perfect will.
It is the way of the cross.
It is the way of Jesus.

Luke 24:39 NIV "Look at my hands and my feet. It is I myself! Touch me and see; a ghost does not have flesh and bones as you see I have."

John 20:17 NIV "Jesus said, 'Do not hold on to me, for I have not yet returned to the Father.'"

1 Cor. 15:50 NIV "I declare to you, brothers, that flesh and blood cannot inherit the kingdom of God, nor does the perishable inherit the imperishable."

Ephesians 3:16 Amp "May He grant you out of the rich treasure of His glory to be strengthened and reinforced with mighty power in the inner man by the [Holy] Spirit [Himself indwelling your innermost being and personality]."

Religion never works!

75

Many of us attempt to approach the things of God by using our own reasoning and strength. That is one of the main reasons that our attempts to approach God and affect our world fail. The things of God are spiritual, not religious; and certainly not of the flesh.

When Mary met with Jesus at the tomb, He had not yet gone to the Father. He could not be touched or contaminated by anything of the world. He was on His way to complete the most wondrous event ever. Jesus was about to seal everything that had been done in the perfect blood covenant with His Father. This act was an unbreakable, spiritual covenant made for every one of us. The life of Jesus, the cross, the tomb, the resurrection, all led to what was about to take place.

The removal of our flesh and the entering into the power of our covenant with God, (in any equation with God for that matter,) always follows the pattern established by Jesus.

It is first the cross - an initial submission of our entire being to the Lord, with subsequent submissions each time our flesh intrudes upon our new life.

Then comes the tomb - the waiting on God as if dead, so that Lordship is completed in us.

Finally, there is the resurrection – the empowering of our spiritual being by the Holy Spirit, that new inner man that receives spiritual power and might, and responds in spiritual ways. The result is the ability to flow in the compassions of Jesus through the perfection of God's established ways.

Prayers and thoughts

From Our Father's Heart
Audio Tape #6
"There is a Time to Come Forth"

The Tomb

When Jesus was dead in the tomb,
it was just a matter of time before I said, "Come forth."
My intervention was inevitable.
Remember, it was absolutely necessary for Jesus to die.
It was also mandatory that He overcame death.
So it is with you.
When you submit to the absolute Lordship of Jesus,
your old form of living ceases to exist.
You die to who you were.
If any area of your life has not fully submitted to that death in Him,
I must complete that work in you.
I cannot leave you as you are.
When the time is right, however,
when the work that needs to be done is completed in you,
I will say "come forth" to you just as I said it to Jesus.
I will raise you up to a renewed life in Him.
One more step has been completed for you to serve Me fully.
I will intervene in your life to complete
what has been started at the cross.
It is inevitable.
It is because I love you.

Rest in the fact that God knows where you are.

He will call you when the time is right.

In the mean time, delight in Him!

Psalm 106:12-15 Amp   *"Then [Israel] believed His words [trusting in, relying on them]; they sang His praise.*

13) But they hastily forgot His works; they did not [earnestly] wait for His plans [to develop] regarding them,

14) But lusted exceedingly in the wilderness and tempted and tried to restrain God [with their insistent desires] in the desert.

15) And He gave them their request, but sent leanness into their souls…"

John 11 The Message Bible   *"A man was sick, Lazarus of Bethany, the town of Mary and her sister Martha. This was the same Mary who massaged the Lord's feet with aromatic oils and then wiped them with her hair. It was her brother Lazarus who was sick. So the sisters sent word to Jesus, 'Master, the one you love so very much is sick.'*

When Jesus got the message, he said, 'This sickness is not fatal. It will become an occasion to show God's glory by glorifying God's Son.'

….Then Jesus became explicit: 'Lazarus died. And I am glad for your sakes that I wasn't there. You're about to be given new grounds for believing. Now let's go to him.

....Then he shouted, 'Lazarus, come out!'"

Galatians 2:20 Amp "I have been crucified with Christ [in Him I have shared His crucifixion]; it is no longer I who live, but Christ (the Messiah) lives in me; and the life I now live in the body I live by faith in (by adherence to and reliance on and complete trust in) the Son of God, Who loved me and gave Himself up for me."

The heart revival that is being implemented all across this land in those who are submitting to the will of the Lord is a renewal of the absolute Lordship of Jesus in our lives, and absolute trust in God. That means an absolute death to our own lordship in every aspect of our lives and a death to doing anything in our own strength. It means a conscious submission of all that we are to the cross.

True crucifixion means that a death must happen. We are called to be dead in Christ, so that His life can be lived through each of us. The hardest thing about being dead in Christ is lying on the slab as if dead until He calls us forth.

Have you ever become impatient with God?

Most of us, instead of patiently waiting for the Lord to intervene in our lives, get up off the slab, pace around the tomb, kick at the stone; and yell at God to roll away the stone because we feel we've been there long enough. When our patience wears out, we take a pry bar, move the stone ourselves (doing whatever we can do in our own strength to get us out of our pressure situation,) and go forth in very much the same manner as we did before - powerless, fully alive to our own strength, and "lean of soul" in the work of the Lord. We have no real power to give others, because we have not allowed Christ's power to be formed in us.

Can you recall any time that you have "worked" to get out of any refining fire in which the Lord placed you?

Do you realize that the Lord sent other challenges your way to complete the refining process in that area? Amplify!

There is a little ditty, (I didn't even know I knew the word "ditty,") that goes like this: "I anticipate the inevitable, the supernatural intervention of God, I expect a miracle..."

As the Lord completes the needed work in you, lay on the slab of your spiritual grave as if fully dead, anticipating the supernatural intervention of God in your life. Expect a miracle. Let Him remove the stone. He will call you forth! He will raise you up in His power, in His time! He will fully live His life through you after He has removed every trace of your old life completely! It is His way. It is inevitable.

Prayers and thoughts

From Our Father's Heart
Audio Tape #1
"I Will Roll Away the Stone"

The Resurrection

A new season is at hand.
To those of you who understand
that there must be a crucifixion of your flesh,
you must also anticipate the joy
that is your heritage after your resurrection.
Understand that I am taking you to a death
of everything that you were,
all that you own, and all that owns you.
I must do this, so that you can be trusted with My presence.
You must be an empty vessel,
so that My presence is all that is in you after I call you forth.
There will be a resurrection.
I will roll away the stone of your grave.
I will raise you up for this end-time work.
Here is what must happen.
You must die to yourself.
That work is in progress as we speak.
Submit to My hand and the trials that you are encountering.
They are refiner's fires
that will allow you to embrace the cross as Jesus did.
Next, you must rest as a dead person would rest,
waiting for Me to move in your situation.
Your submission will have planted the seed in you
of the anticipation of My resurrecting hand upon you.
Then in My time, when all is ready,
I will once again bring forth My light to the world.
It will be in you as fully as it was in Jesus.
Consider this the holy work that it is.
Soon, I will call you to come forth.

Galatians 2:20 Amp "I have been crucified with Christ [in Him I have shared His crucifixion]; it is no longer I who live, but Christ (the Messiah) lives in me; and the life I now live in the body I live by faith in (by adherence to and reliance on and complete trust in) the Son of God, Who loved me and gave Himself up for me."

Phil. 3:10-11 Amp "[For my determined purpose is] that I may know Him [that I may progressively become more deeply and intimately acquainted with Him, perceiving and recognizing and understanding the wonders of His Person more strongly and more clearly], and that I may in that same way come to know the power outflowing from His resurrection [which it exerts over believers], and that I may so share His sufferings as to be continually transformed [in spirit into His likeness even] to His death, [in the hope]

11) That if possible I may attain to the [spiritual and moral] resurrection [that lifts me] out from among the dead [even while in the body]."

Ouch!

So many of us desire to have all of the good stuff without going through the suffering that conforms us into the image of the Lord. We also miss the suffering that Jesus feels for those who will be separated from Him for eternity. We don't really care about the souls of those who are going to hell for eternity. Consequently, we take our head knowledge to those around us. The further consequence of that is that few, if any, people are changed by head knowledge.

God is right this moment calling for a holy generation - a resurrection generation, one that has embraced the cross, waited as if dead to our own abilities to push the gravestone aside; and allowed the Spirit of God to completely eliminate our flesh and renew our spirits. We are a remnant, waiting as if a bride for the Lord to complete His work in us.

There are no shortcuts to completing the work that needs to be accomplished in each of us. Our Lord is very good at placing us in situations and circumstances that are intended to change us. He wants all of us. That's how much He loves us.

Only by Your strength, Lord!

God weaves Himself into our lives and all of our actions as we surrender to His will.

Please note: The themes of the Cross, the Tomb, and the Resurrection have been continually interweaving and overlapping in the last few Father's Heart messages. So it is in our own lives as the Lord weaves Himself into them if we have sincerely desired to be totally His, living as if a waiting bride for the soon return of her Groom, Master, and Lord – Jesus!

If we are to learn of our position in Christ while we wait for Him, we must study Him. There is no clearer example of the posture that we should be taking than that of the betrothed woman of old as she accepts her responsibilities as a waiting bride. Her posture and attitude for living is a type of life that we are to embrace while we wait for the return of Jesus.

The Bridal Call

The bright light of the moon gently touched each corner of the small room, highlighting every object that for many years had been so important to Sarah. Now, however, as she sat at the open window, looking past the beautiful meadow to the small grove of trees owned by Benjamin's father, she felt distanced from them. "It's funny," she thought to herself. "Things that for so long meant so much to me are no longer important at all. It's almost as if they had always belonged to someone else." She was amazed at how much her heart had changed toward the familiar and the comfortable in every area of her life, since she had accepted the cup of betrothal offered her less than six months ago.

Lying covered in the corner, one item in the room had become pivotal in most of her thoughts and preparations for her upcoming marriage. Under several layers of protection from dust and light, her fine, linen wedding garment was fitted and ready. Countless hours of preparation, peaceful moments of meticulous examination to make sure every stitch, every bead, every thread was perfect, had been lovingly spent. To make sure that all was in order, the garment had become the outward testimony of the inward changes she had made over recent months.

In the tradition of previous brides, under the loving guidance of her mother, Sarah learned the importance of preparing herself while she waited for Benjamin to come for her. As he was being taught patience, thoroughness, and responsibility by building their wedding chamber under the tutelage of his father, she prepared her heart for him. The requirement that her garment be spotless and without blemish was a catalyst for her to look for any hidden darkness, selfish motive, or uncleanness of any kind that might hinder her ability to devote herself completely to her new husband. "What dishonor I would bring to Benjamin if my heart was not fully his, completely devoted to his needs," she thought to herself.

Moving from the window seat, Sarah lit the oil lamp near the table where the garment lay. In the dim, flickering light, she gently smoothed a small corner of the protective cover. As she did, she offered a silent prayer to her Lord, asking again if there was any kind of blemish in her heart. A quiet peace settled on her; she was ready.

On her way back to the window seat, Sarah again checked to see that the jar of lamp oil they would take with them was full. Assured that it was, she rested expectantly, her eyes straining to see through the darkness, her ears attentive to the smallest sound, hoping that it would be that of the groomsman heralding the coming of Benjamin and the wedding party.

In the silent beauty of the late evening, Sarah waited, knowing that all was in order. Across the meadow just beyond the small grove of trees, an excited Benjamin stepped out of the completed bridal chamber. With the approval of his father, who earlier that day had decided that all was finished, he had given permission to his groomsman to go ahead and announce his arrival. Soon, he would follow. His heart leaped for joy.

The traditional Jewish wedding of old, with its bridal chamber being built by the groom while the bride prepares herself, is a perfect analogy of our time of preparation as we wait for our Bridegroom, Lord, and Savior, Jesus Christ.

John 14:1-3 Amp "Do not let your hearts be troubled (distressed, agitated). You believe in and adhere to and trust in and rely on God; believe in and adhere to and trust in and rely also on Me. 2) In My Father's house there are many dwelling places (homes). If it were not so, I would have told you; for I am going away to prepare a place for you. 3) And when (if) I go and make ready a place for you, I will come back again and will take you to Myself, that where I am you may be also."

Jesus Was Speaking to Tax Collectors and Hearty Fishermen as a Bridegroom Would Talk to His Prospective Bride

To understand the full impact of what Jesus was really saying, it is vital for us to examine His words through betrothal covenant eyes. Jesus spoke to His followers using language they could understand. The terms He used and the illustrations He gave were clear pictures for those living at that time. After His death and resurrection, early generation Christians clearly understood their position and its requirements, privileges, and benefits because of the terms He used and the way He spoke.

The covenant and its characteristics, the wedding and its significance, fully explained the purposes of God to them, the mission of their Lord, and their standing in Him because of His great love. Most of these terminologies and the intensity of their meanings have been lost over time to the point that they are relatively meaningless to this modern generation. We have, therefore, in this day lost the impact of many of the words Jesus was saying and the truth He was imparting.

This is the story of us waiting for Jesus

If you get this, your life will make sense as never before

We've lost the wealth of His meaning.

Does This Sound Familiar?

1) The bride and groom of old would make a binding agreement.

2) The groom would go away to prepare a place for them to live together.

3) Only the father of the groom could say when the place was completed, so that the groom could go to get his bride.

4) When the father said that all was finished, he would give the groom permission to go and get his bride. The bride would not know when he was coming; she just had to be ready.

5) The groom would "steal" her away to be with him at the marriage supper.

6) They would return after about seven days to greet those whom they knew.

7) Their return would confirm who the bride and groom were and what had taken place.

One more time:

John 14:1-3 Amp *"Do not let your hearts be troubled (distressed, agitated). You believe in and adhere to and trust in and rely on God; believe in and adhere to and trust in and rely also on Me. 2 In My Father's house there are many dwelling places (homes). If it were not so, I would have told you; for I am going away to prepare a place for you. 3 And when (if) I go and make ready a place for you, I will come back again and will take you to Myself, that where I am you may be also."*

Now He's talking to us.

Prayers and thoughts

The Wedding - a Legal Agreement or Covenant

Our examination of the characteristics of the wedding traditions of Jesus' time will amplify the position we have with our Lord and Master. (Please note: This study is from the perspective of a perfect agreement with perfect responses to that agreement. The human factor, with its selfish need for personal gain, ulterior motives, and any other human frailties, has been avoided for clarity's sake.)

To begin a betrothal covenant agreement, the prospective bride would be approached by her future husband - either the one she loved or the one chosen by her father - with a binding, lifetime contract stating the terms of the marriage and the price that would be paid for her hand.

"You were bought with a price..." I Cor. 6:20

If everything was agreed upon, this covenant or betrothal agreement would be written down and signed by all parties involved. The groom would then present a cup of wine to his prospective bride.

The bride's acceptance of this "cup of betrothal" signified her willingness to fulfill all the terms and sealed the agreement. This was no small matter, for in doing so, she no longer was her own person; but was now a devoted property of her husband. By law, she had been bought with a great price, ceased to live for herself; and now lived only for him from that time on.

Note: We are going to concentrate more fully on the bride's part of the betrothal agreement and its significance because it is a portrait of our part of the agreement we have made with our Lord.

The Biblical definition of something devoted to another includes the fact that the object is now set apart, no longer the property of the former owner. Something devoted was to be utterly destroyed, no longer existing as it once was. The bride, by accepting the cup of betrothal, had voluntarily chosen to die to her own desires and fulfill those of her new husband.

Acts 20:28 Amp "Take care and be on guard for yourselves and the whole flock over which the Holy Spirit has appointed you bishops and guardians, to shepherd (tend and feed and guide) the church of the Lord ... which He obtained for Himself [buying it and saving it for Himself] with His own blood."

I Cor. 6:20 Amp "You were bought with a price [purchased with a preciousness and paid for, made His own]. So then, honor God and bring glory to Him in your body."

Although there was no cup present, we accepted a covenant agreement when we gave our lives to the Lordship of Jesus Christ.

All of the terms and agreements have been spelled out in the Bible.

The prospective bride shows us the principles of living passionately for Jesus

The bride's commitment to the betrothal set her on a course to utterly destroy her independent life.

I Cor. 7:23 Amp *"You were bought with a price [purchased with a preciousness and paid for by Christ]; then do not yield yourselves up to become [in your own estimation] slaves to men [but consider yourselves slaves to Christ]."*

Anyone who is truly surrendered to Jesus has taken of the "cup of betrothal" and has entered into a binding covenant with God, whether it has been stated formally by that person or not. In absolute truth, we have been paid for by the very expensive blood of our Master, Jesus Christ, and our lives are no longer our own to do with as we please.

We now belong to God in a binding, legal contract, which is accomplished and on file in the heavenlies. The Lord has a legal right to do whatever it takes to make us cease to exist as we were before. That is part of His contractual promise to us. We are to submit to this process willingly and out of love. If we choose not to, the Lord has a legal right to do what it takes to get us to submit.

We agreed to this process by receiving all of the other benefits given at our surrender, including our salvation; and willingly or unwillingly, we are being formed into the image of the proper bridal heart of Christ. This process is slow and tedious for those who have a rebellious heart. It is the ardent desire of the submissive heart.

The initial stage of that process has already taken place upon our acceptance of Jesus as our Lord. We were changed, so that we would be able to live in the spirit realm with Him forever.

This change signifies new ownership. We are made completely new, so that we can understand the communication that God desires with us. Our Father is now the same Father that Jesus has, so that we can hear His words. Before we gave our lives to Jesus, we could only understand our old master, the devil.

John 8:42-44 NIV *Jesus said to them, "If God were your Father, you would love me, for I came from God and now am here. I have not come on my own; but he sent me.*
43) Why is my language not clear to you? Because you are unable to hear what I say.
44) You belong to your father, the devil, and you want to carry out your father's desire. He was a murderer from the beginning, not holding to the truth, for there is no truth in him. When he lies, he speaks his native language, for he is a liar and the father of lies.
45) Yet because I tell the truth, you do not believe me!
46) Can any of you prove me guilty of sin? If I am telling the truth, why don't you believe me?

We are devoted property and, therefore, have covenanted to no longer exist as we once were.

The Lord has promised to change us into the image of Jesus and we have agreed to submit to that change.

This was every one of us before we gave our lives to Jesus.

Our father was not God and, therefore, we did not choose to listen to Him.

47) He who belongs to God hears what God says. The reason you do not hear is that you do not belong to God."

We Have Been Made Totally New Because of Jesus

II Cor. 5:17 Amp "Therefore if any person is [ingrafted] in Christ (the Messiah) he is a new creation (a new creature altogether); the old [previous moral and spiritual condition] has passed away. Behold, the fresh and new has come!"

This is us now.

John 3:5-7 Amp "Jesus answered, I assure you, most solemnly I tell you, unless a man is born of water and [even] the Spirit, he cannot [ever] enter the kingdom of God. 6 What is born of [from] the flesh is flesh [of the physical is physical]; and what is born of the Spirit is spirit. 7 Marvel not [do not be surprised, astonished] at My telling you, You must all be born anew (from above)."

I Peter 1:23 Amp "You have been regenerated (born again), not from a mortal origin (seed, sperm), but from one that is immortal by the ever living and lasting Word of God."

Instead of fighting God and making Him orchestrate things to get our hearts right, we have the potential to be brought to the place of full cooperation and submission by the Holy Spirit.

This bridal heart response stage into which you have entered - the heart devotion to serve only the Master and to have His singular desires in mind – is in process at this very moment.

Hebrews 12:1-2 Amp   "Therefore then, since we are surrounded by so great a cloud of witnesses [who have borne testimony to the Truth], let us strip off and throw aside every encumbrance (unnecessary weight) and that sin which so readily (deftly and cleverly) clings to and entangles us, and let us run with patient endurance and steady and active persistence the appointed course of the race that is set before us. 2 Looking away [from all that will distract] to Jesus, Who is the Leader and the Source of our faith [giving the first incentive for our belief] and is also its Finisher [bringing it to maturity and perfection]. He, for the joy [of obtaining the prize] that was set before Him, endured the cross, despising and ignoring the shame, and is now seated at the right hand of the throne of God."

The Time Of Waiting

John 14:1-3 NIV "Do not let your hearts be troubled. Trust in God; trust also in me.

2) In my Father's house are many rooms; if it were not so, I would have told you. I am going there to prepare a place for you.

3) And if I go and prepare a place for you, I will come back and take you to be with me that you also may be where I am."

Once the marriage covenant was sealed by the taking and drinking of the cup, the groom would begin to prepare the bridal chamber. Before leaving the bride, he would promise her that he would return for her at some undisclosed future date upon completion of the bridal chamber (a house or a room in his father's house.)

The groom could not give her a specific date for his return because it was the groom's father who determined when the bridal chamber was complete; and therefore, when the groom could return for his bride. This tradition was established so that the groom, in his enthusiasm, would not return too soon. If he would come to get his bride before the wedding chamber was complete, she would not have the protection and comfort that he had pledged to provide for her as part of his agreement promise.

The groom's father would oversee the construction process. There were several reasons for this other than the one stated above.

The bride, in concert with the groom's preparation of the chamber, would begin preparing for the wedding and its requirements. The truly wise bride understood that the position of her heart was of far more concern than all of the physical tasks at hand. This was a process that could not be rushed. From childhood, she had been instructed in the Scriptures and steeped in the traditions regarding her role as a wife. Now that she knew who her husband would be, she could directly address all of the issues in both of their lives that would facilitate a proper marriage.

Proverbs 31:10-31 Amp "A capable, intelligent, and virtuous woman - who is he who can find her? She is far more precious than jewels and her value is far above rubies or pearls.

11 The heart of her husband trusts in her confidently and relies on and believes in her securely, so that he has no lack of [honest] gain or need of [dishonest] spoil.

12 She comforts, encourages, and does him only good as long as there is life within her.

13 She seeks out wool and flax and works with willing hands [to develop it].

14 She is like the merchant ships loaded with foodstuffs; she brings her household's food from a far [country].

This is where we come in.

We should be preparing in earnest just as the bride would prepare.

Are you ready to do so?

15 She rises while it is yet night and gets [spiritual] food for her household and assigns her maids their tasks.

16 She considers a [new] field before she buys or accepts it [expanding prudently and not courting neglect of her present duties by assuming other duties]; with her savings [of time and strength] she plants fruitful vines in her vineyard.

17 She girds herself with strength [spiritual, mental, and physical fitness for her God-given task] and makes her arms strong and firm.

18 She tastes and sees that her gain from work [with and for God] is good; her lamp goes not out, but it burns on continually through the night [of trouble, privation, or sorrow, warning away fear, doubt, and distrust].

19 She lays her hands to the spindle, and her hands hold the distaff.

20 She opens her hand to the poor, yes, she reaches out her filled hands to the needy [whether in body, mind, or spirit].

21 She fears not the snow for her family, for all her household are doubly clothed in scarlet.

22 She makes for herself coverlets, cushions, and rugs of tapestry. Her clothing is of linen, pure and fine, and of purple [such as that of which the clothing of the priests and the hallowed cloths of the temple were made].

23 Her husband is known in the [city's] gates, when he sits among the elders of the land.

24 She makes fine linen garments and leads others to buy them; she delivers to the merchants girdles [or sashes that free one up for service].

25 Strength and dignity are her clothing and her position is strong and secure; she rejoices over the future [the latter day or time to come, knowing that she and her family are in readiness for it]!

26 She opens her mouth in skillful and godly Wisdom, and on her tongue is the law of kindness [giving counsel and instruction].

27 She looks well to how things go in her household, and the bread of idleness (gossip, discontent, and self-pity) she will not eat.

28 Her children rise up and call her blessed (happy, fortunate, and to be envied); and her husband boasts of and praises her, [saying],

29 Many daughters have done virtuously, nobly, and well [with the strength of character that is steadfast in goodness], but you excel them all.

30 Charm and grace are deceptive, and beauty is vain [because it is not lasting], but a woman who reverently and worshipfully fears the Lord, she shall be praised!

31 Give her of the fruit of her hands, and let her own works praise her in the gates [of the city]!"

At that time in history, the wife was the completion of her husband and destined to be in total accord with his every emotion, desire, and need. As seen in the above verses, the wife is the helpmate of her husband in the truest sense of the word. She represented him with every one of her actions, as if he were there himself. Her actions would either bring honor or dishonor, glory or disgrace to him.

The bride, knowing this, became a study of her future husband during the time of waiting. By the time he came to get her, she - to the best of her ability - knew not only his daily needs; but every wish, desire, care, and cause that he had. She was "like" him in her heart. Because of that heart position, she could represent him properly.

He, on the other hand, was about to bestow on her the highest honor he could give to anyone - his name. With the sharing of his name, he was also bestowing the power-of-attorney in all of his household affairs to her. He was actually giving away who he was and all that he had. She, knowing the impact and importance of his commitment to her, took this time very seriously, looking out for his best interests.

Note: The seriousness of the act of giving away a name, the representation of another as if you were that person, and being joined together have lost their impact in today's throw-away society. To really grasp these representations, you will need to study and discuss their true meaning until you understand their importance.

Take the time now to ponder these concepts. Later in this study, we will be discussing what a covenant is and its impact on the participants to help further your understanding. Do not allow the magnitude of these studies to go by unnoticed. They will make a vast difference in your ability to function in the covenant into which you have entered.

Today, we violate the trust of another and go about our business as if nothing has happened. We leave him/her wounded and hurting, giving little thought to the consequences of our actions. Violation of these vows in past times could mean stoning, imprisonment, or the horror of total rejection by a society, a fate sometimes worse than death.

God was showing His future intentions for us by using the marriage betrothal illustration of those times, clearly stating its seriousness and importance - unlike our watered-down, selfish "commitments" of today. Our shallow comprehension of commitment according to today's standards is a true deterrent to our spiritual growth and to understanding what our relationship with God actually entails.

This is where you are heading with Jesus.

We will be like Him.

He has already done this.

We are known as "Christians," followers of Christ.

This is important stuff to God.

Ponder on what has been given to you so far. What has surprised you about the marriage betrothal and its picture of your relationship with the Lord?

Do you see your end of your relationship with the Lord in need of change? Explain!

Do you see the comparisons, the intents, and even the words of the Lord being brought to life as you learn about the betrothal process? What are you feeling?

You are not in a hurry.

Neither is God!

Now might be an opportune time to stop and talk to your Lord. Share the things that have risen up in your heart. Repent of your attitudes and your nonchalance regarding your relationship with Him. Thank Him for all that He has done! Maybe even write a short letter to Him, expressing your heart.

Prayers and thoughts

We Are Waiting for Our Master

As the bride waited for her master, lord, and husband to return for her, we wait for ours. The command to occupy until He comes (Luke 19:13) is little different than the maiden – who was veiled to show that she was set apart and spoken for – going about her days with the single heart-purpose of learning to please her future husband. For the devoted bride, the distractions of each day could not sway or dissuade her from her mission of knowing only him, so that she might be of great pleasure to him.

The prospective bride's study of her groom would become a continuous source of joy to her husband after the wedding as he would observe her going about the business of managing his affairs with practiced ease and knowledge of his ways. In the times of companionship and intimacy, he would be able to savor the fragrance of true devotion as his every need and desire were lovingly and knowingly met, thus enhancing his joy.

Her pleasure during the time of waiting would be fulfilled with the anticipation of his pleasure in the time of completion. She understood her commitment to live no longer for herself and only for him. Ours should be no less as we wait for Jesus.

Note: The concept of living for the best interests of another is foreign to most of us. Few of our actions are selfless, even when we're following hard after the Lord. To think that the highest pleasure one could achieve for oneself would be to help someone else attain happiness or fulfillment eludes us.

We may do something for someone else, which makes us feel good for a while; but to desire nothing but the pleasure of another and to commit our way to achieving the best for another as a lifetime process and priority for the rest of our lives seems impossible. Our thoughts eventually migrate to "What's in it for me?"

Still, that was the heart of Christ. He left heaven, walked as a lowly man, and died for those who hated Him, all so that they could have eternal bliss.

Praising Jesus with our mouth is hypocritical, if we do not choose to praise Him by emulating His life before others

The highest pleasure for Jesus was to bring us back into the Father's presence.

He knew that nothing would please His Father more and that what He was doing would also be very good for us.

95

Could you spend your whole life for the best interests of someone other than yourself? Could you do it with a joyous heart if that person hated you, maligned you at every opportunity, and had no inkling of your service to him/her? What about living for the best interests of everyone else who ever comes in contact with your life as Jesus did? Why not?

----

1 John 2:5b-6 Amp "...By this we may perceive (know, recognize, and be sure) that we are in Him:
6) Whoever says he abides in Him ought [as a personal debt] to walk and conduct himself in the same way in which He walked and conducted Himself."

The Foolish Bride Would Think of Herself

In the deepest, surest sense of reality, the Master of all things, Jesus Christ, is coming very soon for those who are truly His. Upon the command and approval of His Father that all things are complete, Jesus will send forth the Holy Spirit to herald His imminent appearance. (We are convinced in our hearts that the heralding has been present for several years, and is increasing in intensity each day. The Holy Spirit has directed those who have ears to hear to prepare in earnest.)

Jesus will look for those who look like Him in every way.

If we are wise, we will have prepared ourselves for His good pleasure.

While the foolish perceive the time of waiting in this present day as a time to learn only of the ease and comforts they have inherited because of the wealth and love of their Lord, those with a bridal heart – you, the waiting ones – are choosing to study and learn only of Him for His delight when He comes for you. You are studying and applying heart lessons, so that He will be pleased and glorified.

As the unconcerned boast of their position in Christ by attempting to change their surroundings with their authority, the devoted hearts see their need to be changed from within that they might truly please their Lord. As the foolish rest in the promised wealth that is theirs, the true bridal heart reexamines her wedding garment over and over to make sure all is in order to honor and glorify her approaching Bridegroom. Her heart has considered the cost of His approval and has covenanted to do whatever it takes to please Him.

Before you go deeper in this study, write down what you think it means to follow Jesus.

Write down your perception of what you committed to when you said that you would make Jesus your Lord.

Prayers and thoughts

From Our Father's Heart
Audio message #11

"Foundations"

Do you really believe what I have told you in My Word?
Do you understand how important it is to Me
that you submit to My Spirit,
so that I might reveal truth to you?
Some of you have become so involved
in your own perceptions of My plans and purposes,
that you are weak, vulnerable, and helpless to overcome.
Your life is useless in bringing others to Me.
The time is now to repent and turn back to My true ways.
There is an absolute plumb line that I have established for you –
My Son, Jesus Christ.
Become a study of Him by drawing close.
Go back to the basics.
Study the absolutes in My Word.
Be confident again of My sovereign power.
Be assured of My willingness to draw near
and impart Myself to you,
if you choose wholeheartedly to draw near to Me.
Start over.
Start fresh, and pursue the intensity of first love.
Abandon all outside, worldly influences
and make My Son, Jesus Christ, your only love.
We can then again be with you in power.
Come now; let's walk together.

James 4:8-10 Amp "Come close to God and He will come close to you. [Recognize that you are] sinners, get your soiled hands clean; [realize that you have been disloyal] wavering individuals with divided interests, and purify your hearts [of your spiritual adultery].

9 [As you draw near to God] be deeply penitent and grieve, even weep [over your disloyalty]. Let your laughter be turned to grief and your mirth to dejection and heartfelt shame [for your sins].

10 Humble yourselves [feeling very insignificant] in the presence of the Lord, and He will exalt you [He will lift you up and make your lives significant]."

I Chronicles. 29:5 Amp "... Now who will offer willingly to fill his hand [and consecrate it] today to the Lord [like one consecrating himself to the priesthood]?"

The Contract

The bride and groom signed and sealed a contract that reduced to writing all the promises and agreements that their union entailed. We have that same agreement with God in the form of our Bible. Its pages define all the terms and commitments into which we enter.

As it was mandatory that both parties agreed or covenanted to live by the dictates of the marriage contract, which meant that all of its statements were now law to them, so must we. You are going to sign some agreements in this section.

You may already know this, but you have agreed to every one of the following statements as far as God is concerned. You must also realize that from the moment you said "yes" to the Lordship of Jesus Christ, Father God has been creating ways for you to become aware of your lack of commitment, so that you can fully surrender to His ways.

Note: The signature on a document is simply stating in written form what your heart intentions are. To hesitate to sign or to avoid the signature altogether when entering into an agreement means that something is wrong. If you can't sign these commitments now, continue on with the study. Sign the document as the Lord softens your heart into submission. You must one day be able to sign them freely and joyfully, or your commitments to the Lord and your intentions of service are hazy to say the least.

II Sam 14:14 Amp "*...God does not take away life, but devises means so that he who is banished may not be an utter outcast from Him.*"

As you begin to understand what is required of you and submit this knowledge to the Lord, you will be provoked to repentance by the Holy Spirit for your lack of commitment to God. This is a very good thing, not something to fear. You are pleasing God every time you see any error in your ways and come to Him for forgiveness.

Most people who call themselves Christians do not know that they have made commitments and need to live up to them.

As far as God is concerned, you and I have made promises to surrender our lives fully.

Your Signature Is Required

I believe that the Bible is the absolute truth; that God has covenanted with me through the death and resurrection of His Son, Jesus Christ. I further believe that this detailed agreement is the only and completely accurate record on which I can base every decision for every area of my life.

I accept all of the Bible's truth and disregard all other knowledge, circumstances, situations, and tradition that may dictate differently. I believe that there is no other wisdom or direction given to me for my life, and rely on all of its truths alone. I freely invite the Holy Spirit to lead me to the absolute truth of the Word of God, separating me from all falsehood in any form.

Signed: _____ Date: _____

Read the statement above again and again if necessary. By signing your name, you are saying that you believe all of the Bible's truths and submit to its agreements. If you cannot do so, it almost guarantees that the full, bridal intimacy that God intended for you will be short-circuited. There is no way that you can live passionately for Jesus unless you believe that every word of the Bible is absolute truth.

By basing all of your life on anything other than the truth of the Word, you can be assured that hindrances - such as untruths from the past, man-made traditions, and erroneous doctrines - are stopping you from going on with God in freedom.

Big! Big!

Very important truth.

You must agree that you will believe only what the Bible says; or else wounds, sins, former teachings, and formed, invalid opinions will dictate your actions and color your perspective on God's love and promises. Allow the Lord to deal with them throughout this study and every day of the rest of your life. Submit to the truth that the Bible is God's inspired Word to you and for you, for His glory.

Write down the hesitations that you feel about signing the above statement, should you have any.

Mark 4:24 Amp "And He said to them, Be careful what you are hearing. The measure [of thought and study] you give [to the truth you hear] will be the measure [of virtue and knowledge] that comes back to you - and more [besides] will be given to you who hear."

Do You Accept the Cup of Betrothal?

In signing her agreement letter (betrothal covenant) and accepting the cup of betrothal, the bride agreed to walk in her master's steps. A high price had been paid for her, and she made a conscious decision to live no longer for herself, but for him alone.

Her internal death, the death of her singular ways, began her new life. Her old life passed away at that instant, and the betrothed life in her lord began.

2 Cor. 5:17 Amp "Therefore if any person is [ingrafted] in Christ (the Messiah) he is a new creation (a new creature altogether); the old [previous moral and spiritual condition] has passed away. Behold, the fresh and new has come!"

Now It's Your Turn

I fully accept that Jesus Christ is the only Lord of all. I submit that He is my Lord, and I fully surrender all areas of my life to Him. He is now the unchallenged Lord over every breath that I take, every thought that I think, and every move that I make. His glory is my reason for doing all that I do from now on. I willingly give Him unquestioned mastery over all my causes, needs, desires, everything that I own, and all that owns me.

I resolve, by His power, to submit fully to His every desire as stated in His Word, my covenant agreement; and choose to lose my every desire if it does not line up with His.

I recognize that through this agreement, by the terms set forth in His Word, I am submitting to being conformed into His image. I am no longer my own; I have been bought with His blood and choose to live for Him alone by His mercy and grace. I embrace the fact that He has a right from this time forth to live His life through me by the power of the Holy Spirit.

Signed: _____ Date: _____

Lordship means that you are no longer lord over any area of your life.

You are now sold to Jesus.

Romans 10:9 Amp *"Because if you acknowledge and confess with your lips that Jesus is Lord and in your heart believe (adhere to, trust in, and rely on the truth) that God raised Him from the dead, you will be saved."*

Note: It is impossible to keep any of the agreements that you make with God, or with anyone else for that matter, if you intend to keep them in your own strength.

Your relationship with God is His extended hand of love toward you. As you understand the concept of Jesus living His life through you, you will realize that God's extended hand holds the power for you to receive the life, power, and available character of Jesus to accomplish all that needs to be done to fulfill God's plan for your life.

Has the Issue of Lordship Been Dealt with Once and for All in Your Life?

Have you submitted to His hand to change you, instead of becoming more like Jesus by doing good stuff and trying harder?

It is suggested that most weakness, impurity, and loss of integrity in God's church could be traced to this issue of whether or not we have truly submitted to the Lordship of Jesus. In times past, times when full knowledge of the impact of a commitment was understood, the time of conversion truly settled the issue. The converted individual knew what it meant to commit his life to God.

In those times, a simple walk down the aisle, the asking of forgiveness for our sins, and jubilant hugging of those around us was unheard of. During times of true heart revival through the Holy Spirit's conviction, a person went to be alone, or in later days, stayed at the tarrying bench or at the altar until the issue of the Lordship of Jesus Christ had been fully dealt with in the life of that individual. Just as the bride became one with her new master, the newly converted knowingly became one with Jesus Christ, and only Him, at the altar. They were informed that ownership of anything - their rights, loves, material possessions, and even their lives - was to be placed under the Lordship of Jesus. They were bought with the blood of Jesus and were no longer their own.

Whatever you own in your heart has not been surrendered to Jesus.

That even includes your right to be right or your right to have your own way over the Lord's way.

In contrast, today's conversions are mostly centered around the aspect of forgiveness and its freedoms. Today, the new convert is told that he/she is forgiven, and the word "lordship" is used, but rarely fully explained or understood; so he/she proceeds with the new life thinking that all is in order. This kind of conversion is actually one-sided, and without power in times of difficulty.

The individual that surrenders only for forgiveness, believing that the relationship is mostly for the answers to his/her needs and comforts, is soon disenchanted when all prayers are not answered in the way that he/she deems proper. There is no understanding that at the time of conversion, God Himself promised to do His part to fulfill the covenants of the relationship according to His Word, and deals with the relationship as Lord, just as He promised.

Because of this lack of understanding, most of the self-focused convert's days are spent unfulfilled, confused about God, and wondering "What's wrong?" as God begins the refining process that He promised to do. God's time is spent wooing the person into true submission to His Lordship, instead of being able to use that person productively for His work of showing others a true picture of Jesus through his/her life.

You cannot be passionate about your life with Jesus and desire to live only for Him if you are in this relationship for your good!

Do you know for sure that Jesus is the absolute Lord over every aspect of your life? Have you ever purposefully placed yourself, all that you are and all that you own under His Lordship, knowing that in doing so, you are no longer the owner of any of it? Can you do it now? If you can't, why not?

Do You Trust in a Living God?

All other so-called gods are dead. They have always been spiritually dead, and eventually are physically dead. However, we have the assurance of God that Jesus Christ is very real and alive. He is the Bridegroom who will soon come to bring us into His presence for eternity.

The full acceptance of this fact, the understanding of His very real presence with us now, allows us to trust completely in His continual interaction in our lives. This acceptance ensures God's invoking of the bridal covenant to bring about the new birth, sanctification, and the subsequent holiness that God promises to us as Christ's dedicated ones, waiting for Him as if a bride.

Probably the most important decision you will ever make!

Do You Choose to Renew Your Covenant with God?

I fully trust and rely on the fact that Jesus Christ is alive now. He is my soon coming Master, Bridegroom, and Lord; and I resolve to prepare myself to submit to Him, study His ways, and live only for Him by His covenant power until He returns for me.

Signed: _____ Date: _____

You Have Entered into Covenant with God!

You have read the above agreement, proclaimed it to be absolute truth, and signed it, agreeing that Jesus is your unchallenged Lord.

You have taken the cup that your Lord has offered to signify your acceptance of His desire for you to have His bridal heart forever and you have agreed to it.

The Groom, Jesus, has gone to prepare a place for you and has promised to come back for you when all is ready there and also in you, the one with His heart.

The Father has assured you that in the fullness of time, all would be ready. He will oversee all of the preparations. From now on, all of His dealings with you are as the loved and accepted chosen of His Son. You are now in the family. Your agreement to no longer remain as you are enacts His promise to make you like His Son. He will accomplish it all. You are as the waiting bride and His disciple, the student of your Lord.

The Prelude

My children,
you are the righteousness of My Son, Jesus Christ.
All that He is will be formed in you to My glory.
From the beginning,
I have planned all that is taking place throughout the world.
Each of you, My children, has a specific role for which to prepare.
Each task is very important to Me.
I ask you to persevere and prepare.
Submit to My Word at work in you, and My hand upon you,
as you are being developed for your part.
I am forming you.
I am changing you.
I am molding you to represent Me properly.
The plumb line of righteousness has been moved;
not by Me, but by your traditions, doctrines, and personal habits.
I am, however, bringing it back to My center in your life.
For too long, what I consider to be a normal way of life
has been looked upon as extreme to many in My church.
No more!
Normal is absolute purity, devotion, dedication, and zealous love.
It is a heart that is broken for those that are lost.
Normal is Our restored, intimate relationship
from which spring holy works,
which allow people to see My glory in you.
Normal is joyous self-sacrifice and an ardent desire
to be purged from all unrighteousness at any cost.
Normal is an eternal perspective
on all that you do and on everyone that you meet.
You are being made normal again,
so that I might be able to trust you with My Word
in all circumstances.
It is My great joy that you be excited, encouraged,
and at peace, for I AM at work
and aware of all of your needs.
Know that I am training you to live a normal life as I see it.
Your life will then be a plumb line.
Those who choose My ways will observe you
and come to Me because of how you live.
My Son showed you how to live a normal life.
Now I will empower you to do it.
Devote yourself to Me.
I love you!

Being normal is to be passionate about following the ways of Jesus.

Abnormal is following the one who has been defeated at the cross - in any way, shape, or form.

How are you doing? What hesitations do you have so far?

Has your perspective about God changed any?

Are you concerned at all about any part of your relationship with Him?

Quietly rest in the fact that you have placed your entire being in the loving hands of your heavenly Father, a Father who loves you with a holy love.

*Note: Remember that you are valuable to God. You are greatly loved, so whatever is being exposed in you - such as your inabilities to be all that you are called to be - is no surprise to your loving Father God. The road to freedom is honesty with God and subsequent repentance to Him, acknowledging who you are not. This allows the Holy Spirit to do a completed work in you. Your repentance is freedom. The eventual outcome is intimacy, and a passion for His heart as you continually go to Jesus.

Prayers and thoughts

How Do People Really See You?

The following is a letter written as if from someone who has encountered a bigoted Christian.

"You call yourself a Christian. Why would I want to know you or listen to what you say? I have been observing you. You condemn me for sinning, but your Bible says your hate condemns you for murder. You act like you are better than I am, but your Jesus told you to esteem others higher than yourself. You say you serve a God of peace, but you fight against those who don't see as you see; and I see no peace in your heart. You talk of the joy of knowing God; but there is only fear, sorrow, and sadness in your life. You say you represent Jesus, but I see no love for me or for others in you. If you represent what Jesus is like, I don't like Him; and I won't serve that kind of God. Good bye."

This is not the way Christ lived.

It is not the way that we have been called to live.

Jesus Wants All of His Disciples to Follow in His Steps

Thousands of years of promises came to pass before the disciples' eyes, all in their lifetimes. The Messiah, the Christ, had come and walked among men. The Rhema of God Himself was made visible to fallen mankind as He walked through the society of those days. His presence was undeniable to even the most skeptical. His teachings about love, life, wisdom, foolishness, real strength, and real weakness caused even the foolhardy to at least take note that He was different.

The hardened of heart hated all that He was and all for which He stood. Even in the presence of miracles - the feeding of the five thousand and the four thousand, the many unexplained healings; and the preaching of the Scriptures under the anointing of having come directly from the Father - most could not understand who He really was.

The World Could Not See

Some said He was John the Baptist returned from the dead. Some said He was Elijah or some other prophet. The rumors ran rampant as unbelieving man attempted to find out who Jesus really was.

The Bridal Heart Saw

To whom do we go, Lord?

You are the Christ, the Son of God.

However, those who had been chosen to see at that time - Peter, first, and then the others - knew it to be true. He was Jesus, the Christ. They were privileged to see, as it were, "on the other side of the cross," and call Him the Messiah, the Christ of God.

His life, His love, and His actions all exhibited the undeniable. He was more than some mere prophet revisited, some prophet of old come back to life. When He was with them, they could only have a glimpse of revelation, but even that glimpse was enough to seal them in the truth and make them hunger after more. Even though they could not fully understand, they studied Him; then did what He did.

After Jesus' resurrection, it came time for them, however, to walk, preach, and live as He did to their own generation. Walking in His steps became their standard. Empowered by the Holy Spirit, who had tabernacled Himself in the flesh of mankind, they exhibited the living Christ to a lost world.

People by the thousands "saw" who He, the Messiah, was through them. Thousands were able to believe that Jesus was the Christ through the likes of fishermen, tax collectors, lawyers, and common citizens, as they lived His life before them.

Peter Understood That He Had Taken the Cup of Betrothal

In Acts 3:6 NIV, after a crippled man had asked for some money, Peter said, "Silver or gold I do not have, but what I have I give to you. In the name of Jesus Christ of Nazareth, walk."

You have been given authority in the affairs of God just the same as Peter.

You need to know the terms of your covenant.

Peter was given authority in the affairs of God on this earth as part of the covenant into which he had entered. He did what Jesus did because he became a study of who Jesus was and allowed the character of Jesus to flow through him.

Just as the bride of old did, he willingly chose to eliminate his own life to take on the life of the Christ with whom he had covenanted. He could give what Jesus gave because he had what Jesus had.

Many Have "Seen" Jesus Among Them

For centuries now, the light of the gospel has been presented to the lost through the presentation of that same life in Christ to those who will listen. For generations, people have said that Jesus is the Christ because the veiled bride, the true follower

110

of Christ, has lived the life of her Bridegroom in the midst of them. They could accept the Christ of God in spirit as that Spirit was presented to them by God through the lives of those who were dead to themselves.

It's Now Our Turn to Walk as Jesus Did

As Jesus asked the disciples then, as the Spirit of God has asked through the centuries, He is asking each of us today, "Who do you say that I (Jesus) am?" More to the point, "Who are you saying that I am?" Who are you exhibiting as Jesus to your neighbor, the broken, the poor, and the lost by the life that you live in their midst?

Do people see the traits of your Master and Lord in you because you have studied and prayed to become like Him? Have you spent enough time with your Father in Heaven to have Him impart Himself to you to the extent that it oozes from every pore of your existence? Is your love so apparent for the One to whom you have given your life, the One who owns you, that others crave to know more about Him?

Do people "see" Jesus when you are in their midst?

Who are you saying that Jesus is?

How many people in your life have had a difficult time resisting Jesus as their Lord because your presentation of Him has been so clear? When was the last time someone begged you to show him/her how to receive Jesus? If you need more room, please use the margin.

We Must Become a Study of our Master and Spend Time with Him to be Able to Walk in His Steps

The only way to truly emulate someone is to experience, first hand, who he is, how he feels, and what he does. In addition to setting an example for us, Jesus Himself walked like us, so that we could know that He fully understands our needs because He experienced our feelings, weaknesses, and temptations Himself. He knows us, not only because He has made us, but also because He has been like us. In the same manner, we can only learn the true heart of God by spending time with Him and by being submissive to His ways and walking in them.

How can you tell others who Jesus is, if you do not know Him and how He would act if He were here in the form of man today?

111

*Have you
determined
to act like
Jesus in
every
situation?*

After the glow of the agreement wore off and the realization of the promises for the future and the anticipation of the treasures that were now hers became somewhat quieted, the traditional bride began to place herself in her husband's shoes (sandals.) The responsibilities that she had accepted became a reality. In her own way, she would ask herself or her counsel how her new husband would respond in a given situation.

How would he desire his household to be run? What were his desires for the treatment of his family, friends, and neighbors? What were his tastes in food, clothing, and living accommodations? She placed herself in his circumstances, that she might know what pleased him.

Then She Had to Deny Herself

She was in covenant. It was for life, and held her accountable to her betrothal agreement. There was no backing out. More than likely, her deep love did not allow her to even think of refusing to modify or completely deny herself of her own desires in order to take on her husband's desires, that he might be pleased.

*We are not
Him!*

In the process of this study and commitment, however, she would soon painfully realize who she was not. She was not him. Asking what he would do in any given situation made her confront her own ways; and in seeing them, allowed her to see what needed to be modified, so that her ways became like his.

The task of true death to personal traits, desires, and habits - which was not easy, except to the highly motivated - became her daily reason for living until her groom's return. Her only goal was to fully understand him and live with his heart desires in mind.

At the juncture of realizing that the fulfillment of her commitment meant the death of all of her desires, how do you suppose she had the strength to continue on?

What would motivate you to continue on?

Remembering the hazards of breaking covenant, would love hold you to it, or would you submit to the agreement because of the legal aspects of that covenant? Discuss!

What is really motivating you to continue on now?

Note: We won't examine covenant in depth until later. If you would really like to understand the anatomy of a covenant, you can listen to the tape entitled "The Covenant" on our Web site, www.christspassionatelife.com.

Prayers and thoughts

What does motivate you to follow the Lord?

Is it really love for Him?

Or is it just because it is good for you?

From Our Father's Heart

My child,
are you going to do what I tell you to do?
Are you going to live before people
as the finest example of mankind did –
in total obedience to His God and Lord?
If not, what is your relationship with Me all about?
Why do you come to tell Me how much you love Me –
that you will serve Me –
and then function according to the dictates of your fleshly desires?
Why do you tell Me that you have made Me your priority
and then allow your own will to be the god you serve?
The world lies,
but they have never said that they could be trusted.
Their father is the father of lies.
They break their commitments,
but they always have and always will be like that.
But you... You are Mine.
You represent Me.
You have taken My Name as your God.
You have proclaimed aloud that you are Mine
through My Son, Jesus,
and still you go about breaking all of the commitments you make,
even to Me.
It is now time to repent.
Turn from your ways
and become a student of the ways of My Son.
Be known to others as He would be known.
Walk in His integrity, no matter what the cost may be to you.
Your continual choosing of His ways over your ways
will bring the fragrant oil of the Holy Spirit
to those who need to savor it.
That oil will be with you, because it will be needed
to heal the wounds you encounter through your obedience.
If you say that you follow My Son,
you will acquire the scars that He did.
Those scars will be the testimony of your commitment to Me.
The desires and compassions of Jesus
will be given only to those who have walked and conducted
themselves as He did.
Through the denial of who you are,
I will make you who He is to others.
Those who are lost will again see who Jesus
is because you will be in their midst as My waiting bride.
Turn away from your ways to My ways, now.
Deny yourself of all that is not like Jesus.
Come to Me to be changed
and We will walk together with one heart.

*I can't count
the number
of years that
I lied to the
Lord.*

*Repentance is
the answer!*

Romans 8 The Message Bible "This resurrection life you received from God is not a timid, grave-tending life. It's adventurously expectant, greeting God with a childlike 'What's next, Papa?' God's Spirit touches our spirits and confirms who we really are. We know who he is, and we know who we are: Father and children. And we know we are going to get what's coming to us– an unbelievable inheritance."

Colossians 3 The Message Bible "So if you're serious about living this new resurrection life with Christ, act like it. Pursue the things over which Christ presides. Don't shuffle along, eyes to the ground, absorbed in the things right in front of you. Look up, and be alert to what is going on around Christ - that's where the action is. See things from his perspective.

Your old life is dead. Your new life, which is your real life - even though invisible to spectators - is with Christ in God. He is your life."

Your full commitment will expose you for who you really are, if you allow the Holy Spirit to do so.

To fully embrace the concept of the Lordship of Jesus will expose our every sin and every area in which we are unlike Jesus. We will also be confronted on every side to conform to the world's way of facing each situation. Resisting the world will mean pressure and persecution.

What safer place is there than to function in the probable actions of Jesus Christ? What better way to show our commitment? It is a form of high praise. What a gift it is to acquire first-hand knowledge of understanding His ways, so that our ways might be eliminated. It is God's way to refine us, while we wait for the return of Jesus.

Prayers and thoughts

Agreement

Father,

I choose to walk and conduct myself in the same manner in which Jesus did while He was on this earth. I choose to study His ways and come to You, so that You can impart Yourself to me and I may become like Him before people, all so that they may be saved and You may be glorified.

I choose to ask the questions, "What would you do, Jesus?" and "What would Your desires be?" in any given situation. By Your power and strength, I choose to carry them out, no matter what the cost or consequences to me.

I do this, knowing that the suffering and denials that I encounter will help to conform me into His image. One day all of my decisions will be in conformity to His Word through Your continued wisdom and wise counsel.

As I wait and anticipate Jesus' return for me, I desire that You use me in any way that You wish. I surrender fully to You and choose Your will for my life, not mine, realizing that I can follow through with my heart's desire only through Your strength.

Signed: _____ Date: _____

The Understanding

From Our Father's Heart

You, My people, have destroyed My Name
in the eyes of the world.
Your powerless prayers, selfish lives,
self-serving gospel, and your disloyalty
have made you weak and powerless to represent Me.
My love for you has allowed trials in your life
to change you, so that you might become like My Son,
Jesus Christ.
I want you to be endued with His power.
I want to be able to trust you with My presence.
Why do you resist suffering and the denial of your desires?
Why do you seek your own comfort,
while others go without knowing Me?
How did your eyes become focused on your own needs,
instead of on My desires?
You have denied My purposes and ways,
and have lost intimacy with Me in doing so.
Repent.
Turn now, and We will walk together in full accord.

Isaiah 30:18 The Living Bible "Yet the Lord still waits for you to come to him, so he can show you his love; he will conquer you to bless you, just as he said. For the Lord is faithful to his promises..."

Rev 3:19 Amp "Those whom I [dearly and tenderly] love, I tell their faults and convict and convince and reprove and chasten [I discipline and instruct them]. So be enthusiastic and in earnest and burning with zeal and repent [changing your mind and attitude]."

A Better Understanding of God's Ways of Changing Us
Will Help Us When We Are Weary

If we understand the ways in which God is going to refine us, we will not give up or give in when we are weary.

God is not as concerned about what we are doing for Him as He is about who we are becoming. Most of us take the Word of God and loosely interpret it as a guideline on how we should function. We take selective chapters, verses, or sentences that fit our needs or conform to our beliefs. We even minimize, or completely eliminate, some verses from our life's study, if they particularly offend our desired way of living.

There is no way that we can shortcut or circumvent God's ways of dealing with us to eliminate our sin nature so that His presence might be with us to accomplish any given task. He will have His way. He is our covenant keeper.

II Sam 14:14 Amp "...God does not take away life, but devises means so that he who is banished may not be an utter outcast from Him."

Amos 3:3 NIV "Do two walk together unless they have agreed to do so?"

God's Idea of Walking Together with Him is Very Different from Ours

Eph 4:12-13 Amp "His intention was the perfecting and the full equipping of the saints (His consecrated people), [that they should do] the work of ministering toward building up Christ's body (the church),
13 [That it might develop] until we all attain oneness in the faith and in the comprehension of the [full and accurate] knowledge of the Son of God, that [we might arrive] at really mature manhood (the completeness of personality which is nothing less than the standard height of Christ's own perfection), the measure of the stature of the fullness of the Christ and the completeness found in Him."

His purpose for walking with us is to perfect the character of Christ in us, so that we will be like His Son in our hearts.

Moses Understood and Submitted to God's Plan

Moses said that God had better equip him (change him.) He understood that only God's power would allow him to make it.

Exodus 33:12 Amp "Moses said to the Lord, See, You say to me, Bring up this people, but You have not let me know whom You will send with me. Yet You said, I know you by name and you have also found favor in My sight."

Only a deep, intimate knowledge of God and His ways would do.

Exodus 33:13 Amp "Now therefore, I pray You, if I have found favor in Your sight, show me now Your way, that I may know You [progressively become more deeply and intimately acquainted with You, perceiving and recognizing and understanding more strongly and clearly] and that I may find favor in Your sight. And [Lord, do] consider that this nation is Your people."

God came to Moses because of his submissive heart.

Exodus 33:14 Amp *"And the Lord said, My Presence shall go with you, and I will give you rest."*

If only we would always talk to God like this!

If only we understood how important it is to have His presence with us in all that we do!

Moses once more knew that he needed to rely completely on God if he was going to succeed. He wasn't foolish enough to go it alone in his own strength and wisdom.

Exodus 33:15 Amp *"And Moses said to the Lord, If Your Presence does not go with me, do not carry us up from here!"*

Only God's hand-in-hand presence and the fullness of His power would make the task successful.

Exodus 33:16 Amp *"For by what shall it be known that I and Your people have found favor in Your sight? Is it not in Your going with us so that we are distinguished, I and Your people, from all the other people upon the face of the earth?"*

Moses could only see and function from the other side of the cross of Christ. Paul, however, understood the same message and knew that God's way was for him to have God's presence with him in all that he did.

God brought His man for that hour to the point of full submission through the circumstances and trials that were allowed in his life in order to refine, mold, and make him totally sold out to God.

II Cor 12:7 Amp *"And to keep me from being puffed up and too much elated by the exceeding greatness (preeminence) of these revelations, there was given me a thorn (a splinter) in the flesh, a messenger of Satan, to rack and buffet and harass me, to keep me from being excessively exalted."*

Great credentials!

II Cor 6:4-10 Amp *"But we commend ourselves in every way as [true] servants of God: through great endurance, in tribulation and suffering, in hardships and privations, in sore straits and calamities.*
5) In beatings, imprisonments, riots, labors, sleepless watching, hunger;
6) By innocence and purity, knowledge and spiritual insight, longsuffering and patience, kindness, in the Holy Spirit, in unfeigned love;

120

7) By [speaking] the word of truth, in the power of God, with the weapons of righteousness for the right hand [to attack] and for the left hand [to defend];

8) Amid honor and dishonor; in defaming and evil report and in praise and good report. [We are branded] as deceivers (impostors), and [yet vindicated as] truthful and honest.

9) [We are treated] as unknown and ignored [by the world], and [yet we are] well-known and recognized [by God and His people]; as dying, and yet here we are alive; as chastened by suffering and [yet] not killed;

10) As grieved and mourning, yet [we are] always rejoicing; as poor [ourselves, yet] bestowing riches on many; as having nothing, and [yet in reality] possessing all things."

Prayers and thoughts

The easy ride is never for the dedicated Christian.

God's refining hand, however, is motivated by a heart of compassion

Phil 3:10-11 Amp *"[For my determined purpose is] that I may know Him [that I may progressively become more deeply and intimately acquainted with Him, perceiving and recognizing and understanding the wonders of His Person more strongly and more clearly], and that I may in that same way come to know the power outflowing from His resurrection [which it exerts over believers], and that I may so share His sufferings as to be continually transformed [in spirit into His likeness even] to His death, [in the hope]*

11 That if possible I may attain to the [spiritual and moral] resurrection [that lifts me] out from among the dead [even while in the body]."

Most people are determined not to be passionate about anything, unless it benefits them.

You're going to have to get your course set on gaining the heart of Christ and submitting to the mind of Christ.

A breakdown of the above verses reveals the way to a heart that God can use.

1. *"My determined purpose"*

Jesus had a single purpose. Paul had a single purpose. Any person that was truly used by God was, first and foremost, sold out to God. God moves on behalf of one who is determined to be in line with His causes. Most of us aren't willing to pay the price; and therefore, never receive the joy of knowing the powerful hand of God in our lives.

What is your determined purpose in life? Really, for what do you get up every day and pine?

Do you think that your purpose in your life pleases God? Do you believe that the pursuit of that purpose could possibly be why there is an emptiness deep down somewhere that you have not been able to fill? What do you think would help you?

Paul's Determined Purpose!

2. *"That I may know Him"*

Jesus came for many reasons, one of which was to show us how to act on behalf of the Father in a world that is dying. The only way one can act like or emulate someone is to study and embrace the life, loves, and true purposes of that individual.

Remember the bride of old? She set her mind to really know the one to whom she was betrothed. In the same way, the beginning of a true alignment with God's purposes, so that we can represent Him, is to become a study of the One who walked perfectly on this earth. To know Jesus and His motives allows us to know God and His plans. Anything else is empty and futile, with no real life, no real fulfillment.

Big! Big!

The pursuit of Jesus usually begins for our good and pleasure. He meets our needs, brings us to salvation, and makes us feel good every time we go to Him. That's good for us. There comes a time, however, that we understand the Father's plan more clearly.

He shows us that this relationship is not only about us and our needs. He brings us to an increasing level of maturity. As we begin to understand His character better, we understand and move with His heart more often. As this action, response, action, response relationship continues, we gain more of His heart, and love more and more as He loves. We also begin to identify with His heart so closely that it becomes our heart.

It's a process.

We move in the direction of love.

The closer we get, we actually fall in love with His ways and move from admiration of Him to a love for Him. Getting to know Him and His ways leads to increasing love for Him, because we are changed more and more from being in His presence. Once we know Him, we act in a way that pleases Him because of the love for Him that has been placed in our hearts.

The closer we get, the more we admire His ways.

A second reason for knowing Jesus is in the realization of the great privilege we have been given - to personally and intimately know the King of Kings and the Lord of Lords, the Ruler of all things. It is easy to become passionate about something so wonderful. The enemy of our hearts would love to put out the fire of our zeal and dumb us down.

This is only the King of Kings Who has invited us to get to know Him!

As in any relationship, it is paramount that we never forget what has been done for us and given to us. What more need be said, other than to comment on the astounding foolishness of not maintaining our zeal and proclaiming the wonders of God with passion.

Do you really "know" Jesus?

Why can you say what you said?

----

3. *"That I may in that same way come to know the power outflowing from His resurrection which it exerts over believers"*

It's all because of the cross and the astounding wealth that happened there.

Paul, unlike us, never forgot that all that he was, did, and became were possible only because of Christ's resurrection power, made available to and flowing through him because he belonged to God. When he believed who Christ was, he had access to all of it.

To not fully understand what his covenant held for him was unthinkable. How could he function properly if he had no idea of the extent of the covenants, gifts, promises, commands, God-like purposes, desires, power, and astounding love that he owned because of Jesus? How can we?

What kind of spiritual wealth do you really walk in?

Own this!

Note: Unless you realize that the same power that raised Jesus from the dead is available to raise you and me from our dead, compassion-free lives, we will become frustrated religious fools, striving to become something we will never be. The change of our heritage was a spiritual thing. What it takes to make us like Jesus is also spiritual, only accomplished by the Holy Spirit.

4. *"And that I may so share His sufferings as to be continually transformed in spirit into His likeness"*

We don't like to hear it; but it is, nonetheless, true. To become like Christ, it will cost you everything that you desire in the flesh. To finally renounce everything that hinders you from becoming like Him, you will experience the death of those things one-by-one. The trials that come allow us to choose the sufferings of Christ in order to deny those hindrances any place in our lives.

Let's talk about two kinds of suffering - suffering for Christ, and suffering with Christ.

To care only about what Jesus cares about means you willingly die to what you value. (Did you really hear that with your heart?) God's trials and purging in our lives bring about this heart in us - His heart with all of its characteristics, passions, and zeal. It is the only way to be transformed into His likeness.

We must die to what we value and live for what Jesus values.

Paul knew it and accepted it fully. It then became a lifelong joy. He joined God in killing his "flesh" man to become like Jesus. His joining with God against everything that denied Christ in his life, instead of fighting God over those issues (sin,) allowed the Lord to flow unhindered through him.

Paul joined God in killing everything that denied Christ in his life.

Because he did not cling to fleshly desires, he could take on the desires of his Lord. He felt the pain of those who would be separated from his Father for eternity. He understood the desperate needs of those around him. He had compassion on those who were in desperate need. After putting aside his flesh through the power of the Holy Spirit, he could take on the heart of Jesus that his heavenly Father willingly offered while they were in communion.

Note: Study Paul's life and see how God was able to mightily use a very ordinary man, who had few communicative skills and little physical prowess in person, to do extraordinary things and express supernatural wonders that ring from centuries past into today's world - as alive with the power of God as when they were first penned.

Remember the covenants that required your signature? Remember the heart of the bride of old? She was motivated by the love of her groom as she learned of him, and not because of the stipulations of her contract.

Note: Later in this study you will understand the spirit of suffering. Apply these pages to that portion of the study.

Could it be that the best interests of Jesus have not been the motivation for your coming to salvation? Could that heart motive be the reason that your walk with Him is less than fulfilling, and not really anointed?

What do you think that you should do about it?

Paul knew that he was dead in his heart. He knew that only God could lift him out from under the weight of dead religion and a works-oriented, fruitless lifestyle.

5. *"That if possible I may attain to the spiritual and moral resurrection that lifts me out from among the dead even while in the body"*

Nobody can kill a dead man. Nobody took Jesus' life; He willingly gave it away. Nobody took Paul's life. Through his suffering (willing denial of self motives,) he found the freedom that Jesus possessed. He was free from the holds and fears that any man could put on him. The love that Jesus exhibited to him and through him overcame any and all other reasons for living.

The perfect love and life of Christ flowed through him, so the most horrible sin to him would have been disobedience to his Father God, not anything that was done to him in the flesh. He walked in heavenly places, above the death and decay of the world, while still in the body. So can we.

Do you really desire to have your life be in perfect alignment with the intensions of your Father God? Elaborate!

It's time to really assess why we are doing what we are doing.

Jesus never owned His life, it belonged to His Father.

Paul had grown to no longer own his life.

Do you really want that, or is the way you have been seeing your association with God working well enough for you, giving you total peace with God and freedom from fear? How do you think it's working for God?

Do you care if God is able to use you fully? Do you want to be part of His heart for your generation? Does it matter to you at all if your existence is counted as a positive component in God's eternal plan? Elaborate!

Getting honest with God.

What a concept!

Get honest with yourself and with God. Really take the time to wait on God to reveal your heart to you. Journal your findings for future reference and comparison while He works in you.

So... God has determined to conquer you, so that He can bless you with the life of His Son in you and flowing through you.

Jesus joyously existed for the good of His Father and of others. To say that you are following Him, you must have the same heart motives. You can no longer have even the slightest notion to resemble who you are at present or who you used to be, and still say you are a true follower of Christ.

Prayers and thoughts

THE TURNING

Do you hear it?
Do you hear the call to remove all that stops My life
from totally eliminating your life of sin?
You have called yourself by My Name for some time.
Now I desire you to look, act, and truly be like Me from your heart.
Submit to Me and I will change you.

I John 2:6 Amp "Whoever says he abides in Him ought [as a personal debt] to walk and conduct himself in the same way in which He walked and conducted Himself."

I Peter 2:19-21 Amp "For one is regarded favorably (is approved, acceptable, and thankworthy) if, as in the sight of God, he endures the pain of unjust suffering.

20 [After all] what kind of glory [is there in it] if, when you do wrong and are punished for it, you take it patiently? But if you bear patiently with suffering [which results] when you do right and that is undeserved, it is acceptable and pleasing to God.

21 For even to this you were called [it is inseparable from your vocation]. For Christ also suffered for you, leaving you [His personal] example, so that you should follow in His footsteps."

For how much of your life have you attempted to be good before the Lord in your own strength? So far, how much of your walk with Him has been about you and your needs? Explain!

How have you fared?

Mr. Baxter

Tony walked around the newly completed house for one final inspection. As he turned the corner on the north end of the building, he saw Mr. Baxter's new Lexus pull up into the driveway. An intense hatred for this man who had been his boss for twenty years swelled in his heart.

"Twenty years of my sweat bought that car," he said to himself.

The last straw and the determining factor that caused him to finally submit his resignation was Mr. Baxter's audacity in building this stupid house. "I want it built first-class," Baxter said in his usual, condescending tone. "It's important to me that it be well-built, so spend what you think is necessary to get the job done right."

Because of his already hectic schedule and his work overload, Tony was furious that he was asked to do this additional task. "Today is the day. Today, I'm going to tell him that it's all over. I can't stand him anymore!"

As he neared the car, Tony remembered all of the subtle ways he had used the construction project to vent his anger for the times over the years that he was expected to work long hours for nothing; or how, when he did get a raise in pay, it hardly met his increased living expenses.

"I can't even buy my own house," he thought. "And even if I could, I wouldn't have the time for it."

Although this house looked beautiful to the untrained eye, Tony made sure that the people for whom he had built it would one day look at Baxter with disdain because of the trouble they were having with it. The use of inferior products wherever they could be hidden, and marginal contractors, hired solely for their low bids, insured premature deterioration and guaranteed aging. Although everything looked in order, plaster cracks, leaks, and a myriad of other problems would eventually be the plight of whoever lived there because of corners that were cut to defy Baxter. That didn't matter to Tony, however. He would be gone, and it would be Baxter's problem. That simple thought gave Tony the quiet satisfaction of personal revenge.

By the time Tony reached the car, Mr. Baxter had gotten out and was looking at one of the discount shrubs near the driveway. It was already showing signs of wilting.

"Is everything completed to your satisfaction?" Mr. Baxter spoke, just as Tony was about to tell him of his decision to quit, now that the project was over.

"Yes, sir," was Tony's immediate, somewhat off-balance response. Tony resisted his almost overpowering need to vent all of the built-up hatred he felt for this man, who was always in control.

"So, it's finished first-class," Mr. Baxter continued, before Tony could again say anything.

"Yes, sir, it is," Tony assured him. Knowing the truth about how shabbily the house was really built brought a smile to his face. Mr. Baxter, misinterpreting the smile, smiled back.

"Well, then," Mr. Baxter began, "it's yours. Thank you for all of the loyal service you've given me over the years."

Mr. Baxter handed Tony the keys to his new house, patted him on the back and drove away, leaving Tony speechless; staring open mouthed at the retreating car.

Note: Stop now and really ponder this situation. What is your immediate comment on the story?

Oops!

Now think the story through and bring it to some possible conclusions, relating it to our relationship with the Lord. Picture Tony living in the house and knowing its condition. Think of him talking to his wife in weaker moments when she possibly wants to talk to Mr. Baxter about the horrible house that he gave them. What is Tony going to say to Mr. Baxter should he find out about all of the trouble the house is causing?

If you were Tony, would you desire to face your sin one day? Yes or no. Why?

Have you ever been mad at the Lord for allowing you to go through some difficult times?

Do you see a parallel attitude there somewhere?

It Was All for Tony

What astounding foolishness on Tony's part. Think of it. The house that he was building was really for his benefit. All along, his master's plans were to provide a safe, comfortable haven for Tony and his wife and family - people for whom Mr. Baxter truly cared.

Mr. Baxter, his master, gave Tony the freedom to build it in any way he desired. Tony, however, in his blindness and foolishness, was unable to see past his own needs and selfish desires in order to understand the true purpose for all that he was doing. His hardships were, in essence, for his own good.

How Foolish We Are

Herein lies one of the most wonderful truths of our association with God because of Jesus. God's part of our covenant is to make sure that we do not remain unlike Jesus. He is continually reminding us that we have sold our old life to Him. (Actually, He bought it from us. The price was the blood of Jesus.)

If we attempt to hold on to our lives, striving to maintain any semblance of control over them, we will lose their real value. If we voluntarily lose our lives, willingly taking the posture of Jesus by giving everything away to God, we gain more than we could ever believe possible. When we choose to make these fleeting moments in time that we call our lifetime all about the glory of the Lord, He shows us that He has far more for us than if we had been concerned only for ourselves.

It works like this: If we really do give everything away, He draws so close to us that our nature is superseded by His nature; and consequently, we care less and less about our own needs the more we come to Him. (Supersede – to force out of use as inferior, to take the place, room, or position of.) Our surrender causes the Lord to develop in us the character of Christ - a nature that is deeply in love with the Father and wanting only His desires - in place of our selfish, carnal character. The freedom achieved through our submission is the really good news of the Gospel of Jesus Christ. God lovingly brings us out of the horrors of our fleshly nature.

God, our Father, is at all times showing us that intimate fellowship with Him is the position for which each of us has been created. We are made to function hand-in-hand with our Father in Heaven. The guidelines on how to function that way have been made available to us in His Word. His constant urgings to be like Christ, to lay our lives down, to deny ourselves, to take up our cross, and to make God first in our lives are love messages to the

God is allowing you to build your life any way that you desire.

He places His life in us when we come to Jesus; then He adds and adds Himself each time we surrender.

133

bridal heart of Jesus. He also promises to do everything to initiate and accomplish those changes.

True intimacy is our privilege. If we look to our own needs and place our Lord somewhere behind them, our precious, loving Father promises to bring His priorities back in order in our lives. He has committed to do so. We have committed to need Him to do it.

How do you really feel about an invitation to get intimate with the God of the universe?

What are you feeling now?

Why do you think that we are failing to live in the freedom ordained for us?

Haggai 1:2-14 Amp "Thus says the Lord of hosts: This people say, The time is not yet come that the Lord's house should be rebuilt [although Cyrus had ordered it done eighteen years before].

3 Then came the word of the Lord by Haggai the prophet, saying,

4 Is it time for you yourselves to dwell in your paneled houses while this house [of the Lord] lies in ruins?

5 Now therefore thus says the Lord of hosts: Consider your ways and set your mind on what has come to you.

6 You have sown much, but you have reaped little; you eat, but you do not have enough; you drink, but you do not have your fill; you clothe yourselves, but no one is warm; and he who earns wages has earned them to put them in a bag with holes in it.

7 Thus says the Lord of hosts: Consider your ways (your previous and present conduct) and how you have fared.

8 Go up to the hill country and bring lumber and rebuild [My] house, and I will take pleasure in it and I will be glorified, says the Lord [by accepting it as done for My glory and by displaying My glory in it].

9 You looked for much [harvest], and behold, it came to little; and even when you brought that home, I blew it away. Why? says the Lord of hosts. Because of My house, which lies waste while you yourselves run each man to his own house [eager to build and adorn it].

10 Therefore the heavens above you [for your sake] withhold the dew, and the earth withholds its produce.

11 And I have called for a drought upon the land and the hill country, upon the grain, the fresh wine, the oil, upon what the ground brings forth, upon men and cattle, and upon all the [wearisome] toil of [men's] hands.

12 Then Zerubbabel son of Shealtiel and Joshua son of Jehozadak, the high priest, with all the remnant of the people [who had returned from captivity], listened to and obeyed the voice of the Lord their God [not vaguely or partly, but completely, according to] the words of Haggai the prophet, since the Lord their God had sent him, and the people [reverently] feared and [worshipfully] turned to the Lord.

13 Then Haggai, the Lord's messenger, spoke the Lord's message to the people saying, I am with you, says the Lord.

14 And the Lord aroused the spirit of Zerubbabel son of Shealtiel, governor of Judah, and the spirit of Joshua son of Jehozadak, the high priest, and the spirit of all the remnant of the people, so that they came and labored on the house of the Lord of hosts, their God..."

But We Don't Get It

Few of us realize the magnitude of harm we are doing to the representation of Jesus to others by our inferior Christ-likeness. Our false spirituality and hardened hearts not only harm us, but also those who are brought in our path.

God has asked us to build the temple, our bodies, for His full presence; and we spend most of our time avoiding the true cost of the building process. The reason we are supposed to breathe is for the Lord to bring His very breath to others through us.

Do you have anything to say to Jesus at this time? If He were standing in front of you discussing your life, what would be the gist of the conversation - on His part, on your part? Journal your communication elsewhere if needed. It is something that would be very important to have available in the future.

Nothing's really working because our priorities are wrong.

Did you ever think that even though you were doing the typical Christian stuff, you might really be doing harm to the work of the Lord because you weren't representing Jesus properly?

135

The World Misses Jesus in Us

Hebrews 12:12-13 The Living Bible "*So take a new grip with your tired hands, stand firm on your shaky legs,*
13 and mark out a straight, smooth path for your feet so that those who follow you, though weak and lame, will not fall and hurt themselves, but become strong."

The plan of God is that we be removed from the world, trained in the ways of Christ through trials and subsequent total submission; and then return to those who don't know Jesus with our wealth. Our lives should be exhibiting Him to them in order to bring them out of darkness, all for God's praise and His glory.

It's time to step back and take a real good look, isn't it?

Our pursuit of comfort and the selfish fulfillment of our own needs override the plans of God for our lives. Most of the time, it doesn't even register in our minds how far we've fallen. It's time to step back from everything, and take a strong look at what the Lord really requires of us and what we committed to long ago.

Hosea 13:6 NIV "*When I fed them, they were satisfied; when they were satisfied, they became proud; then they forgot me.*"

This is where most of us really are.

So… Here's where most of us are standing at present. We are beginning to realize that God is calling us to a deeper walk with Him. He is wooing our hearts to become holy vessels of service and Christ's love for the times in which we live. We have looked around and found that most of those who say that they are following Jesus are really trying to make God follow their own plans. What has become painfully obvious is that we realize that we are included in that lot of poor, empty souls.

Do you believe that Father God is mad at you at this time, or is He delighted that you see what you are seeing in yourself?

Those who choose to hear and see what the Lord is doing are becoming more and more aware that the times in which we live could very well be the end of the end times. Most of what is needed for Jesus to return has been Biblically fulfilled. Almost everything is in place, so it could happen at the next twinkling of an eye. Even if we are mistaken about the urgency of the times, the calling to holiness is very real and becoming increasingly clear.

What is so disarming is that with the heralding we are hearing, we are also painfully aware that we are not prepared for whatever is planned on God's calendar. We are very much like the betrothed bride who one day came to the painful realization of who she was not. She was not like her groom. Our "business-as-usual" Christianity has a stench about it that reminds us of the rottenness of the world of which we are supposed to have come out, but we seem helpless to do anything about it.

How clear is the call to holiness in your life? Are you really aware of the heralding that is ringing in the ears of those who have ears to hear it? Do you really care if the world has a clear picture of Jesus through your life?

If your answer is no, you really are on dangerous ground. You need the Lord to change your heart to even want His will and His way in your life.

Get real with God. Ask Him to give you a heart of repentance. Don't give up until you get the proper heart attitude with God. It may take a while, so don't become discouraged.

Remember, this is no surprise to the Lord. He knew of this day and is very pleased with you if you come to Him honestly. If you don't, you can be assured that the Lord will devise means in your life to get you to repent of your hardened heart.

God will keep His end of the covenant He has entered into with you, and yours, too, because it is humanly impossible for us to do so. (Refer to the section on covenant later in this study to understand why.)

Prayers and thoughts

Let's Look at Some Reasons Why We May Be Hindered from Selling Out Completely to God

In our pride, we believe that we are well fed because God has given us morsels of His presence. The cost of becoming like Christ appears to be far in the distance, for somebody else, or too high a price to pay. Little do we know the overwhelming benefits of walking in intimacy with our God and the comparative loss involved in not doing so.

The view is incredible from your knees at the foot of the cross.

We will never be able to draw close to God unless we deal with the sin in our lives. All sin must be dealt with, so that it can be forgiven by God. Everything starts when we once again kneel at the foot of the cross. It is a reserved position for anyone who desires to go deeper with God. It is the mandatory position for the remnant bride in preparation for the return of Jesus.

Only from the cross can we see clearly the plan of God for our lives and the price we need to pay for the honor of presenting His life to those who are dying in their sin. It is, in essence, the same situation that Jesus faced. He had to die, so that others could live. We must die to our old nature, so that His nature can be seen in us - all so that others might see Jesus through us and embrace life.

Psalm 32:5 Amp "I acknowledged my sin to You, and my iniquity I did not hide. I said, I will confess my transgressions to the Lord [continually unfolding the past till all is told] - then You [instantly] forgave me the guilt and iniquity of my sin. . ."

Repentance is fun!

It's sort of like being bathed in clean water and getting "squeaky" clean.

Do you believe that an attitude of repentance indicates condemnation? Why or why not?

Are you seeing that the knowledge of our need for repentance is the first step to healing? I am not talking about our personal healing, but the healing needed in our relationship with our Lord? Why or why not?

Repentance Brings Freedom

Don't confuse God's intended life of continual repentance, the continual washing of God's forgiveness, and the freedom it leads to on a daily basis with a position of continually dwelling on your sins and subsequent feelings of worthlessness. The first brings a joyous life, while the second denies your full acceptance by God through the shed blood of Jesus. The denial of that atonement brings depression and fear.

Did you really hear this?

Note: Repentance is not scary. In fact, once you realize the freedoms that an attitude of repentance brings, it becomes a pleasant continual process, bringing continual washing and cleansing. Paul stated that he always remained in right standing before God and man. He lived a life of repentance, continually being on guard for any offense that would stand in the way of his freedom with his Lord or those around him.

Living a life of repentance brings freedom from any form of condemnation.

Acts 24:16 Amp "Therefore I always exercise and discipline myself [mortifying my body, deadening my carnal affections, bodily appetites, and worldly desires, endeavoring in all respects] to have a clear (unshaken, blameless) conscience, void of offense toward God and men."

I love to be free from any hindrance in my relationship with my Lord. I also hate any distance between fellow believers and me. It is absolutely necessary to attempt to make all wrongs right. If the other party cannot forgive, or cannot see the need to reconcile, the Lord will cover that. Make sure that all is in order between you and everyone as best as you can. Liberty is a wonderful experience.

Do you really believe this? Explain!

If You Have No Desire to be Right with God
and Right with Others,
You Need to Examine Yourself for the Sin of Unforgiveness

You will have no passion for Jesus, if your only passion is to be in control of everything and everyone around you.

Unforgiveness is a controlling sin. Along with its root sin of pride and its companion sins of anger, hatred, and murder, it causes more weakness in the body of Christ than most have imagined. The Bible says that if you ask with the wrong motives, you will not receive.

> *"[Or] you do ask [God for them] and yet fail to receive, because you ask with wrong purpose and evil, selfish motives."*   James 4:3a Amp

Hidden beneath many prayers are motives driven by the sins that accompany unforgiveness. Therefore, because of His integrity, God cannot move on your behalf.

Let's Examine the Sin of Unforgiveness
Before We Go Any Further

The root sin of unforgiveness is pride. Because that is rarely recognized, it is never really dealt with as such; and we evade submitting the root sin to the kind of total Lordship we presented previously in this book.

I Will Remain in Charge –
the Antithesis of Submission to the Lordship of Jesus Christ

Playing God is a frightening and dangerous position to occupy.

Anyone harboring unforgiveness toward another has, in essence, determined to hold that sin (real or imagined) over that person and has chosen to be the "lord" of that incident or grieving situation. The dominance and control exercised by the unforgiving party denies all that was promised to God when he/she committed to the Lordship of Jesus in all areas. This area, therefore, remains under the dominance of Satan. Pride caused him to be expelled from the presence of God, and he is delighted when we follow his lead in any area of our lives.

If God has forgiven the person who has offended you but you won't, are you not telling Him that your position is loftier than His? In light of the truth, that's not possible, is it? What do you need to do at this point?

God demands that we forgive if we desire to be truly free. He even shows us, in Luke's account of the crucifixion, that Jesus forgave all those who harmed Him; and also the repentant thief just before he died. We must do the same.

Unforgiveness, although often deeply masked by wounds, scars, and self-pity, is one of the greatest causes of weakness in the body of Christ and it will cripple any attempt to draw close to the Lord if left unconfessed. Once this main stronghold is acknowledged and confessed, a tide of healings and freedoms are able to surface and it can be brought under the Lordship of Jesus Christ.

Do you have any unforgiveness toward anyone in your life?

What about forgiving yourself?

Have you even forgiven yourself for failing God so many times? (Remember, you are totally forgiven by Him when you repent. You are under the blood. Remember also, God knew how many times you would fail Him and He still asked you to be His through the Holy Spirit. Your sin is no surprise to Him.)

If God forgives you, but you won't accept His forgiveness by holding that sin over yourself, so to speak, have you not told Him that your perspective carries more weight than His? In reality, that's not true, is it? What are you going to do now?

141

I Cor 11:26-32 Amp "For every time you eat this bread and drink this cup, you are representing and signifying and proclaiming the fact of the Lord's death until He comes [again].

27 So then whoever eats the bread or drinks the cup of the Lord in a way that is unworthy [of Him] will be guilty of [profaning and sinning against] the body and blood of the Lord.

28 Let a man [thoroughly] examine himself, and [only when he has done] so should he eat of the bread and drink of the cup.

29 For anyone who eats and drinks without discriminating and recognizing with due appreciation that [it is Christ's] body, eats and drinks a sentence (a verdict of judgment) upon himself.

30 That [careless and unworthy participation] is the reason many of you are weak and sickly, and quite enough of you have fallen into the sleep of death.

31 For if we searchingly examined ourselves [detecting our shortcomings and recognizing our own condition], we should not be judged and penalty decreed [by the divine judgment].

32 But when we [fall short and] are judged by the Lord, we are disciplined and chastened, so that we may not [finally] be condemned [to eternal punishment along] with the world."

Eating of the bread and drinking of the cup is making covenant as God sees it. Most of the church has fallen into the sleep of death. As a dead person cannot be awakened, there is very little that can stir the hearts of most people who call themselves Christians.

The saying that approximately twenty percent of the church performs like the church when called upon is no joke, but an abomination. The unforgiving, sin-filled church is truly asleep as if dead. Even many of those who are attempting to move with Jesus are weak and sickly, either spiritually or physically, because of sin.

Just like one who is feeble due to illness has little power for warfare, most of us stagger about having little effect even on our family, neighbors, or friends who aren't saved, let alone on the enemies of the gospel. It is impossible to love or be passionate with such hindrances.

Did you know that you were lying to God?

We are under the judgment of God (His hand is bringing us to repentance) for covenanting with Him, while choosing to remain in some of our sins. Our pride, unforgiveness, anger, hatred, selfishness, worry, fear, etc., judge us before Him. No wonder the world can't see Jesus in us! We don't even mean what we say to God.

Note: Take the time now to sit quietly and reflect on your attitude about communion and all of its wonders. It is covenant. We get to restate our desire to be in covenant with God each time we participate. In covenant with God, it's easy to remember that all He is and all He has is ours, too; but what about that part of the covenant where all we are (or aren't) and all we have are His, too? And consequently, He is free to do what He wants with us, making any necessary changes. That's what we agreed to when we came into relationship with Him through Jesus. Those little words, "Yes, Lord," pack a mighty big punch!

Our Words Have Lost Their Meaning Through Loose Usage, but God's Haven't

Read God's Word through His eyes. He means what He says. When He talks about salvation through the blood of His Son, He means it. When He says that we should devote ourselves to Him as our life's purpose, He means it.

When He says that if we call ourselves Christians, we should walk in this world as Jesus did - full of passion, limitless love, and spiritual power, always, in whatever circumstances - He means it. No matter how often we might choose to misinterpret or realign the Word of God to prove that we can somehow remain comfortable, at ease, and self-serving; God has said that He will do all in His power to bring us to repentance, so that we might become like Jesus so that the world can see Him in us - and He means it!

Determine this very moment to walk only in truth.

Note: Before you move on to the next lesson, allow the Lord to examine your heart in any area that we have discussed. Wait on Him to reveal any hidden agendas, false notions, and harbored sins even if it takes days. Get everything right with Him. It is foundational for any further study of His Word and His ways.

Write down any areas that you think are not completely dealt with, even though they have been submitted to the Lord. This will allow you to reference this section to see if any of these are in the way, as you continue walking with the Lord, submitting to His will in what He shows you. It will also allow you to watch the power of the Lord at work in your heart. You will be surprised at how much your honest heart pleases Him.

Make sure that you have been able to sign all of the agreements that we have covered. If you cannot do so, something is still wrong in your commitment to God. To go any further in this study would be playing religious head games. You will gain nothing and possibly deeply offend your God in the process. Do whatever it takes to get things right. Forgive everyone. Mend fences. Fix every relationship that you can. Accept your Lord's love for you.

You are valuable.
Remember that you are intensely loved by God.

Be blessed as you go on to the different lessons in this guidebook.

Prayers and thoughts

From Our Father's Heart

May I tell you one of the wonders of Our relationship?
I am always with you!
I understand that you have heard that saying so often
that it has lost its real meaning,
so please listen with an open heart.
The work of the cross accomplished many wonderful things.
Some are so wonderful
that your mind cannot comprehend what they are,
so I am not going to share them with you until you are with Me.
One completed work that you can understand, however,
is the fact that I have become near to you once again
because of what Jesus did.
Spiritual law separated us before the cross.
That law has been fulfilled in Christ
and now We have free access to one another.
That means that nothing can separate us again.
This fact makes the difference
between you being limited to your miniscule, human limitations
and having full access to My boundless, spiritual nature.
I now reside in you.
You have been made alive in your inner being
by My Holy Spirit.
I bring My world to your world through you.
If you ever really comprehend what that means,
you would never again
choose to dabble in the limitations of your world.
You would become a study of the cross
to find out what has been provided for you
and why I have provided it.
You would seek real wisdom and flee from listening
to your old, selfish nature, which limits your perspective.
You would rejoice in Our relationship as I flowed through you
with wonders that have limitless, spiritual impact
on everything and everyone with whom you come in contact.
You would be free in a world that continually attempts
to place bondages on you.
You would be able to rise above every limitation
because of the freedom that I have given you.
I am with you, in you, and for you.
Come to Me and allow Me to show you
how wonderful that really is!

*Can you hear
the joy
resounding
through this
message?*

*Wow!
God is
really for
us!*

145

Ephesians 3:16-19 Amp "May He grant you out of the rich treasury of His glory to be strengthened and reinforced with mighty power in the inner man by the [Holy] Spirit [Himself indwelling your innermost being and personality].

17) May Christ through your faith [actually] dwell (settle down, abide, make His permanent home) in your hearts! May you be rooted deep in love and founded securely on love,

18) That you may have the power and be strong to apprehend and grasp with all the saints [God's devoted people, the experience of that love] what is the breadth and length and height and depth [of it];

19) [That you may really come] to know [practically, through experience for yourselves] the love of Christ, which far surpasses mere knowledge [without experience]; that you may be filled [through all your being] unto all the fullness of God [may have the richest measure of the divine Presence, and become a body wholly filled and flooded with God Himself]!"

This spiritual stuff often gets confusing and far beyond my comprehension, if I try to figure it all out with my pea brain. My mind gets so cluttered that I almost become immobilized with it all. That is why my mind is not the place to discern spiritual things. That is also why most of the body of Christ gets bogged down with contentions, judgments, and disagreements. We are trying to grasp the spiritual with our carnal minds. It doesn't work.

Because of our acceptance of the work of the cross, we have become spiritual. Our bodies are dying daily, but our spirits have been made alive. Our inner man – the eternal, spiritual person that we really have become - comprehends, accepts, and thrives on things of the Spirit. It has been made alive through Christ, and will continue with Him throughout eternity. That is where we should allow ourselves to be guided daily by the Holy Spirit within us, not in our thinking and reasoning abilities.

At times, I am almost paralyzed by my inabilities. I look at those around me and sometimes become hamstrung with who I am not, in comparison to who they appear to be because of their worldly presence and achievements. To my mind, and by the world's standards, I am a failure. In those times, I realize that my incapabilities are exactly what drive me to God's capabilities. He is my power. He is my dwelling place, my real life - not what I see and feel.

I am delighted when I am strengthened with power and might by the power of the Holy Spirit in my "inner being."

The Beginning
(At Least as Far as We Are Told)

This is important to know, so that we can understand how privileged we really are. It is time to become grateful!

Long before mankind ever came upon the scene, God was busy at work unfolding His plans and His purposes. In the Bible, we are told of two creations, the angelic creation and the mankind creation (Adam and Eve.)

We are told very little about the angelic creation. We do know that there was a great rebellion and one third of the angels were separated from God for eternity. Some were cast down to this earth where they are used in the refining process of mankind, functioning as demons; others are chained in utter darkness until God's determined time. They had no chance to repent and come back to God as far as we know.

The second creation - mankind - committed the same rebellion. In fact, that same rebellion was stimulated in Adam and Eve by the same fallen angel leader. He had committed rebellion in the timeless past and it got him kicked out of fellowship with God. This time, however, even though the same sin of rebellion was initiated by him and committed by the mankind creation, God chose to make a way for all of mankind to be reconciled to Himself.

Same guy, same old trick.

Only this time God really fooled Him.

His foul deed set in motion his permanent defeat.

God pursues mankind to this day to bring as many as will come back to Him. Most of us call this the mercy of God, His "salvation plan." It came through Jesus Christ.

II Sam. 14:14 NIV "God … devises ways so that a banished person may not remain estranged from him."

Why don't you pause for a while to find gratefulness in your heart for your loving heavenly Father? Write down what your inner man wants to express to Him. Mark these two pages, so that you can keep a running account of what the Holy Spirit shows you. Come back here when you grow weary or discouraged.

The Covenant - a Prelude to Jesus

For an in-depth study on
covenant, listen to the audio message,
"The Covenant,"
on our Web site,
(www.christspassionatelife.com)

"The Covenant"

Our present day Bible is divided into two testaments or
covenants – the old and new covenants. Each apply to man's
relationship with God. Throughout the Old Testament, or old
covenant, God would make agreements (or covenants) with
people who had a heart for Him. These agreements would be
entered into to fulfill some purpose that God had in mind.

Most of these agreements would be broken due to man's
inability to keep them. When one covenant failed, God would find
another honest heart to agree with and function through. During
these times, God would also have man make covenants with one
another, when it would fulfill intermediate steps in His plan in
posturing all of creation for the arrival of Jesus. These agreements
combined - those with God and man and those man to man -
would further the cause of God until the proper appointed time,
when He would make an unbreakable agreement with Himself
(Jesus.)

*This will
show you
the "why"
of the
cross.*

Enter Jesus

Have you ever wondered why Jesus had to be born of a
woman? Most of us would say so that He could be part of
mankind to experience all that we go through. That is correct, but
only to a point.

This is so cool!

Have you ever wondered why the seed that allowed Him to
become man was planted by God through the Holy Spirit in
woman instead of being planted by man (Joseph?) The common
answer would be because He had to have God's nature to claim
to be the Son of God. That too is absolutely true, but that is also
only part of the answer.

Have you ever wondered how these two factors, Jesus
being born of mankind (woman) and fathered by God, completed
God's unbreakable agreement with mankind? We basically
understand the "God being man" part, but does the phrase "man
in God" ever cross your mind when you observe Jesus?

149

Have you settled in your heart that this godly agreement is all that is needed for your assurance of eternal association with God, if you've fully surrendered to the personal Lordship it has created for you? It should, and here's why.

Anatomy of a Covenant

You need to own this.

We are going to first study the laws and characteristics of covenants made between two parties and show that God established them to be a "type" of the final covenant He made with Jesus. Covenants were binding agreements on the parties involved and also on all future generations represented by those participating in the covenant – in other words, all of the unborn seed in the loins of the covenant makers.

To break covenant would mean, in most cases, death to the violating party. Depending on the terms of the covenant agreement, that death sentence, or whatever consequence was agreed upon, would apply to every generation stipulated in the agreement.

If, for example, the covenant agreement stated that all of the terms of the covenant applied to the person who initially made covenant and the four generations that followed, each of those succeeding generations was bound by the covenant as if they had made it themselves. They would be recipients of all of the benefits, but if they violated the covenant, they would also receive whatever consequences were part of the agreement.

This was an unbreakable, life-involving commitment that was enforced by the law of the land. It was no small thing to enter into covenant with someone and of great consequence to anyone who took the terms lightly.

Whenever a covenant was entered into, there were many elements that needed to be fulfilled and many formal, significant actions taken before it was binding on both parties. First and foremost, both parties had to have a desire to enter into covenant and then had to agree to its terms. It would be foolish to commit to something this binding and not like the terms and consequences to which you were committing.

For example, one reason for two parties to enter into covenant would be for the sake of protection and survival. If one person had extreme wealth, but no one to protect his money, it would behoove him to enter into covenant with someone who had a vast army of warriors, but no money to feed and equip them. The money of one party would be used for the equipping of the other's army. That person's army would always be available to protect the other's money.

150

It is important to note at this point that each party became legally "one" as far as covenant law was concerned. The man with the army could go to the bank and withdraw whatever he needed for his troops as if he was the other party. *He would go in the other party's "name"* and legally take whatever he needed without asking permission of the other party, if he chose to do so. Because of covenant, all the money was his as much as it was the property of the original owner. The bank recognizes him not as himself, but as the person with whom he is in covenant. He came in the name of His covenant partner.

(Notice our prayers to God. We come to Him in Jesus' Name, not our own. This has become a ritual as we say it, but God recognizes our coming as if Jesus was coming with requests, praises, and petitions.)

In the same manner, the wealthy man could command the troops of his covenant partner whenever needed within the terms of their agreement, because they had become legally his. He had purchased authority over them. He was free to do anything with them that was necessary to protect his money. (Please ponder these situations as they are presented and begin to see how crucial it is to know of this authority when you are learning about our covenant with God because of Jesus. Also observe what God means when He says that the marriage covenant is a picture of the mystery of Jesus and His church.)

Each party mutually "owned" the "wealth" of the other in accordance with the terms stated in the covenant agreement. (Every future generation represented at the covenant commencement had the same rights if either party died, but only if the first party died. The covenant automatically passed down to the specific generations stated. The one making covenant had to die in order to have the next generations receive the benefits of the covenant terms. Think through what is being said and begin to understand the need for the cross of Jesus Christ as He was making covenant for us with the Father!)

Upon entering covenant, there were formal steps taken to assure its validity and formalize its terms. Whenever the terms were agreed upon, it was done in front of witnesses, usually at a banquet or supper of some sort. At that meal, the terms, conditions, and reasons for the covenant were stated and usually sealed by drinking a cup of wine. (Remember the cup of betrothal earlier in this study, and the cup that Jesus presented at the Last Supper. Jesus' cup was the cup of the new covenant!)

Most covenants were blood covenants, meaning that blood would be shed in one form or another to seal the agreement. In covenants person-to-person, a cut on the wrist or across the chest

The two became one.

The closest we have today is the marriage covenant, and it is so diluted that it is unrecognizable as a covenant.

This just gets "gooder."

There had to be a death of the covenant maker, so that the terms and privileges of the covenant could be passed on to the others mentioned in the original covenant agreement

would be made and then the parties would hold the cuts together while stating and agreeing on the terms. After this ritual, usually black pitch or dark coloring would be placed in the wound, so that the wound would remain visible for the life of the covenant makers.

In the case of the parties who made the above agreement, if robbers should ever confront the wealthy man, all he had to do was show his scar to them. Whoever was foolish enough to pursue foul play was automatically confronting the man with the armies. His covenant partner was committed to avenge any confrontation unto his own death, if need be.

Remember, everyone present - either physically or represented as future generations - would not be able to "walk" in the covenant while the original covenant makers lived. As soon as they died, the next in line and everyone in succeeding generations included in the original covenant automatically inherited and became obligated to the covenant, with all of its power and promises, as if they had made it themselves. (Everyone who eventually comes to Christ was "in" Christ when He made covenant just as any unborn generational seed was in the covenant makers when they covenanted one to another.)

Back to Jesus

Jesus had to be 100% God to have the integrity to be able to make an unbreakable covenant with His Father. Therefore, He had to be "Fathered" by the Holy Spirit.

He had to be 100% man to be able to represent all of mankind (man and woman) when the covenant in heaven was made. Therefore, He had to be "born of a woman."

Contemplate on that last statement. If that concept was not powerful enough for you, get ready to be really blessed.

When Jesus and His Father entered into the everlasting covenant, He and His Father stood there for Themselves – God with God and also God with all of the spiritually unborn seed that were in Jesus (you and me.) That means that Jesus was not only our representation on the cross; but we, according to the terms of covenant, were with Him as He and the Father agreed that "all was finished." Jesus took the blood that He shed - not the blood of goats and cattle as in the passing covenant, but His very own blood - to the mercy seat in heaven and placed it there to satisfy all of the requirements for fallen man to be reconciled with His Father.

Jesus had to die, so that we could inherit His life!!

Are you excited yet?

Jesus!

100% God and 100% man

He could take our place and make covenant for us as God.

152

In the place of His tomb, after He had been raised from the dead - when Jesus would not allow Mary to touch Him - He was saying that He had not yet gone to the Father with His redemptive blood. To have been touched in any way before that happened would have defiled the blood offering and nullified the cross.

His death assured us that all of the promises that He made with His Father God would be "legally" fulfilled. Every one of us who has been, or will anytime in the future be, "born of Him" (Jesus) inherits those promises because he/she was "in" Him as part of His unborn spiritual seed. That applies even now and any time in the future before He comes for His own.

To assure that all of the covenant promises are as fresh as the day they were made, Jesus now is alive as the mediator of the covenant promises. He makes sure, as it were, that we inherit the promises that He and His Father made.

Do you really understand the implications of you being "in Jesus" when He and His Father sealed the covenant for eternity?

What an Astounding Arrangement!

The Bible states that in the heavenlies, a day is like a thousand years and a thousand years are like a day to the Lord. To God, Jesus died only two days ago, so to speak. That blood is fresh.

Why did God the Father spend hundreds of generations, the death of His Son, over two thousand years since the resurrection of Jesus, and who knows how many more years in the future to bring rebellious, fallen mankind back into fellowship with Himself? Being God, He could have willed it into being. He also could have found more convenient, quicker ways to accomplish the forgiveness of man.

Why do you think He did it?

153

Why did He even provide forgiveness for us? He didn't do it for the angelic creation. Why us?

God has eternal plans that are much bigger than we could ever imagine.

Our job is to get in line with those plans in the way He desires.

If we observe all that has been accomplished through Jesus as "about us" and that God simply "loved us enough to do all of that" as the only reason, we will become self-centered recipients of an astounding gift, with a heart that craves that the Giver continue to bestow more gifts on us because we somehow must deserve it. Why, we must be the center of all of His plans. Oops! That is how most of us really feel - that we are the only object of God's ideas, God's devotion, and God's plans.

Where Then, Do We Put This?

Eph. 3:9-12 NIV "… this grace was given to me; to preach to the Gentiles the unsearchable riches of Christ, and to make plain to everyone the administration of this mystery, which for ages past was kept hidden in God, who created all things.

10) His intent was that now, through the church, the manifold wisdom of God should be made known to the rulers and authorities in the heavenly realms,

11) according to his eternal purpose which he accomplished in Christ Jesus our Lord.

12) In him and through faith in him we may approach God with freedom and confidence."

This will change the positioning of your thoughts, actions, and motivations forever if you fully get this.

It will give you an understanding of how very important it is for you to flow with the plans of God and embrace your reason for breathing.

The above verses had as much impact on my understanding of the plans of God as any other single segment in the Bible. It was almost like the Damascus Road experience that Saul must have felt. That experience stopped him in his tracks and changed the direction of his life forever. These verses have done the same for me and will do likewise for you, if you are willing to receive the message through the Holy Spirit.

As precious as you are to God, all of this is not only about you. It is also about the eternal plans of God and their impact on heavenly beings.

When the angelic beings fell, they were given no mercy. They were cast from the presence of God, experiencing firsthand His boundless power and authority.

154

At present, some of those who remain with Him can only lie prostrate before Him crying "Holy, Holy, Holy," because He is so magnificent. Others, especially those who were cast from His presence, to this day understand His power and authority. To them, He is undeniably "Almighty God."

Enter puny mankind! Limited to functioning within the five senses, frail in comparison to even the lowest order of angel, incredibly ignorant concerning spiritual things, and so on and so on - you get the picture…

Since the cross, when the veil before the Holy of Holies was ripped in two, puny mankind - who previous to this time was truly on the outside looking in - has the kind of access to God that the angelic creation will never have. We can now come directly into the presence of God anytime we desire to go there and are accepted as if Jesus Himself entered. (Stop and ponder that, and then ask yourself why in the world we don't spend the majority of our time in His presence. That is how limited and puny our thinking is! Of course, the Lord did say that His thoughts and ours are two different things, and this example certainly proves it. We settle for so little, and it must grieve the heart of God how often we miss what He's made available.)

We now have complete access to Father God.

Because of the covenant that Jesus established, we go into the presence of God in His Name, not our own. God accepts us just as He would accept Jesus because we were "in" Jesus when covenant was made. After Jesus died, we were the full recipients of His kind of access to the Father.

To the angels, God providing this access for us was only one of the many facets of God that they had never seen. Each time He flows His wondrous privileges toward us, they see other facets about Him in which they are not allowed to participate.

This is probably a great revelation to some of you. I know that it was to me. Maybe it's time to get a little more excited about what has been provided for us! Here is that verse again.

Eph. 3:9-12 NIV "… this grace was given to me; to preach to the Gentiles the unsearchable riches of Christ, and to make plain to everyone the administration of this mystery, which for ages past was kept hidden in God, who created all things.
10) His intent was that now, through the church, the manifold wisdom of God should be made known to the rulers and authorities in the heavenly realms,
11) according to his eternal purpose which he accomplished in Christ Jesus our Lord.
12) In him and through faith in him we may approach God with freedom and confidence."

What are you thinking now?

How has your understanding about your covenant place in Christ changed?

As you read the account of the Last Supper, the death and resurrection of Jesus, and His promises to us through covenant eyes, how has your understanding changed? (This could take a while.)

Let's Talk About Some Perceptions as to Who We Are in Christ

We observe three separate heart positions functioning in the church body today, all called "Christianity." There is the infant heart, the growing heart, and the mature heart - one that symbolizes the bridal heart, or more simply, the kind of heart that Jesus has. You will need to know and understand these three distinctive heart positions, so that you can function properly with the Lord's help as you encounter them – either in yourself or others.

The Infant Heart

The infant heart beats only for itself. All of the things that God does center around their needs in some way. The salvation process was for them alone. It was put in effect by God specifically for them, to make them safe after they die.

The Bible is simply a book of promises that they can call upon to relieve their hurts in time of need. God is perceived as this wonderful benefactor, who is waiting for their next need to occur, so that He can help them through it; and prayer is solely a channel by which they can make their needs known.

In essence, everything that God has done, is doing, and will do hinges upon the perception that mankind is at the center of it all; and they have somehow tapped into this incredible opportunity. So, God is all about them and for them alone. There is no need to go any further; it is enough, and it is very good. Sadly, a lot of today's church functions in this religious arena.

God has also been brought down to their size, perceived as functioning for them and in service to them. To be with most infant hearts is a roller-coaster of highs and lows, happy and sad, good days and bad days, all of which are determined by how they perceive their prayers are being answered, or how much of an "attack" they might be under.

Very much like infants in diapers who are not capable of understanding that the world around them is not about them, these spiritual infants cry when they have need, demand when these needs are not met; and are only truly satisfied when they are comfortable in all areas, without giving the slightest thought to the importance of anything going on around them. Everything that they can do to make themselves comfortable is done without question. What they own is all theirs. God has some rights to their money, but never more than 10%. The importance of anything else or the needs of anyone else mean nothing when there is personal need to be addressed.

What kind of heart do you think you have?

How far from a mature heart do you think you are?

Everything is about them.

God exists to serve their needs.

157

The bottom-line thinking of this kind of heart is that God has put Himself in a position to serve its needs only. Preaching topics on this kind of life include phrases like "holding God to His promises" or "We're King's kids" or "God wants you happy and blessed." All of this is about those who have been saved for their good and their good alone.

This kind of heart is forever wanting to know about God, which seems wonderful on the surface. It is usually an enthusiastic "attender" at all church functions. It is continually in Bible studies and fellowship meetings.

Some infant hearts never grow up

On the surface, this activity looks impressive and makes the believer appear to be growing; but because the basic motive is self-preservation and personal safety and security, there is little fruit other than "pre-digested food," manna that someone else has received and the infant heart tries to devour as fresh food. Just as "junk food" will not sustain a good quality of life, other people's revelation of God will produce weak, immature spiritual infants, if the hearer does not dig in for himself in order to know God – for His reasons.

Association with the immature heart that refuses to grow up will eventually bring spiritual complacency to you.

This kind of "devotion" is a warped use of all that Jesus has done on the cross. Most of the slanted doctrines, such as the name–it-and-claim-it studies come from this false mentality. This mindset deteriorates into the foolish notion that God is in the business of serving us, rather than us serving Him. It culminates in sluggish, lazy Christians who cannot be stirred from self-centeredness, even when their friends and neighbors are on their way to hell.

How close to this kind of heart do you function? What areas in your life need to grow away from this pattern? (If you have things that are out of order, rejoice that you have finally found them! Now is the time to surrender to the Lord.)

The Lord points these sins out because He intends to change you if you choose to cooperate. He's always ready when you are and He'll even give you a push to get you started!

The Growing Heart

This second kind of heart, the growing heart, is the heart that is open to learning more about the truth of the Gospel in its pure form. It is in the process of understanding that diapers are not standard apparel for the Christian and that there might be more to the walk with the Lord than having one's needs met.

People on their way to hell are given some notice, and this heart is beginning to question if Jesus really cares about the unsaved as much as He cares about them. This heart cherishes the things of God somewhere hidden under traditions, man-made doctrines, fears, wounds, and confusions. It has bought into the promises of the unscriptural, cold church, however, and is not free to move in a direction of holiness, because it does not - as of yet - believe the promise that holiness is available to it. It is thought to be for someone else.

In some of the sporadic moments of "pressing in," the growing heart experiences taste buds for more of God. Seasons of searching, alternating with seasons of relative complacency, make the growing heart the "unhappy wanderer" of Christianity.

It sees the possibility of more to the life in Christ, but finds it difficult to grasp. Often, it longs to sell out completely but can't because of the hold that the world, personal fears, and material possessions still have on it.

Although fully loved and accepted by God, this heart is to be pitied if it never grows up.

Unfortunately, this is where most of today's church desires to be.

The pressures of the world keep this heart at bay. Continually unsatisfied with where it is at present, but fearful to move to the deeper things of God because it would cost a price that is presently too high to pay, this heart is continually in a state of borderline happiness.

To go where it knows it needs to go with God might mean sacrifice, ridicule from friends who don't feel the same way; and in general, stepping into an uncomfortable zone of the unknown world of absolute trust in God. Of the three kinds of hearts, this is truly the one to be pitied. It can see the truth, but it desires not to change because it will cost too much or feels that it is impossible to obtain; so it remains in a state of Christian mediocrity.

List the elements of this kind of heart that are in you. What would it take to have you sell out completely? (With God, all things are possible!)

The Visitor

Perry and his wife of twenty years were relaxing after a hard day in the comfort of their spacious den. They decided that they had had enough of the day's events and they simply wanted to stretch out, hoping that no one would bother them for once. Monica had her fill of meetings, driving their two children, Dale and Ashley, back and forth to private school, plus the myriad of other incidentals that made for a very busy day.

Even her Thursday morning Bible study seemed to take too much of her time, which was at a premium these days. That worried her a bit, for she usually looked forward to getting together with her friends to discuss the Word; so she pushed her negative feelings aside, attributing them to overload.

Getting up from his favorite maroon leather chair, and pushing aside the matching ottoman as he walked toward the theater system to retrieve the remote, Perry took a moment to notice the beautiful hues cascading from the lake as the setting sun performed its daily gift for him. He was often doubly blessed as he got the privilege of seeing the colors change as they were mirrored in the backyard pool located between the house and the lake. He loved his Lord for prospering him so abundantly.

As he watched the final rays of the sun hide behind the stand of trees on the other side of the lake, which left behind it a warm glow of evening peace, he gave a quiet thank you to Jesus. There was nothing Perry could think of that he needed. He was truly blessed.

"Do you need anything?" he asked in Monica's direction, as he picked up the remote and headed for his chair. In his mind, it would hopefully be the last time that he had to get up - except to go to bed, of course.

"No sweetie," she responded, without looking up from the home decorating magazine that she had purchased a couple of days ago and hadn't had time to read. "I'm fine," she said quietly, almost as an afterthought. She turned the page, her thoughts already engrossed in the challenge of redecorating the sun room. It had been almost three years since she had given it any attention, so it was way past the time for its makeover. Several lawn parties with the neighbors was sufficient reason for change.

Surfing through the channels on the wide screen TV, Perry found a movie listing that caught his attention. Rated PG-13, he felt it would be safe enough to watch. "Probably just some swearing or some kissie-face," he thought to himself as he settled a little deeper into the overstuffed chair.

For about an hour, the two reveled in the quiet of the evening. The only interruptions to Perry were Monica's requests for his thoughts concerning a decorating scheme she had found on one of the pages of the magazine. He voiced a half-hearted response, not really seeing what she had shown him. Picking up on this, Monica decided not to interrupt him any more; his interests were obviously in other places.

"Is that the doorbell?" Perry queried, looking at his watch as he got up. "It's 10:30 at night. Who would be here at this hour?" he thought again, as he crossed through the cathedral-ceilinged living room and expansive foyer to the front door. Before opening the door, Perry flipped on the outside front light switch and glanced through the narrow window beside it.

Whoever was there was standing so close to the door that it was impossible to see anything but the back of his coat. Without giving a thought to the oddity of someone wearing a wool sport coat in the middle of July, Perry opened the door to greet his guest.

"Hello, Perry," the figure, who looked very much like a vagrant, said quietly, almost knocking the startled man to the floor with the power and love emitting from the friendly voice.

Perry had to hang on to the door. "Master," he gasped. No, it couldn't be. His knees were weak and he was about to fall. Perry gripped the door tighter. "Master," he said again to the smiling face of the man standing on the front porch. "How could this be?" he thought to himself.

Perry's mind raced. He could feel his heart pumping fast to the point of fear that it would burst. Cold chills were traveling up and down his back and to his shoes so fast that he could no longer tell what was a chill or simply part of his body shaking.

"I can't be seeing this," he thought, his shirt now wringing wet with perspiration. Perry's face was feeling as if all of the blood had left it; and his hands were clammy, almost slippery, against the doorknob. The man at the door took Perry's hand and held it gently. A peace began to fill his entire being instantly. Strength enough to stand flowed into his body.

"Who is it, dear?" Perry heard his wife's voice as she crossed the living room floor. "Who..." Perry heard a thud, the sound of a body landing on thick carpet. Forcing himself to look away from the most loving eyes he had ever seen, Perry turned in the direction of the living room. Monica had fallen just next to the grand piano. She lay there motionless.

In reaction to what he saw near the piano, Perry forgot his guest and moved toward Monica to see if she was OK. On his way to help her, he turned toward the kitchen for some water. Everything was simultaneously in slow motion and high speed. Returning to the living room, Perry stopped short, spilling some of the water on the Italian marble foyer floor. Jesus had situated Himself in a sitting position near Monica and He had placed her head on His leg, and was lovingly stroking her hair. He looked up and smiled at Perry.

About then, Monica began to stir a bit. She opened her eyes, met the eyes of her Savior, and immediately fainted again. Jesus laughed quietly and touched her head, bringing her to consciousness. Not knowing what else to do, Perry knelt down, never taking his eyes off the Man who was comforting his astounded, mesmerized wife. It didn't even bother him that his knees were soaked from the spilled water. He stayed there for a moment, holding the glass almost sideways as he stared at the unbelievable scene in front of him - Monica, the love of his life, was being comforted by the Savior of the world in his living room. It was too much to comprehend. With his mind overloaded, he felt himself starting to faint. Everything went dark.

Perry had no way to justify or explain anything that was happening. He was sitting at the breakfast room table with his wife and Jesus, the Risen Christ. Was he dreaming? Had he gone nuts?

Slowly, he moved his arm under the table so it wouldn't be noticeable when he pinched himself. It hurt. He wasn't dreaming. The going nuts part was yet to be determined. Jesus was sitting there, right in front of him, in his outdated, threadbare suit and dirty, scuffed work boots, talking to Monica. Somehow, they were given the power and ability to be in His presence. The Bible verses where Jesus prepared a fire and ate fish with the apostles came to Perry's mind. "They talked with the Master at that time," he thought. "It must be possible." Then he immediately wondered, "How did I get from the foyer to the table?"

Jesus looked away from Monica long enough to include Perry in His conversation. "I would like to spend a few days with you," Jesus told them. "I won't be a bother. Just go on with your normal routine; I simply desire to be with you." Looking at Perry and then back to Monica, who had withdrawn her hand from His, he continued, "I've come to bless you."

This turn of events hit Perry and Monica like a fast-moving train barreling straight toward them. It was as if they had been working in the middle of the tracks and didn't have time to do anything else before the impact except jump.

Jesus spending time with them! What were Dale and Ashley doing? What was on their schedules that would offend Him? Who would stop by to embarrass them? All of a sudden, the movie that was still playing in the den was too loud. Words about God damning something, said by one of the actors, now resonated throughout the house as if they were shouted through a bullhorn. Perry looked at Jesus immediately. He was expressionless, almost as if He hadn't heard them.

Perry noticed His Master's hands. The scars he expected, located in His wrists just above the heel of each hand, healed from what must have been vicious wounds. What Perry didn't expect were the calluses, the grime, and the dust. These were the hands of someone acquainted with hard work. The muscular arms, the sun-darkened face, the cropped, unkempt hair - all brought the reality of a first-century man to Perry's mind. His clothes - covered with dust as if He had come from some desert country. Perry mused that he would not normally let someone in his house who looked like this man. Monica would certainly never have allowed Him to sit on her white living room carpet.

Jesus listened quietly as Monica expressed her surprise and gratitude, savoring the glass of water He had been given as a connoisseur would savor a fine wine. This Man was gracious and strong; but so gentle, so quiet, yet consuming every element of the room. This Man was Jesus.

As the evening wore on, Monica began to run out of expressions of love and thankfulness. She became agitated and increasingly nervous. Jesus did nothing to make her feel uncomfortable. In fact, His every move, every statement were reassuring and full of love. Finally, when the Master asked if He could use the guest room and retired for the evening, she broke down into uncontrollable fits of crying.

"Why would He do this to us? I don't think I can handle having Him watch my every move for the next few days. Perry, do you know what that means? It means that our friends will think we've gone crazy. We're going to have to act differently. It scares me. Where do we take Him? What does He eat? Does He eat? I'm so...."

She continued on through the night even after Perry went to bed. He heard her toss and turn for hours. He must have been awake much of the night asking himself the same questions, for he knew each time she got up to pace the room at the foot of their bed.

The next morning, Jesus accompanied Perry to the law firm. He had showered and cleaned up somewhat, but refused Perry's Armani suit when offered. The Master chose to wear the dust-covered suit and work boots everywhere He went. Once, when Perry asked himself the question of why that should be, Jesus responded to his thoughts by saying that He was wearing His work clothes, just as He did before He was crucified. He said that more than Perry could ever imagine was being accomplished with that outfit. It was perfect for the job at hand.

It was true. After the first day, Monica and the kids - who incidentally were not told that their houseguest was the Savior of the world - left to visit her mother across the state. The pressure and fear simply became too much for her to bear. Monica found herself embarrassed to be seen with Jesus. Some of her friends took her aside to warn her of the dangers of allowing "that kind of person" to stay with them. Some even demanded that He leave "for the good of the neighborhood."

Perry found that after a while, he too wished that their visitor would leave. All Jesus did was serve, help, and be a good friend to everyone, in every situation; but it just got tiring being on guard all the time. Introductions became disconcerting. People at work laughed or got angry that a "man like this" would hang around all day.

Club officials wouldn't let Perry in, if he insisted that his friend come along. Perry's golfing partners, some of whom were part of his Bible study, expressed their relief at the decision and rushed to make the next tee time. Even the board members of the foundation that Perry and a few of his friends had set up to help the poor did not allow Jesus to sit in on their meeting. He sat in the hall, while decisions about donations and money grants to ministries in the community were made. Jesus smiled when Perry remarked on the way home in the car that they had disbursed almost five hundred thousand dollars to the needy that night.

The ride back to Perry's house on the way home from church Sunday morning was quiet. Jesus sat in the front seat, His head down most of the way. Perry fought the desire to ask Him why He had to make everything so difficult. He felt very uncomfortable having Jesus sitting next to him during Pastor's sermon on God's promises, and our ability as Christians to request our covenant rights from Him. Even the people who normally stopped for lunch at Figaro's Deli after church asked Perry not to come today. It caused him to want to ask Jesus a lot of questions.

Jesus broke the silence. "Perry, why don't you pull into that park over there? Let's talk, OK?

Perry pulled the shiny, new Lexus into the park and stopped near the play area. They both got out of the car and walked to a grassy area next to the swing set. Jesus squatted down and picked up a few blades of grass and smelled them, savoring the aroma with obvious delight. Moving to the swing set and resting Himself against one of the swings, as if he were ready to use it, Jesus asked, "Perry, do you know how serious I want you to be about My Father's plans?"

The question caught Perry by surprise. Before he could respond, Jesus continued in answer to His own question. His voice was soft and full of love. "I want My Father's plans and desires to be the only reason that you breathe. There should be no other purpose for getting up each morning except to do the will of My Father every moment, every day." Perry could only stand there speechless.

Jesus took one swing on the play set, then got off and stood in front of Perry for a moment as He looked into his eyes and smiled. "Let's take a walk over here," Jesus said, putting His arm around Perry's shoulder as they headed in the direction of a vacant baseball diamond.

"Can you imagine how it grieves Our hearts to see you waste any of the resources that We give you?" He began as they walked. "I'm not only talking about money, but that is a big issue with Us and completely misunderstood by My church."

Jesus stooped down to observe a tiny hill swarming with industrious ants. Remaining in a squatting position while looking up at Perry, He continued. "Let me ask you a question. When you gave the money from your foundation to those ministries, it was a free gift, wasn't it?"

Perry nodded, and said, "It was, but we do hold them accountable to make sure that they are good stewards of what has been given to them. After all, it is your money."

"Exactly," Jesus said with a smile. Standing up and walking to the outfield fence, Jesus turned around and faced Perry again. "Perry, who holds you accountable for the stewardship of the time, money, and other resources that I give you? Who determines how much you are allowed to keep for yourself or do with as you please?"

Perry was somewhat taken aback by the very direct inquiry into his accountability. No one had ever done that to him since he was a child; and frankly, he didn't like it. His mind raced to remember the vast amounts of money that he had given to the work of God over the years. He wanted to tell Jesus that he had given probably more to the work of God than most of the rest of his church combined. He spent countless hours on church committees and volunteer groups. What more could he do?

As he was about to mouth his thoughts, Jesus spoke again. "Do you remember when I was in the temple with My first team, the guys you call "the Apostles," and marveled at the love that the widow showed by giving Me everything that she had; and how it meant more than all of the wealth that those with much gave?" Perry nodded. "Well, nothing has changed." Jesus looked directly into Perry's eyes as He spoke.

After several moments, Jesus again started walking along the fence line, touching the fence periodically. He picked up a blade of grass and put it in His mouth, which He removed as He talked. Perry followed, walking next to Him, his spirit quieted, remembering the verses. He had never before considered himself of the same spirit as those in the temple.

"Perry, living in a wealthy society and earning much does not mean that you should join the world in its sin." Jesus held up his hand to quiet Perry, knowing his thoughts and his desire to defend himself and take issue with the word "sin."

"The difference between having Me added to your life and having Me as the center of your life stems from what you hold on to, or own with your heart. That is manifested most prominently by money; but really everything is included - time, talents, everything.

"My church elects good businessmen to its boards. Does it seem unusual to you that those who have little of this world's goods are rarely elected? Aren't they the ones who are constantly seeking Me to know My heart? Aren't they the ones who need Me for every morsel of food, or they would not be able to exist? Haven't they become accustomed to moving by My Spirit every day?

"That misguided attitude has only brought the wealthy to more prominence, leaving the poor - those dressed less stylishly and having little..." He stopped and had Perry take notice of the clothes that He wore, "considered lower in stature. It would seem to Me that those who are aware that they need Me every day, for everything, would have the godly wisdom needed for church direction and the power to represent Me properly to their community."

Jesus stopped and turned to face Perry. "My friend, I'm deeply concerned for those whom I have prospered. You think that you have done much because you have given out of your abundance. In My eyes, you have given very little; in fact, much less than the widow. Gifts from a place of comfort have little weight in heaven. They only continue to emphasize a need to realize how poor you really are, and how much you have kept of My provision which should have been used for My work.

"You've only given gifts to Me from a place which allowed you to remain where you are. You've never given anything that would put you in a place of needing Me for your next provision. I require the same heart motive from those who have very little to give to Me. They are not exempt from the truth of My Word.

"Because I have given you the wisdom to make money and orchestrated every event so that you could do so, does not mean that I love you more than anyone else; or that any of it is yours to keep unless I say so. There are times that I allow some of My people to have finer things, of course; but it is for My reasons, not because they themselves feel that they have somehow earned them.

"Good things are to be enjoyed if I allow you to keep them, but I am much more concerned that My Father's work is done than I am about you being comfortable. I desire for you to be blessed. In fact, you will be overwhelmed by what I have prepared for you when we get together in My home, but obedience to Me and My Word are what I require now. I want you to take on My heart in everything you do and all that you have been given."

Jesus observed two young men passing a football near them. As the ball was overthrown, Jesus jogged over to pick it up and threw it back to them. Perry noticed that neither thanked or even acknowledged Him for the effort.

Undaunted, Jesus continued. "Why would you think that you have a right to live any way other than the way I choose for you to live? I own the cattle on a thousand hills as it says in My Word. Do you think that you have the right to take even one without asking Me first? That would be theft. That is, however, what you've done if you use My resources in any way other than My will for your life. Carrying out My Father's plans is His priority and should be yours, too.

"Search My Word and find out whom I esteem as truly wealthy. Is it not those who desperately understand their need of Me and trust Me for everything? What example did I set in showing you how to live when I was here? Could you even hear Me clearly if My desire for you would be to give everything that you make to My work, keeping nothing for yourself? Read about My Laodicean church. It is alive and well in your midst."

Jesus looked into Perry's eyes and cupped his face with His hands. "Please understand that I'm not angry with you. I am, however, deeply concerned for you. You are not wealthy in My eyes at present because you don't really need Me I desire that you become extremely prosperous by living the life patterns that I have established for you. Begin to move in faith as you once did. I want you to arrive in heaven with many crowns to lay at My feet. I don't want you to be empty-handed. It would grieve My heart. Don't let that happen, OK?"

With those words, Jesus kissed Perry on the cheek and hugged him. "Please tell Monica that I love her very much. I do understand, and I would love to talk to her anytime she wishes. Tell her that everything will be OK and that she will do fine."

Jesus smiled again, looked deep into Perry's eyes; and turned and walked toward the open field. Perry knew that he was not to follow, so he just watched. After a few steps, Jesus turned around with a broad smile on His face. "I really enjoyed being with you these days. You are very valuable to Father and Me. We have a lot to accomplish through you. Let's have fun, OK?"

Perry waved in unconscious reaction. He watched His Lord until he could no longer see Him because of the trees near the golf course. Then he drove home knowing that he would never be the same.

Story Bible Verses

9) I have no need of a bull from your stall or of goats from your pens,

10) for every animal of the forest is mine, and the cattle on a thousand hills.

11) I know every bird in the mountains, and the creatures of the field are mine.

12) If I were hungry I would not tell you, for the world is mine, and all that is in it.

Psalm 50: 9-12 NIV

1) My brothers, as believers in our glorious Lord Jesus Christ, don't show favoritism.

2) Suppose a man comes into your meeting wearing a gold ring and fine clothes, and a poor man in shabby clothes also comes in.

3) If you show special attention to the man wearing fine clothes and say, "Here's a good seat for you," but say to the poor man, "You stand there" or "Sit on the floor by my feet,"

4) have you not discriminated among yourselves and become judges with evil thoughts?

James 2:1-4 NIV

13) Now listen, you who say, "Today or tomorrow we will go to this or that city, spend a year there, carry on business and make money."

14) Why, you do not even know what will happen tomorrow. What is your life? You are a mist that appears for a little while and then vanishes.

15) Instead, you ought to say, "If it is the Lord's will, we will live and do this or that."

16) As it is, you boast and brag. All such boasting is evil.

17) Anyone, then, who knows the good he ought to do and doesn't do it, sins.

5:1) Now listen, you rich people, weep and wail because of the misery that is coming upon you.

2) Your wealth has rotted, and moths have eaten your clothes.

3) Your gold and silver are corroded. Their corrosion will testify against you and eat your flesh like fire. You have hoarded wealth in the last days.

4) Look! The wages you failed to pay the workmen who mowed your fields are crying out against you. The cries of the harvesters have reached the ears of the Lord Almighty.

5) You have lived on earth in luxury and self-indulgence. You have fattened yourselves in the day of slaughter.

6) You have condemned and murdered innocent men, who were not opposing you.

James 4:13-5;6 NIV

17) You say, `I am rich; I have acquired wealth and do not need a thing.' But you do not realize that you are wretched, pitiful, poor, blind and naked.

18) I counsel you to buy from me gold refined in the fire, so you can become rich; and white clothes to wear, so you can cover your shameful nakedness; and salve to put on your eyes, so you can see.

Revelation 3:17,18 NIV

"But without faith it is impossible to please and be satisfactory to Him. For whoever would come near to God must [necessarily] believe that God exists and that He is a rewarder of those who earnestly and diligently seek Him [out.] "

Hebrews 11:6 Amp

"... However, when the Son of Man comes, will he find faith on the earth?"
Luke 18:8b NIV

How did that story make you feel?

Of the two kinds of hearts explained so far, what kind of heart did Perry have – infant or growing? Why?

What kind of heart do you think Perry's wife had? Why?

Would you have felt under scrutiny spending your day with Jesus or would you have been able to totally relax with Him going everywhere you planned to go?

Jesus talked to Perry about His concerns on how he spent his time and money. What would He have discussed with you? What is out of order in your daily life?

What areas of your life would you be embarrassed to have Jesus be a part of?

What requests would you ask Jesus if you had the kind of chance Perry had?

Would you enjoy the kind of experience Perry had? Why or why not?

Prayers and thoughts

The Mature Heart

The mature heart is a wonder to behold. This is the passionate heart of Jesus. It is also the bridal heart, prepared and waiting for Christ, the one that will overcome and even prosper during the perilous times ahead. As Jesus is one with the Father, the mature or bridal heart beats in unison with Them both.

This heart sees only the Father's will as important, only the Father's plans as worth addressing throughout life. The world, the cold church, and all else in the physical realm hold no audience with this heart. There is no purpose but God's purpose, no plan but God's plan, no future but God's future. This heart is untouchable in its alliance with God. It is in total freedom in its chosen "slavery" to only the Father's will.

I want this heart!

This heart has put aside most of its elementary sins against God, those choices of the flesh that have carried over into the Christian walk, the choices of doing good things vs. going deeper and deeper with the Lord. It has set aside fleshly temptations and ponders over the things that concern Jesus. Improper spiritual choices, such as moving ahead on anything without waiting for everything to develop properly in the spiritual realm, cause this heart to understand its dishonor of God and bring it to repentance for its disobedience.

Phil. 3:10b-11 Amp "...and that I may so share His sufferings as to be continually transformed [in spirit into His likeness even] to His death, [in the hope]
11 That if possible I may attain to the [spiritual and moral] resurrection [that lifts me] out from among the dead [even while in the body]."

Because this dedicated heart is growing in the character of Christ as a priority, functioning in the world holds no promise for it. Its only desire is to be in fellowship with its source for beating - Father God, its "Abba."

No price is too high to pay to remain in intimate fellowship. Even moving on assigned and directed missions is done only because it pleases the Father. As soon as the task is completed, this heart only wants to move back to the posture of intimacy.

This should be the normal Christian heart.

It is available to anyone who is willing to pay the price to receive it.

Any outward expression of this heart to the world comes directly from the throne room. It does nothing of itself, but only the Father's will. It is the heart that will come out of the refiner's fire and beat steadily in unison with the heart of Jesus as the bride of Christ. This kind of heart should be your goal.

Colossians 3 The Message Bible "So if you're serious about living this new resurrection life with Christ, act like it. Pursue the things over which Christ presides. Don't shuffle along, eyes to the ground, absorbed in the things right in front of you. Look up, and be alert to what is going on around Christ - that's where the action is. See things from his perspective.

Your old life is dead. Your new life, which is your real life - even though invisible to spectators - is with Christ in God. He is your life."

How much do you long for this kind of freedom and devotion? What kind of price are you willing to pay for this kind of heart?

----

2 Cor. 6 The Message Bible "People are watching us as we stay at our post, alertly, unswervingly ... in hard times, tough times, bad times; when we're beaten up, jailed, and mobbed; working hard, working late, working without eating; with pure heart, clear head, steady hand; in gentleness, holiness, and honest love; when we're telling the truth, and when God's showing His power; when we're doing our best setting things right; when we're praised, and when we're blamed; slandered, and honored; true to our word, though distrusted; ignored by the world, but recognized by God; terrifically alive, though rumored to be dead; beaten within an inch of our lives, but refusing to die; immersed in tears, yet always filled with deep joy; living on handouts, yet enriching many; having nothing, having it all.

Dear, dear Corinthians, I can't tell you how much I long for you to enter this wide-open, spacious life. We didn't fence you in. The smallness you feel comes from within you. Your lives aren't small, but you're living them in a small way. I'm speaking as plainly as I can and with great affection. Open up your lives. Live openly and expansively!"

This is the wide-open, spacious life according to Paul.

He believes that everyone should function here with this kind of heart.

Before you go any deeper into this study, take the time to ponder what you have learned. Don't minimize any opportunity to go to God when He calls you. Wait on Him to give you His heart. Review your journal notes and add the Lord's words to you as you do.

You are valuable!

Remember that you are very valuable to God. He has done all that He has done, so that you can know Him in a richer way. As you see who you are not, allow Him to reveal how He sees you and who He desires to make you. This is a love relationship. You are greatly loved.

174

Living Out Christ's Love

Previous sections gave us the reasons why we should be passionate about our relationship with our Lord and what has been provided for us. Fully understood, what God has done for mankind is the most wonderful action ever taken for the sake of another. We were helpless and without hope. Instead of leaving us in our misery, mercy is extended to any one of us who chooses to accept it.

By accepting the extended hand of God, we enter into a relationship unparalleled since the Garden of Eden. As wonderful as it is to have a knowledge of what has been provided for us, we find ourselves unable to love as Jesus loved and follow the Father's will as our only desire.

Seeing what we are to become is a far cry from becoming what God has shown us we can be. Because He makes it clear in His Word who He desires us to be, most of us attempt to become better in our own strength, striving to please Him and struggling to eliminate the sins that so easily entangle us. (Heb. 12:1)

How often do you attempt to take matters into your own hands, when God doesn't move fast enough for you? (Would you like another sheet of paper?)

What would you like to tell the Lord now?

God is calling for the mature bridal heart to be accepted by each of His children. He is bringing to those who will hear a desire to sell out completely, so that the passionate life of Jesus can function through us, exhibiting His character to a dead and dying world.

Is this you?

Experience has shown us that any attempt to become like Jesus through knowledge, personal determination, and purposeful human strength ends in dismal failure. It is impossible to achieve spiritual maturity through physical means. We are told not to attempt to complete in the flesh what was begun in the Spirit.

In this section, we are going to examine some of the ways that Father God has established to complete the work of living Christ's passionate life in us, allowing us to attain a submissive bridal heart, which is prepared for the coming of our Lord. Although we are fleshly participants, we must remember that this is a spiritual work being accomplished in us by the Lord Himself. He is the one transforming us. We are the ones required to submit to that work. Even our ability to submit, however, is accomplished by His power, the power out-flowing from Christ's resurrection.

All relationships are very important to God.

What God is basically doing in each of us is eliminating the power of our flesh and replacing it with the life and character of Jesus. Once we understand that it is God's plan to basically eliminate us and all that does not serve Him, so that Jesus can live His life through us, we find new motivation for all that we do - if we choose to comply with the will of God. Our prayers take on a repentant tone. Our desires begin to change. Our hearts start to become submissive.

Very important to note. Read this paragraph as many times as you need to do so, until you own it.

*The following pages are designed to develop taste buds for the Lord to accomplish His work in us by allowing us to revisit our motives for living the way we do in our relationships with God and with others - all the while leading us to develop a passionate life, which is devoted to the Lord. We will also see how our vertical relationship with God and our horizontal relationships with others, when entered into properly, are designed to make the changes in us that are required to attain a mature bridal heart.

Do not minimize the importance that God places on our relationship with Him and with those He has provided in our lives, even those who hate us and those who are difficult for us to love. Do not underestimate the monumental work that these relationships will do in us as we submit to the anointed power instilled in them by the Lord.

Our Communion with God

Because of what Jesus has done, our relationship with God has been restored back to what it was before Adam and Eve sinned. We once again have unrestricted access to Him. How and why we use that access determines our real motives for that relationship.

God has provided specific ways to allow us to be changed into the image of our Lord. He has provided the vertical relationship with Him (prayer,) and the horizontal relationship with others (those in the world, church fellowship, marriage, and family.)

Own this

All of these relationships are designed to allow us to see who we are not, who we are to become; and the necessity of having any change in us implemented through His power. They are also catalysts to bring about needed changes in us as they drive us to repentance - as we see our sin and our total bankruptcy and inability to act like Jesus to people when they sin against us.

and this!

Prayer
(Our Vertical Relationship)

Our vertical relationship with God is the first part of the complete relationship that Jesus has provided for us at Calvary.

What do you think is the purpose of prayer?

In general, what do you desire to accomplish through prayer?

How do you think God views prayer?

What do you believe that God would like to accomplish through your prayers?

Prayer Changes the One Who Prays

This vertical relationship with God (prayer - communication with God, worship, waiting on God, reading His Word, petitioning, interceding, etc.) allows us to get to know Him. By presenting ourselves to Him in prayer, we begin to understand who He is - His majesty, sovereignty, and all of the magnificent attributes that make Him the only God. This knowledge also establishes our position as someone who is in submission, a posture very much needed if we are to grow in our relationship with Him.

Through continued fellowship, we also gain insight into His nature, as He imparts Himself to us when we seek Him. With that knowledge, confirmed by the Word, we also have insight into His plans of the past, present and future. Eventually we are shown our specific participation in those plans.

Communion with God is His design for us to receive mature growth.

Every means God uses to allow us to communicate with Him, i.e. His Word, praying, waiting on Him, provides for and comforts us as He adopts us as His own. As our fellowship with Him allows us to get to know Him, He enjoys His intended purpose of fellowshipping with us and imparting Himself to us, His creation of future priests and kings. When we allow Him and His Word to change our very nature as promised, it equips us for all of His work that is ahead.

He imparts Himself to us.

I John 1:3b Amp "And [this] fellowship that we have [which is a distinguishing mark of Christians] is with the Father and with His Son Jesus Christ (the Messiah)."

Do you really believe in your heart that the Creator God truly desires to have fellowship with you, whom He has created? Explain!

Do you believe that fellowship has been restored to the intimacy that Adam and Eve had? Explain!

Our relationship with God is dynamic in nature, constantly changing as He imparts more of Himself each time we are with Him!

From Our Father's Heart

Compare your petitions to Me
with those who have gone before you!
Include those who were passionate to bring glory to Jesus
on their way to the arena
that was filled with waiting lions and jeering crowds.
Examine your heart and your needs
to see if your requests have value in the light of eternity.
How much of what you request from Me
is for the well-being of others?
How much is for your comfort,
rather than for your desire to go deeper with Me
no matter what the cost?
Is there ever a time that you come to Me
wanting nothing for yourself?
Have you ever had only My plans in mind
and seek Me to implement them in My power?
Have you ever sought Me for the power
to defend My reputation and the reputation of Jesus?
Have you ever wept for how most of the church offends Me
with their weak religion
and carnal presentation of My cherished Word?
Have you ever waited in My presence
until you knew for sure what the desires of My heart were?
Do you think that maybe it's time for you to grow up?
I do!

We Have Access to God

Study the diagram on the opposite page. Observe all of the avenues that communication with God creates.

"Let us then approach the throne of grace with confidence, so that we may receive mercy and find grace to help us in our time of need."   *Hebrews 4: 16 NIV*

Look at the incredible provisions that are designed for our benefit!

Access to the inner chambers of God has been provided for us by the work of Jesus on the cross. His death and subsequent resurrection opened the door of communication for us. We now have unlimited audience with God whenever we have any kind of need, question, or just a desire to spend time with Him. It is one of the covenant commitments God made with Jesus for us. In God's eyes, we have exchanged our old carnal life for a new spiritual life that is accepted by Him forever. The covenant cannot be broken.

In prayer, there is a connection between what God does and what you are to do. Prayer (communication with God) is the vehicle that Father God has established for us to navigate from the physical realm to the spiritual realm and back again to accomplish His will from heaven to earth through us.

Through this communication and because of the work of Jesus, God brings Himself, His plans, and His very being into His established tabernacles – us. Within the communication, we present our requests for all that is necessary for us to become who we need to be. Our Father also communicates His will to us. It is true communication between the Creator and His creation, with Father God all the while fine tuning our encounters with Him through the Holy Spirit.

Our Vertical Relationship
and
Interaction with God

God ——

Fills His heart and is blessed
Fellowship with His creation
Fulfills His plan
Blesses His people

Gives Himself
Shows absolute truth
Gives us life
Adopts us
Transmits His plan

1 Peter 3:12a Amp "For the eyes of the Lord are upon the righteous... and His ears are attentive to their prayer..."

Jer.1:12 Amp "Then said the Lord to me, you have seen well, for I am alert and active, watching over My word to perform it."

The Holy Spirit
(Third Person of the Trinity)

Shows us who Jesus and the Father are

Reveals truth, convicts of sin, teaches

Enables us to walk in all that the Lord is and has provided

Advocate, Comforter, Counselor, Strengthener, Helper

God's Agent at creation with Jesus

Indwells us

The very presence of God in operation in the world

Access to God

Jesus
(the Mediator of the covenant through the cross)

The Living Word

Prayer is the connection from the spiritual to the physical. *(heaven to earth)*

Intimacy is the difference between only knowing about God and personally experiencing the fullness of Him.

Get to Know Jesus

John 14:7 NIV "If you really knew me, you would know my Father as well..."

Heb 1:3a Amp "He is the sole expression of the glory of God... and He is the perfect imprint and very image of [God's] nature, upholding and maintaining and guiding and propelling the universe by His mighty word of power."

Allow Jesus to Live His Life through us

Gal 2:20a NIV "I have been crucified with Christ and I no longer live, but Christ lives in me..."

1 Th. 2:13 "...the Word of God, which is effectually at work in you who believe [exercising its superhuman power in those who adhere to and trust in and rely on it.]"

Also: II Tim. 3:16-17
Heb. 4:12

Acts 10:4b Amp "...Your prayers and your [generous] gifts to the poor have come up [as a sacrifice] to God and have been remembered by Him."

James 5:16b Amp "...The earnest (heartfelt, continued) prayer of a righteous man makes tremendous power available [dynamic in its working]."

Who Jesus is

2 Cor. 4:4
Heb 1:3
Col. 1:13—19

What Jesus Does for us

Saves us
Gives us Himself
Gives us access to the Father
Shows us who the Father is
Is our example
Intercedes for us

Us ——

God's Plan through Jesus

What is His heart?
Eph. 2:11-22
What is our part in His plan?
2 Cor. 5:18-20
Col. 1:20

In Hebrews 1:3 Amp, the writer states of Jesus, *"... and He is the perfect imprint and very image of [God's] nature,..."*

Because of the indwelling of the same Holy Spirit in each of us who are born again, the very nature of God has walked among the people of the world since the resurrection of Jesus. In us, to us, and through us, God once again communicates His perfect will to mankind through mankind renewed.

I John 4:15 Amp "Anyone who confesses (acknowledges, owns) that Jesus is the Son of God, God abides (lives, makes His home) in him and he [abides, lives, makes his home] in God."

Col. 2:9-10 Amp "For in Him the whole fullness of Deity (the Godhead) continues to dwell in bodily form [giving complete expression of the divine nature].

10) And you are in Him, made full and having come to fullness of life [in Christ you too are filled with the Godhead – Father, Son and Holy Spirit – and reach full spiritual stature]. And He is the Head of all rule and authority [of every angelic principality and power]."

II Pet. 1:3-4 Amp "For His divine power has bestowed upon us all things that [are requisite and suited] to life and godliness, through the [full, personal] knowledge of Him Who called us by and to His own glory and excellence (virtue).

4) By means of these He has bestowed on us His precious and exceedingly great promises, so that through them you may escape [by flight] from the moral decay (rottenness and corruption) that is in the world because of covetousness (lust and greed), and become sharers (partakers) of the divine nature."

Note: You really need to have the above verses deep within your spirit. Allow the Lord to reveal this truth to you.

Do you believe in your heart that you have unlimited access to God? Explain!

Do you have that same liberty when there is sin in your life?

Is your access to God ever not covered by the work of the cross? Amplify!

What kind of posture does "approach with confidence" mean?

Matt. 6:9-13 NIV "This is how you should pray: 'Our Father in heaven, hallowed be your name, your kingdom come, your will be done on earth as it is in heaven. Give us today our daily bread. Forgive us our debts, as we also have forgiven our debtors. And lead us not into temptation, but deliver us from the evil one.'"

Matt.16:19 Amp "I will give you the keys of the kingdom of heaven; and whatever you bind (declare to be improper and unlawful) on earth must be what is already bound in heaven; and whatever you loose (declare lawful) on earth must be what is already loosed in heaven."

Matthew 6 The Message "And when you come before God, don't turn that into a theatrical production either. All these people making a regular show out of their prayers, hoping for stardom! Do you think God sits in a box seat?

Here's what Merry and I want you to do: find a quiet, secluded place so that you won't be tempted to role play before God. Just be there as simply and honestly as you can manage. Allow the focus to shift from you to God, and you will begin to sense His grace. (We are in no way encouraging you to let your mind become blank. That is an occult method and can lead to voices, thoughts, and experiences you don't want to entertain. Just be mindful of the Lord as you wait to hear from Him. What He shares always lines up with Scripture.)

The world is full of so-called prayer warriors who are prayer ignorant. They're full of formulas, programs, and advice, peddling techniques for getting what you want from God. Don't fall for that nonsense. You are dealing with your Father, and He knows better than you what you need. With a God like this loving you, you can pray very simply.

The Message Bible explains the Lord's Prayer like this: "Our Father in heaven, Reveal who you are. Set the world right; Do what's best - as above, so below. Keep us alive with three square meals. Keep us forgiven with you and forgiving others. Keep us safe from ourselves and the Devil. You're in charge! You can do anything you want! You're ablaze in beauty! Yes. Yes. Yes. "

Remember also that we are going to the Father "in Jesus' Name" because of the covenant that has been established for us. He is receiving us with the same delight as if Jesus came to Him.

How do you approach God - totally accepted, as an unclean outsider, or somewhere in between? Why?

Wait on God to provide these and all of the other answers you need from Him.

How does God want you to approach Him?

As you participate with the Lord to fulfill His plans on this earth, you can be confident that the fullness of His covenant promises with Jesus are at work in you and for you to accomplish any task that is given.

I Thess. 2:13 Amp *"...but as it truly is, the Word of God, which is effectually at work in you who believe [exercising its superhuman power in those who adhere to and trust in and rely upon it]."*

Hebrews 4:12 Amp *"For the Word that God speaks is alive and full of power [making it active, operative, energizing, and effective]; it is sharper than any two-edged sword, penetrating to the dividing line of the breath of life (soul) and [the immortal] spirit, and of joints and marrow [of the deepest parts of our nature], exposing and sifting and analyzing and judging the very thoughts and purposes of the heart."*

II Tim. 3:16-17 Amp *"Every Scripture is God-breathed (given by His inspiration) and profitable for instruction, for reproof and conviction of sin, for correction of error and discipline in obedience, [and] for training in righteousness (in holy living, in conformity to God's will in thought, purpose, and action),*
17) So that the man of God may be complete and proficient, well fitted and thoroughly equipped for every good work."

So, God is sending us out as representatives, the same as when He sent Jesus. When we realize that He never sends us ill-equipped, when we see that He is in the business of making sure that His representation is strong, we can have peace that what was proclaimed to be accomplished in us will be done. He equipped Jesus with everything He needed. Now Jesus, who is God, sends us.

John 20 The Message Bible *"... just as the Father sent Me, I send you."*

Ephesians 5 The Message *"Watch what God does, and then you do it, like children who learn proper behavior from their parents. Mostly what God does is love you. Keep company with him and learn a life of love. Observe how Christ loved us. His love was not cautious but extravagant. He didn't love in order to get something from us but to give everything of himself to us. Love like that... Figure out what will please Christ, and then do it."*

Jesus spent a lot of time communicating with His Father.

Do you think that it's a good idea for us to do the same?

Have you ever thought of prayer as being God's way of establishing His will here on earth through you? (Think that through until it's part of you!)

Jas. 4:2-3 Amp *"… You do not have, because you do not ask. [Or] you do ask [God for them] and yet fail to receive, because you ask with wrong purpose and evil, selfish motives…"*

I John 3:22 Amp *"And we receive from Him whatever we ask, because we [watchfully] obey His orders [observe His suggestions and injunctions, follow His plan for us] and [habitually] practice what is pleasing to Him."*

I John 5:14-15 Amp *"And this is the confidence (the assurance, the privilege of boldness) which we have in Him: [we are sure] that if we ask anything (make any request) according to His will (in agreement with His own plan), He listens to and hears us. And if (since) we [positively] know that He listens to us in whatever we ask, we also know [with settled and absolute knowledge] that we have [granted us as our present possessions] the requests made of Him."*

Prayers and thoughts

Waiting on God

Romans 12 The Message "Take your everyday, ordinary life- your sleeping, eating, going-to-work, and walking-around life - and place it before God as an offering. Embracing what God does for you is the best thing you can do for him. Don't become so well-adjusted to your culture that you fit into it without even thinking. Instead, fix your attention on God. You'll be changed from the inside out. Readily recognize what he wants from you, and quickly respond to it. Unlike the culture around you, always dragging you down to its level of immaturity, God brings the best out of you, develops well-formed maturity in you."

One of the most misunderstood and yet one of the most foundational forms of prayer is waiting on God. The simplest definition of waiting on God would be a continual life devotion to God and an immovable expectation and awareness that He will intervene in your life.

There was no separation between the life of Jesus and the life of His Father in heaven. He did nothing of Himself, and more importantly, He wanted to do nothing of Himself. He had placed His life as an offering before His Father, so the Father could do with it as He pleased.

With that heart position, His life became a continual prayer. The perfect will of His Father in the heavenly (spiritual) realm became manifested in the physical realm unhindered. As the perfect vessel, Jesus imparted the very nature of His Father to the world.

Today, "waiting on God" is our portion of that kind of life, whether for our own needs or on behalf of someone else. As we devote ourselves to our heavenly Father, wanting only His will as our life's purpose, we become the same kind of vessel to accomplish His will to be "done on earth as it is in heaven."

Waiting for the will of the Father to be revealed to us and then waiting for it to be accomplished through us is truly the blessed life. Think of it! In our everyday, ordinary occurrences that we call "life," we are actually conduits for the will of God to be accomplished through us. All we need do is listen and follow as our only purpose for living.

*Waiting on God
by
Andrew Murray*

Very important book to get and use often

The Ultimate Form of Worship

Just as few of us see our emulating Christ as the highest form of praise, few of us see prayer as the ultimate form of worship that it really is. Our limited church experience has allowed us to classify worship as singing the more quiet songs as a congregation, possibly bowing our heads in reverence, or raising our hands in an attitude of submission as we feel a warm presence.

Getting "caught up" does not mean that we are giving true honor to God!

Christian music has categorized its presentations into praise music and worship music. Praise music could mean anything from up tempo songs with lyrics that notice God in any form whatsoever to heavy rock with loud, screaming vocals accompanied by an indistinguishable wall of sound that begs to close down the senses. (I have often wondered how the Lord would feel if He were sitting in the first row of most heavy rock "praise" concerts. The picture of a holy God being presented with screaming electronics as an accepted offering gives me pause, to say the least.)

Think of what prayer really is.

Think of how it could be an expression of the highest honor we are able to give our loving God.

Worship music is usually slower and quieter with words that honor the Lord and give time for the listeners to focus their attention on Him. These ways of praising and worshiping God are the accepted forms of expression that are evident in today's church.

Think of what true prayer is, however. In prayer, as we approach the Lord, we are expressing an understanding of His office as God. We are saying that we understand and fully submit to His sovereignty, His power, and His position as the ruler of all that exists.

As we lower ourselves in our own eyes, making requests or offering heart petitions of love, we are stating that He is God, and we are not. To do so moves us from our normal position of rebellious independence to one of humble submission. It honors Him, whereas our fleshly offerings cannot do so.

Worship is a lifestyle of communicating with our Father, not just an activity entered into so we can experience the "warm fuzzies."

It might be noted here that the Bible records Jesus as stealing away for prayer often. He taught those around Him to pray – they already knew how to sing to the Lord in psalms and hymns. He even stated clearly the importance of doing nothing in our own strength and showed us the importance of submitting to His Father's strength at all times. I am convinced that He was showing us how best to honor His Father by looking to Him for all things. That is called worship! It's a lifestyle, not just one more activity in which we can be involved that happens to incorporate music!

192

From Our Father's Heart

Make sure that you remain diligent
while you are waiting for Me to move on your behalf.
Your time of waiting is also
a time of learning to be obedient in other areas of your life.
Complete those things that I have told you to do.
Clean up all of the relationships that have been neglected.
Become a study of Jesus.
Learn about My heart.
Bring your house to order, so that new assignments can be
completed when I give them to you.
Few understand the importance of waiting on Me.
I am not only completing patience,
diligence, and obedience in you;
I am orchestrating many things concerning your life.
As soon as everything is in order, you need to be ready to move.
There will be work to be done.
Prepare while you can.
When I call you, I will expect immediate responses.
A work of completed patience will bring new faith in Me.
Soon you will walk in it.

Psalm 51:10 Amp   "Create in me a clean heart, O God, and renew a right, persevering and steadfast spirit within me."

Psalm 106:12-15 Amp "Then [Israel] believed His words [trusting in, relying on them]; they sang His praise.
13) But they hastily forgot His works; they did not [earnestly] wait for His plans [to develop] regarding them.
14) But lusted exceedingly in the wilderness and tempted and tried to restrain God [with their insistent desires] in the desert.
15) And He gave them their request, but sent leanness to their souls…"

Acts 12 The Message Bible   "Then the time came for Herod to bring him out for the kill. That night, even though shackled to two soldiers, one on either side, Peter slept like a baby."

Romans 8 The Message Bible "This resurrection life you received from God is not a timid, grave-tending life. It's adventurously expectant, greeting God with a childlike 'What's next, Papa?' God's Spirit touches our spirits and confirms who we really are. We know who he is, and we know who we are: Father and children."

The picture of Peter shackled to two soldiers and snoring up a storm while waiting for the Lord to move on His behalf is probably one of the most descriptive, mature heart positions of trusting in God ever presented. It is a delightful portrayal of absolute trust in a faithful Father God. It can also, however, evoke the wrong picture of what waiting for the Lord to move on our behalf is really all about. Yes, waiting on God most certainly accomplishes quiet, peaceful, steadfast patience in those who are waiting; but much more than that takes place.

Waiting on God can be a very active, productive time.

Waiting on God is never a time of sleeping the days away. In fact, it is the opposite of inactivity. Although the primary focus is always seeking the Lord diligently and repenting of revealed sins - especially those of faithlessness and control - many "clean-up" tasks are accomplished during these times.

Waiting is a time of both heart and physical preparation. It is a time of bringing proper order back to your spiritual and physical house. To wait on God is a settling in with the Lord, cleaning your ears so that you can once again hear Him properly, cleaning your house so that you can move when He tells you to move; and sharpening your tools so that you have what is needed for the important tasks ahead. Waiting for the Father to impart what is on His heart for your life also imparts His life to you in the process.

God imparts Himself to you when you simply sit in His presence. It is a time to commune with the Lord in silence, sitting quietly and peacefully with no agenda on your part except to be there with Him, which allows Him to minister His life to your inner being. Nothing is more important to the Lord. Nothing is more important to you. It is amazing what changes can occur as we are seemingly "doing nothing!"

Our Posture in Prayer

Romans 4 The Message "He (Abraham) didn't tiptoe around God's promise asking cautiously skeptical questions. He plunged into the promise and came up strong, ready for God, sure that God would make good on what he had said."

The effective attitude of true prayer is a study in extremes. On the one hand, every fiber of the Word of God invites each of us who are born again to approach the Master of all things with an absolute confidence because of the work of Calvary. We have been formed to bask in the presence of the Living God without measure or time limit. We are invited to "wait" with Him. It is our heritage.

194

Interestingly enough, the only way to receive that kind of access is to have a humble heart, the heart of Jesus. He and the Father came together with the same heart purpose, accomplishing the Father's will, which left Jesus' own will down the street someplace. Actually, He had given up His will before He even took on the character of man. It was not part of His nature to exercise His own will.

Romans 12 The Message *"Love from the center of who you are; don't fake it. Run for dear life from evil; hold on for dear life to good. Be good friends who love deeply; practice playing second fiddle……….. Make friends with nobodies; don't be the great somebody."*

Romans 15 The Message *"Those of us who are strong and able in the faith need to step in and lend a hand to those who falter, and not just do what is most convenient for us. Strength is for service, not status. Each one of us needs to look after the good of the people around us, asking ourselves, 'How can I help?'*
"That's exactly what Jesus did. He didn't make it easy for himself by avoiding people's troubles, but waded right in and helped out. 'I took on the troubles of the troubled,' is the way Scripture puts it. Even if it was written in Scripture long ago, you can be sure it's written for us. God wants the combination of his steady, constant calling and warm, personal counsel in Scripture to come to characterize us, keeping us alert for whatever he will do next. May our dependably steady and warmly personal God develop maturity in you so that you get along with each other as well as Jesus gets along with us all. Then we'll be a choir – not our voices only, but our very lives singing in harmony in a stunning anthem to the God and Father of our Master Jesus!
So reach out and welcome one another to God's glory. Jesus did it; now you do it!"

Just as our posture in prayer with the Father is one of humility and submission, so should our posture be when praying for others. Jesus came as a servant with love in His heart, influencing the world, and influencing His Father because of His heart. That same attitude should be ours if we are to be a true representative influence in the flow of the Father's Kingdom. The love of Jesus will be manifested on this earth in our lives and in the lives of those for whom we pray as God honors our petitions to Him.

Those who God calls us to pray for are very important to Him.

Our Horizontal Relationship with Others

God has placed us in a world that is actually out to kill us, so to speak. As Christians, we are oil floating on top of water and if we are true to our calling, we'll never mix in because the spirit and flesh cannot function together. God has also called us to overcome that world. Our time spent with others and our responses to them allow us to seek the Father so that we can be changed in order to reflect Christ properly.

Oil and water don't and can never mix.

Working Out Our Salvation

Phil. 2:12b-13 Amp "...work out (cultivate, carry out to the goal, and fully complete) your own salvation with reverence and awe and trembling (self-distrust, with serious caution, tenderness of conscience, watchfulness against temptation, timidly shrinking from whatever might offend God and discredit the name of Christ).
13 [Not in your own strength] for it is God Who is all the while effectually at work in you [energizing and creating in you the power and desire], both to will and to work for His good pleasure and satisfaction and delight."

Once we have given Jesus Lordship over our lives, it is the Father's intent to refine, mold, and develop that salvation in us to the fullest extent. If we are going to tell others about Jesus, we will have to be changed so that we can represent Him properly. Our words alone will usually not be enough for others to see their need of Jesus. In fact, if our lives do not mirror Him, our words will more than likely be cast aside, and rightfully so. The world can spot a phony and they won't listen to one.

Our vertical relationship with God allows us to know Him and know His plans for us. We also go to Him for answers to our needs and the ability to make permanent, spiritual changes so that His plans, which include us, can be accomplished.

Relationships with others are designed to show us how much we've learned or have not learned in responding as Jesus would.

Our horizontal relationships are our training ground so that we can bring the character of Jesus to the world. To show us our need for the character of Christ to be alive and well in us, God establishes divine relationships and initiates continual "setups" for us, so that we become more like Jesus. He is the one who has created the institutions in which we function, i.e. marriage, family, and church fellowships; and our participation in these institutions teaches us to function in love as Jesus would if we keep our hearts open to the Lord.

Have you ever wondered why some people are in your life? Why do you think they are there?

Two Institutions

God has designed two main institutions in which He allows us to participate. One is marriage; the other is the fellowshipping with other believers. Both of these institutions are designed by God to destroy our selfish attitudes and fleshly desires, so that the Spirit of the Lord in us can come forth. (The family unit is also a training ground, but we will confine our study to the other two areas and trust that you will apply what you learn to family relationships.) Study the chart on the opposite page and notice the wonderful flow and purpose that the Lord works in us through relationships.

Did you know that the church is designed by God to teach us to be like Jesus because of the conflicts that occur, and the subsequent forgiveness that must take place? This process builds Christ-like love in us as we submit to His heart when conflicts occur.

In the same way, marriage builds the character of Christ in us as we deny our own needs and live for the needs of our mate. The combined situations and people that we encounter in the church, in marriage, in our families, and in the world create the refining fires that are needed for us to determine to seek God as our only source, and overcome the world through the character of Jesus Christ that is formed in us. Have you ever thought of that person who really boils your potatoes as a wonderful provision of God being used to make you more like Jesus?

Our interaction with fellow believers – fellowship - is a command of God. He said that we should not forsake fellowshipping with others. We take that lightly, but God sees the pressure of refinement through those relationships as very important for our growth.

Notice that God plans relationships with others as both blessings and refiner's fires.

Our Horizontal Relationship with Others

Our relationship with others is the "working out" of God's plan in our lives.

It is one of the vehicles that He uses to make us like Jesus.

This is not an "add on;" it is an integral part of His plan.

You will not be able to pray effectively
until you understand how God uses others to change you

Us

How Do I Become
Like Jesus?

Others

What are Their
Needs?

Relationships Form us into Christ's Image

So that the world can see Jesus in us
and be reconciled to the Father
(Rom 8:29-31; 2 Cor. 5:18-20; 1 Peter 2:9)

Interaction trains us to walk as Jesus did.
(1 John 2:6)

Prepares us for future kingdoms
(Rev. 22:3-5)

Conflicts make us seek God.

Allows us to see who we are not
(Luke 16:14,15)

Gives purpose to our lives
(1 Thes 1:6,7; 2 Cor 1:3,4)

Shows us our need of others

Shows us our place in God's plan
(Eph. 6:18)

Interactions encourage us when
they are fruitful.

Stimulus For <u>Interaction</u>

The Word of God
Needs of people
(1 Jn 3:17)
Commitment, Conflicts
(1 Peter 4:8)
Truth vs. Perceptions

Makes others aware of
a spiritual realm

Allows them to see God's mercy
(Romans 2:4)

Brings them to know about Jesus

Brings them to salvation

Relationships for the good of others fulfill
God's plan for mankind

To glorify Christ

To develop priests and kings
(1 Peter 2:9)

To bring souls into the kingdom
(Matt. 28:19)

To teach angels
(Eph. 3:10-12)

Marriage Covenant

Fellowship
Church Associations

From Our Father's Heart

Have you ever carried the weight of other people's sins?
Have you ever labored for them so intensely
that you thought you would break under pressure?
Have you ever longed that they get right with Me
for their good, for My reasons?
Did the loss of someone's fellowship ever make you mourn
and desire to do something, anything, to restore it?
Was the feeling of emptiness so intense
that you were consumed with finding ways
to bring yourself together with that person once again?
If you see broken relationships with Me and with each other -
which are caused by sin - as the horror that they really are,
you are beginning to understand relationships as I see them
and the reasons for which I have established them.
When someone sins against you, your heart should break,
not necessarily for the offense,
but for the broken relationships -
the relationship with Me and with you.
You must intercede that the fellowships be restored,
that he or she makes things right,
for his or her good and for My glory.
If you have sinned against another brother or sister,
you must drop everything and run to repentance.
I will not allow you to rest until that is done.
If you have hardened your heart and do not crave restoration,
I will begin My process of breaking your rebellion until you do.
You will eventually wonder why your praise is empty,
your eyes are dry,
your prayers are cold; and your life is out of order.
Nothing you do will satisfy you
until you move in the direction of healing.
It is because your "inner being"
knows that something is out of order.
It is My doing, so that you desire restoration.
Don't think that I do not notice violated fellowships;
they are key to My will going forth on your land.
They are important to Me.
I would not allow the broken relationship with My creation to
remain; why would I not require the same from you?
If you see that things are out of order in someone's life,
pray for that person.
If you have been offended,
take the steps necessary to reestablish communion.
If you have offended, don't rest until the offense is gone.
I will wait.

Make every relationship right to the best of your ability!

201

2 Samuel 14:14b NIV "But God does not take away life; instead, he devises ways so that a banished person may not remain estranged from him."

Matthew 5:23,24 NIV "Therefore, if you are offering your gift at the altar and there remember that your brother has something against you,
24) leave your gift there in front of the altar. First go and be reconciled to your brother; then come and offer your gift."

Galatians 4:19 NIV "My dear children, for whom I am again in the pains of childbirth until Christ is formed in you..."

If you are pursuing the bridal heart, there is no place for self-service in any relationship in which you engage.

How do you feel about that?

Are you willing to ask the Lord to have you care more for others than you care for yourself in any and every situation?

Even those who hate you?

List a few of the people you need to forgive or with whom you need to make things right if you haven't already done so.

Don't necessarily go to them now, but be obedient when the Lord directs you to move. It will be great, maybe not fun, but great for your relationship with the Lord.

Christ being formed in you or in someone else is far more than the initial salvation event. It is a continual working out of forsaking our old nature and walking in His new nature, which we received upon establishing a relationship with Jesus Christ (2 Cor. 3:18 Amp.)

If you read the book of Philippians, you will see that Paul labored hard for that. Christ died for that.

Have you ever realized that the members of your fellowship are there so that Christ can be formed in them and in you? Did you know that your lack of Christ-likeness is a refiner's fire to them as theirs is to you? Write down your heart comment.

True fellowship requires something from everyone - tolerance, compassion, time, forgiveness, and continual monitoring. It is not easy, so many interactions fall by the wayside. What is usually never noticed is the broken heart of God when these relationships perish.

Relationships and friendships are no accident. God brings people together for His reasons. He requires us to maintain associations for His good and for our growth.

It is easy to throw someone away because of an offense. Children who do not know any better do that all the time. It requires maturity to pursue love in the midst of and through offenses. It is difficult to go the distance all the way to restoration. Most people are not willing to pay the price; and, therefore, never really grow to God's kind of maturity.

We throw people away when they offend us or become a burden to us.

I firmly believe that most of us in the church are not trusted to function in many of the gifts of the Spirit, because we cannot be trusted with the relationships that God brings our way. Few of us are willing to humble ourselves enough to do what it takes to love others as Jesus loved us.

Laying our lives down for the sake of another is the way of the cross of Jesus Christ. Most of us get off the cross when the going gets tough. We are grateful for the persistence of Jesus, but not humble enough to honor His heart.

Marriage

For an in-depth discussion by Jim and Merry Corbett,
go to www.christspassionatelife.com
and listen to the audio message entitled,
"The Marriage Covenant."

Marriage is the most misunderstood institution ever established by God. Both the world and most of the church are clueless as to the reasons God joins two people together as man and wife.

This is so cool!

Eph. 5:21-31 Amp *"Be subject to one another out of reverence for Christ (the Messiah, the Anointed One).*

22 Wives, be subject (be submissive and adapt yourselves) to your own husbands as [a service] to the Lord.

23 For the husband is head of the wife as Christ is the Head of the church, Himself the Savior of [His] body.

24 As the church is subject to Christ, so let wives also be subject in everything to their husbands.

25 Husbands, love your wives, as Christ loved the church and gave Himself up for her,

26 So that He might sanctify her, having cleansed her by the washing of water with the Word,

27 That He might present the church to Himself in glorious splendor, without spot or wrinkle or any such things [that she might be holy and faultless].

28 Even so husbands should love their wives as [being in a sense] their own bodies. He who loves his own wife loves himself.

29 For no man ever hated his own flesh, but nourishes and carefully protects and cherishes it, as Christ does the church,

30 Because we are members (parts) of His body.

31 For this reason a man shall leave his father and his mother and shall be joined to his wife, and the two shall become one flesh.

32 This mystery is very great, but I speak concerning [the relation of] Christ and the church."

Gen. 2:23,24 Amp *"Then Adam said, This [creature] is now bone of my bones and flesh of my flesh; she shall be called Woman, because she was taken out of a man. Therefore a man shall leave his father and his mother and shall become united and cleave to his wife, and they shall become one flesh."*

I Cor. 6:15-17 The Message Bible "... *remember that your bodies are created with the same dignity as the Master's body. You wouldn't take the Master's body off to a whorehouse, would you? I should hope not.*

There's more to sex than mere skin on skin. Sex is as much spiritual mystery as physical fact. As written in Scripture, 'The two become one.' Since we want to become spiritually one with the Master, we must not pursue the kind of sex that avoids commitment and intimacy, leaving us more lonely than ever – the kind of sex that can never "become one."

In verse 23 of Ephesians 5, the Lord says that marriage is related to Christ and the church. The message that permeates that relationship is one of crucifixion. Christ died for us; we are to lay our lives down for Him and for others, so that He is glorified. Marriage is no different.

Let's study God's ideal heart attitude in a marriage. It would be good to observe here that there are no exceptions when we are in a relationship with Jesus. He calls us all to a walk of the cross in every relationship in which we are involved. He did it, so why would He allow us to enter any relationship for selfish, self-serving motives?

Why do most people marry?

How does that attitude comply with the life attitude of Jesus?

What is the reason that most divorces occur?

The answer to the last question is selfishness. No matter how it is masked, it always boils down to the sin of selfishness. The husband or wife is not being pleased by the other, so he/she acts in a manner that causes separation to occur, or he/she walks away and finds another futile relationship in order to be pleased or satisfied.

Few people equate marriage with being one of God's refining fires and His most precious presentation of His love to the world. Few enter into a marriage for the best interests of the other person. Instead, they enter into marriage for their own pleasure, so they never really learn to love as Jesus loves. (Now don't go find someone who is repulsive to you and ask that person to marry you just so you can be super-spiritual. Listen to the God-heart of what is being said.)

Let's Deal with Some Preliminaries

Because of the work of the cross of Jesus Christ, both men and women are equal in every way in God's eyes. Neither is "more loved" or more "powerful." In marriage, and also in the church, there is a God-ordained office that a man has. It is an office of protection, or covering. Many people have misinterpreted that function as "authority," and have destroyed their marriages and even misused it within the church.

This office is one of absolute service and protection (akin to a shepherd and his covering over his sheep,) designed for the well being of others. In the case of marriage, the man's office is meant for the well being of his wife.

If you get this and devote your marriage to its principles, you will touch more people for Jesus than you can ever imagine.

Because of his office, a man will answer to the Lord for how well he fulfilled his role of providing fertile soil for his mate to grow in Christ. Did he live the life of Jesus in her midst, so that she could see Jesus in all of his actions and dealings with her?

Very serious stuff!!

In the ideal marriage, both parties - as equals - should enter the commitment "for the best interests of the other," not for their own gain or their own needs, whatever they might be. As wonderful as a mutual attraction can be, both parties are called to a commitment to serve the other - for God's best interests for their spouse - before they ever enter into the marriage covenant with each other.

Beauty fades, circumstances change, difficult life situations happen. Honest, godly commitment to serve the other person, no matter what ensues, weathers and overcomes the storms and trials. In other words, both parties are called to die to themselves, their own rights, and all of their own needs; and determine to live for the best interests of the other.

In the beginning of this study, you learned of the bride of old who understood her position and requirements while she was waiting for the one to whom she was betrothed. She waited for her master, as we wait for ours. She prepared her heart, so that he would be pleased when he came. We do the same for Jesus.

The kind of crucifixion of her flesh that occurred in training is no different than what is expected of us as we wait. Likewise, the marriage covenant is not exempt from the same living-for-the-good-of-the-other attitude we have determined to be important while waiting.

Do you believe that God would ask us to always lay our lives down for the good of others and then allow us to enter into a marriage agreement for the good of our own interests? Why or why not?

Eph. 5:21-31 Amp *"Be subject to one another out of reverence for Christ (the Messiah, the Anointed One)."*

So many members of the body of Christ enter into marriage for their own good. They attempt to wait for the perfect partner, meaning the one that really rings their bell. That is opposite of the intent that God has for marriage. He calls us to enter into marriage for the best interests of the other person.

Please don't misunderstand. This is not a morbid, "woe is me" kind of torment invented by our Father to make us miserable. In fact, when fully understood, this is the epitome of a holy life that exhibits the pattern for the world to follow and reveals the nature of Jesus to them. When Christ-like service is at the center of all that you do, especially in your marriage, the only real happiness comes when you are serving, not when you are being served.

Jesus came to serve - especially under difficult circumstances

Now He asks us to do the same.

It develops His character in us.

The mature bridal heart demands that we serve others before we serve ourselves. Subjecting ourselves to another is the way of our Lord. He came to serve; so must we, especially the one that Jesus has chosen as our life partner.

When selecting a mate, pray for the one that the Lord intends for you. Pray, however, that He provides you with the person that you will be willing to serve, through His power, for the rest of your life; not one that fulfills all of your desires. Jesus is the One who is to fulfill those desires. That is how a person can be completely fulfilled whether married or not.

As you pray, whether you are a man or a woman, pray for the heart of God and your ability to submit yourself to the needs of the one He provides for you. When that person enters your life, pray for each other and commit your way to serve the other, even if the other at some time refuses to do so. You must gain the heart position of Jesus; so that your union is for the other's best interests, not your own.

> *25 Husbands, love your wives, as Christ loved the church and gave Himself up for her,*
> *26 So that He might sanctify her, having cleansed her by the washing of water with the Word,*
> *27 That He might present the church to Himself in glorious splendor, without spot or wrinkle or any such things [that she might be holy and faultless].*
> *28 Even so husbands should love their wives as [being in a sense] their own bodies. He who loves his own wife loves himself.*
> *29 For no man ever hated his own flesh, but nourishes and carefully protects and cherishes it, as Christ does the church,*
> *30 Because we are members (parts) of His body.*
> *31 For this reason a man shall leave his father and his mother and shall be joined to his wife, and the two shall become one flesh.*

The Ideal Scenario

Husbands, there is no other reason for you to marry other than to lay your life down for your wife as Christ did for the church. (Read verse 31 again) You are given the mandate to provide an atmosphere of freedom for your wife to become all that she can be in Christ. By your love and service, your wife is to see Jesus. Because of how you act, she is to crave Jesus. By your example, she is to learn to love to follow Jesus.

> *22 Wives, be subject (be submissive and adapt yourselves) to your own husbands as [a service] to the Lord.*
> *23 For the husband is head of the wife as Christ is the Head of the church, Himself the Savior of [His] body.*
> *24 As the church is subject to Christ, so let wives also be subject in everything to their husbands.*

Wives, you are to submit to your husbands as you would to Christ.

How is that really supposed to work? Before reading on, how do you perceive what the Lord had in mind?

209

The Ideal Situation

Partners in marriage are to enter into the marriage covenant as equals in every way, devoted to serving the other's best interests before their own. In the order of God, the man is the covering over the woman as the weaker vessel. (That does not imply less than, lower than, nor less intelligent than.) Remember, every person ever given breath is of equal quality in God's eyes. Jesus considered everyone important enough to die for them.

Because of the office of the covering, (that does not mean better than, more important than, smarter than; and especially, more approved than. It is designated to maintain the order of God that was established in the Garden of Eden.) man - with the woman considered a full equal - will answer to God for the well-being of the gift that God has given him.

Here's How That Submission Thing Works God's Way

As stated before, a man and woman enter into marriage as equals for the best interests of the other, devoted to serving the other. The weight of their lives is equal in every way in God's eyes.

Should there be a disagreement in any decision at any time, the man - because of his office and only because of his office - has the responsibility to determine what decision should be made to bring forth peace. He must lay down his own desire before the Lord and find the decision that is in the best interests of his wife. This is the crucified life.

Absolute freedom!!

He is to take on the same heart that Jesus has, giving up all of his rights for the good of his wife, and find the answer that is best for her. As the answer is presented, the wife submits to that answer, knowing that her husband has the same heart toward her that Jesus has.

Eph.5:33 This mystery is very great, but I speak concerning [the relation of] Christ and the church."

Marriage is one of the ways that the church and the world will see a real life example of Jesus in action.

Do you really see how Jesus is formed in you because of the relationships that He brings into your life? Explain!

What kinds of heart changes do you need to have the Lord make in you so that you can love others?

Is it time to study your marriage in the light of what has been presented here?

What kind of heart changes do you have to make to better represent Jesus to your mate, to the church, to the world?

Prayers and thoughts

Dear Father,

I choose to be willing to do whatever it takes to allow the Word of God to work in my heart as I learn to function in our marriage. I choose to forgive any wrong done to me, any real or perceived injustice, any hurt from neglect, or any time I have felt alone or abandoned by my mate.

I choose to open my heart completely to You, Lord, to learn whatever You desire to teach me. From this day forward, by Your power, through Your Holy Spirit, I lay down all pre-conceived notions that I may have had about marriage concerning rights, positions, duties, roles, and attitudes. I release my mate to do the same. I also release my mate from any control that I may have taken over him/her in any way.

Father, I choose this day to release You to place forgiveness in my heart, and replace any wronged feelings with Your holy love. I choose to serve my mate, and get in line with Your Word as to my responsibility in our marriage.

I choose to turn from all resentments, unforgiveness, anger, and hatred toward .... and surrender to Your perfect will for us.

I lay down my own agenda, secret heart plans, personal motives, and selfish expectations in regard to our marriage. I choose to search Your heart and submit to Your will. If I am holding anything against ....,, I now confess all sin, and come to You to release me from attitudes that may hinder me from being open to Your perfect will. I choose to commit our marriage completely to You.

Signed _____ Date _____

As mentioned previously, we need to become a study of Jesus to fully understand how we are to display the character of Jesus and live His passionate life. As Paul determined to know Him as his priority, so must we adopt that same purpose.

When Jesus was teaching His Sermon on the Mount, He established some definite characteristics as patterns for His life and ours. These were imprinted in the minds of those who heard what He was saying, so that they would recognize what He was doing when He lived them out before them.

The Much Sought After Characteristics of Christ section, which appears a little later in this book, is a study of some of the character traits that each of us will need, so that we can display the life of Jesus to a dying world. These traits were given to us by Jesus Himself in the form of "beatitudes." He called us blessed if we function in them. These beatitudes are patterns for life and epitomize the life of our Lord. They are patterns of His very nature, given so that we can understand them and agree to have them implemented in our hearts as we submit to Father God. We can then display them before the world and each other as a true representation of Jesus.

The book, The Seven Spirits of God, by Ron Auch is a must read.

As we learn that one of the most important reasons the Lord has chosen for us to remain on this earth is to reach others, we find that we need "more of Jesus" apparent in us to do so. How foolish of us, then, to lift up our doctrines, beliefs, and our church fellowships in an attempt to effect any real change in the lives of those who don't know Jesus as Lord.

As Jesus Himself walked among His people, we find that He displayed the traits presented in the Sermon on the Mount and many others as an example of how all of us, who call ourselves His followers, should live each and every day. Although they do not give us an all-inclusive picture of the Lord's holy, completed character; they do, however, show us His heart and give each of us direction and reliable guidelines as we proceed on our way in learning to function like Jesus. In 1 John 2:6 we are told, *"Whoever says he abides in Him ought ... to walk and conduct himself in the same way in which He walked and conducted Himself."*

Living Out Christ's Love
(LOCL)

This is a practical application that will challenge you to live as Christ would by praying for one person. You will need to refer to this section over and over again as challenges and situations come up because of the commitment we will ask you to make of praying for that person for one year. We call it Living Out Christ's Love.

Now is an opportune time to introduce the Living Out Christ's Love (LOCL) portion of this continued study. We will introduce LOCL in detail here before you study the character of Jesus in the next section, because you will need to know and apply His character traits when you find the person for whom you will pray. It will be important to continually link these two sections together as you pursue your prayer commitment.

Living Out Christ's Love is simply making a wholehearted agreement to pray for one year for someone to whom the Lord directs you, using the support system of our Web site and our daily e-mail encouragements. *We are going to ask you to document your prayers in the prayer journals provided, and then give those journals to your prayer recipient each month during that year.*

We have found that this type of commitment to another person is the epitome of a refiner's fire, because it challenges you to deny yourself for someone else as Jesus did for you and helps to prepare your bridal heart. The study of the character traits of Jesus as found in the Beatitudes and the application of them when you pray for another will amplify your effectiveness in showing the one for whom you're praying who Jesus is.

Living Out Christ's Love is a passionate life experience that exhibits the character traits of Jesus to others and forms them in the heart of the participant. Stopping short of walking as Jesus would - for the sake and best interests of another - nullifies all that has been addressed so far in this study.

Anyone can learn *about* God, and Jesus, and the Holy Spirit. It is those who purposefully choose to become involved with God for the sake of others who are entrusted with His heart and passions. This LOCL experience will infuse* Christ's life into you, because of the challenges and situations with which you will deal as you prayerfully and practically focus on the life of someone else who needs more of God. In essence, you will be positioning yourself as an advocate for someone who cannot, does not know how, is too weary because of life struggles, or maybe doesn't even want to petition God himself. * Definition of infuse – implies

This will be a refiner's fire and an incredible blessing at the same time.

Either way, you will bless God.

There comes a time when the Lord calls upon us to put into effect what He has taught us.

In a definitive moment in history, Christ's disciples were transformed from a huddling, fearful mass into bold ambassadors.

Acts 4:29-35

It's time to get involved with God for the good of someone else.

a pouring in of something that gives new life or significance! (See Gal.2:20)

If the person does know how to reach God, you will be interceding along side of him for his best interests. (We will use he/him/his throughout the LOCL section in its all-inclusive sense, meaning that you can substitute with she/her if the person for whom you pray is female. God sees us all as equals, but grammatically this will be easier to read!)

Here's How You Get Started

Seek the Lord so you know for whom He desires you to pray, record your prayers in the way the Lord desires in the monthly journals; and then give the journal to that person at the end of every month for a minimum of one year. Once you have waited patiently on the Lord and know for certain for whom you will be praying, your prayer guidelines go something like this:

A) Wait on the Lord so you know for what you'll be praying.
B) Wait on the Lord to see the results of those prayers manifested in the life of the one for whom you are praying.

Prayer is fun when approached with that kind of freedom. It is God's power that accomplishes everything. He desires for us to find His will by coming to Him, and then enjoys it when we are privy to and participants in His will being accomplished in someone else's life. That's God's kind of prayer.

Keep in mind:

A) The person for whom you'll be praying should be the same gender as you, unless it's someone in your immediate family, i.e. husband, wife, father, mother, sister, grandfather, etc. Prayer forms an intense spiritual bond, and you'll be exercising godly wisdom with this stipulation so that ungodly ties do not result. The flesh has a way of contaminating what is begun in the spirit!
B) You should be approximately the same age as your prayer recipient, meaning that adults pray for adults and children pray for children. Again, wisdom and discernment must be used here. Obviously immediate family members must be free to pray for other members of their family, i.e. parents for children, children for parents or brothers and sisters, aunts, uncles, etc. The goal of our cautions is propriety and safety.

Commit to pray for someone for one year,

write a summary of your prayers in the journals provided,

and then give that person the journal after you pray for him/her each month.

Someone once said: "Testify of Jesus at every opportunity that comes your way, if need be, open your mouth."

218

C) Never take the position of being a counselor or an expert on the needs of people. Your goal is to simply bless someone and live the caring life of Jesus in his midst by your honest concern and heartfelt prayers for him.

D) Don't go it alone. Work with others who are participating in LOCL if possible.

E) Use the resources in our Father's Heart mailings and on our Web site, www.christspassionatelife.com. Use discretion as you communicate with others. We will monitor chat room discussions and eliminate any foolish talk or behavior.

F) Seek the counsel of others as you find out the needs of your prayer recipient. However, do not betray the trust of that person by airing his confidences, especially to those he knows. Prayer has an unfortunate way of becoming gossip if things are not handled in a godly fashion.

G) Implement what you have learned about representing and seeking God.

As soon as you know for whom you are committing to pray, begin to enter your prayers in the first journal as the Lord leads you to pray. You may not have anything to enter on some days, so don't attempt to fill all of the pages just for the sake of filling in all the spaces. You also don't want to overwhelm your prayer recipient with myriads of pages and copious notes. Just relax and love that person before your Lord.

Always remember that your commitment is a gift to the person the Lord has chosen for you. This is not a time to pick him apart, force your beliefs upon him, or attempt to sell him your ideas of how he ought to live. This is done too often in prayer meetings.

Many church people disguise their hidden agendas in the form of prayer. If that is your heart, you should begin this study over again; you have not yet learned some of the things you need to know.

Pray God's love for your prayer recipient. Place yourself in his shoes upon receiving the journal. Depending on where he is with the Lord, this first presentation could be quite a shock. He may never have had anyone give him this kind of gift.

If the Lord has given you someone who hates Him, the idea of prayer may not sit well with the one for whom you are going to pray. Make sure that you have the best interests of your Lord and your new associate at heart. Wisdom and sensitivity are the watchwords as the Holy Spirit directs your steps.

Don't go brain dead with this praying for someone stuff.

Represent Jesus properly.

Never pray to further any agenda you might have.

Never pray to reinforce your spirituality to someone who has doubted your Christianity.

You will only reinforce his opinion and be trapped for a year, or you'll end up violating your commitment.

Be careful of
your interaction
if you do not
know the
person.

After you have prayed for one month, get the journal to the person for whom you are interceding. This again will need prayer and possibly even counsel from someone else who is also involved in the process of LOCL. You may hand the journal to him personally, or mail it. However you transport the journal, you need to remember that you are possibly the only representation of Jesus he has ever really seen.

Any form of communication must be loving and brief, making sure to convey that there is no obligation on his part. How the person receives the journal and the whole idea of someone doing what you are promising him you will do will greatly determine how much you say or write at the time of this and any other monthly presentation.

Some of you may end up holding on to the journals until the Lord releases you to deliver them. There may even be some of you who will not give the journals until the end of the year, which is one more learning experience at the Lord's hand. Make sure that personal fears or foolish leadings do not color your activities.

You must not make any commitment other than to pray within the guidelines of this program. It is of utmost importance to never say or commit to anything that you will not be able to do ten or eleven months down the road. You are representing Jesus.

Do not let your enthusiasm or your zeal overshadow God's wisdom. You are not becoming a counselor, a guide for this person's life, or an answer to all of his needs. You are simply going to pray. Should the Lord have you assist the person at any time in the future, that is for Him to reveal to you and only after you have prayed long and hard about it and have sought wise counsel.

Use wise counsel before each communication, and during all future communication or involvement with the person you're lifting up to the Lord. (Be wise as serpents and harmless as doves. See Mt.10:16.)

A word of caution: It is imperative that you have the proper heart, the mature loving heart of Jesus, when you are dealing with your prayer recipient. Understand, however, that you must guard your heart.

If the Lord has given you someone in the world, or even in the church - someone who takes advantage of others, is a con artist, or simply has no regard for others - make sure that you set boundaries on your interaction with him. You are simply going to pray for him - that is your commitment until you know differently.

Never set yourself up for harm or jeopardize your family because of your commitment. You must do what is necessary to be in control of your interaction until you are familiar with the person for whom you are praying, and know the playing field.

Private meetings with relative strangers is a road to disaster if that person has ulterior motives. Plan your strategies properly and solicit the interaction of your family, friends, and wise counsel in any other communication outside of the journals.

Be careful where and how you interact or meet. The Lord may restrict your communication to just sending the journals through the mail. If you do have limited interaction, find people who understand the type of individual with whom you are dealing and use their prayerful counsel. If you are to meet, we suggest you take a friend with you. In some instances, you might choose to remain anonymous throughout and even after your year of commitment, depending on the circumstances.

Never give money until you have prayed long and hard and have shared your desire to do so with at least several people, those you trust implicitly and who are very familiar with the person you're lifting before the Lord. Heed their counsel.

It is strongly recommended that you "team" with at least one other LOCL member (several would be much better) throughout your commitment time and walk each day in wisdom. Use the chat room on our Web site. Subscribe to the daily Father's Heart messages, if only for the bottom portion that deals with prayer and interaction suggestions.

Remember that Satan will hate what you are doing. He would love to destroy your testimony or compromise you in any way he can. Love deeply, but always use wisdom and wise counsel. We cannot stress that enough.

There is the possibility that the Lord may direct you to pray for one of His bridal hearts in process. It may be someone that you already know and trust, or even someone that is very close to you, like a marriage partner or other family member. Always be very prudent in your dealings with him as well and heed scriptural and proper guidelines, but be free to love as Jesus would.

This experience is designed for you to learn how to love as Jesus loves others and to also show others how He loves. There will be many wonderful opportunities to share that love in ways that the Lord brings about, and also many challenges as you fulfill your commitment to Him and your prayer recipient. No matter who he is, totally enjoy the opportunity to live the life of Jesus before him, knowing that the Lord is with you and very pleased with you.

It's God's job to determine the results of your prayers.

More than likely - maybe at first encounter, or possibly after a few months of presenting the prayer journals to him – the one for whom you're praying may inquire as to why you are doing this. Be prepared to give an answer. Many factors will determine your answer, so it is impossible for us to address every situation and your proper response at that time. Spend time with the Lord as to how you should respond.

What is most important to remember is that you answer his question and every question that follows in truth. The time to deal with this issue is during the initial selection process with the Lord. You should lay all personal agendas down and develop the pure motive of blessing someone. Even having the motive of praying for someone's salvation could color your dealings with your new friend. That may sound noble, but it may hinder that person from open communication if it's presented prematurely.

You need to get your heart right with God and pray in obedience to His desires for the one He's chosen for you. You may not see that person come to the Lord for many years after your one-year investment. He may possibly never come. That has little to do with the decision to pray for him. Your answer to him in regard to his inquiry must be solid in your heart long before he ever sees the first journal.

The Lord will give you what to say about why you are praying. You can be sure that whatever the answer is, it will be for the blessing of the one for whom you are praying in some way. Your answer will determine the tone of the rest of your association. Make sure you clear your heart before you even begin your commitment.

Along the way, you may find that you have a delightful interaction with a sincere, loving person full of integrity or one anywhere in between that and someone with whom you need to be cautious. He may share his prayer requests with you and respond very favorably with what you are doing, or simply tolerate your communication.

Your partnering with him might be a wonderful journey toward his healing, salvation, or whatever else that the Lord intended for your association; or you may not even know why the Lord spent a year of your life investing in him.

The outcome of your association matters far less to the Lord than how you have represented Jesus to the one you lifted in prayer along the journey. Did you really exhibit the character of Christ to him at every turn? Did you show him your freedom to repent when you made a mistake? Did your prayer journals reflect your total acceptance of him, no matter what his station in life is, or were they condescending and judgmental?

Let's revisit a few key points before going on to the next section, which will also be of value to you as you are coming to an understanding of what the Lord would want accomplished through this one-year commitment and how you are to go about doing it. Don't hurry the preparation time as the Lord makes your heart ready to embrace the person for whom you'll be praying. Be sensitive to His timing.

As you become involved in Living Out Christ's Love, remember the following:

A) Find wise counsel and submit to their wisdom.
B) Use our Web site and e-mail support system.
C) Refer to and use all elements of this "Passionate Life" learning series, the Word, and your intimate times with the Father to give you wisdom as you pray.
D) Study, revisit often, and walk in the heart characteristics of Jesus that you will be introduced to in this next section. Use them to regulate your heart position before journaling. (Is your attitude the same attitude that Jesus would have? Is it how He would pray for someone?).
E) Talk to several other people and partner to LOCL with them if you can.
F) Get your heart and motives for your commitment in order.
G) Act responsibly. You are representing Jesus.

By the way: that person that you are sure the Lord has given you as a future mate is more than likely *not* the Lord's prayer choice for you at this time. The one that could really help your ministry if only he knew your heart better could be an incredible stumbling block to you for the next year and maybe longer, because of your improper heart motive at the time of your commitment to him. You get the idea!

Gottcha !!!

Above all, remember that you are making a commitment to God and in His Name to the person you choose. Determine now that you will honor that commitment or do not even begin. The reputation of Jesus is on the line once more in your life and reflected in your decisions. Honor Him and bless someone in His Name. He is with you!

The Much Sought After Characteristics of Christ That Are Ours to Function in Each and Every Day
(The Beatitudes)

Note: We would like to thank Pastor Ron Auch, the author of the book, <u>The Seven Spirits Of God</u>, for allowing us to use some of his ideas and wisdom in understanding these characteristics of Christ as they pertain to the beatitudes.

As authors of these pages, we have taken the liberty of labeling certain traits with descriptive names to amplify their meaning more clearly by using today's language and calling them a "spirit." The word "spirit" is not meant to portray an invisible dominance of some sort, as much as it is intended to mean "to take on or emulate the character of another." As we learn of and emulate the character of Jesus, we will walk in the "spirit" of Jesus, as led by the Holy Spirit.

Also, in your study of these character traits, you will notice that they tend to overlap in some ways, especially when explaining the gentle, merciful character traits of Jesus. I am convinced that the Lord chooses to emphatically amplify these certain characteristics of His Son to us because they are so vitally important.

Please restrain yourself from minimizing the importance of the over-all trait because one or two aspects sound familiar. When you have completed this section, you will see the interweaving flow and complementary interaction amongst all of them, which creates an overview of some of the wonder of our Lord.

Note: It is imperative to remember that none of these character traits can be implemented by us. We cannot change one portion of our character. We may change the way we act for a time, but lasting change can only come through communion with God and allowing Him to change our inner being.

After describing the main characteristics of each trait, we will apply those same characteristics to our position in prayer (our vertical association with God,) and in our dealings with others (our horizontal association with others) in today's modern marriage and also as you live out Christ's love (LOCL) during every interaction with your prayer recipient.

Make sure that you refer to this section often as you interact with others and especially as you journal your prayers and communicate with your prayer recipient.

225

A Spirit of Advocacy
(Those who are poor in spirit)

Matt. 5:3 NIV "Blessed are the poor in spirit, for theirs is the kingdom of heaven."

Matt 5:3 Amp "Blessed (happy, to be envied, and spiritually prosperous - with life-joy and satisfaction in God's favor and salvation, regardless of their outward conditions) are the poor in spirit (the humble, who rate themselves insignificant), for theirs is the kingdom of heaven!"

Matthew 5 The Message "You're blessed when you are at the end of your rope. With less of you, there is more of God and His rule."

Heb. 12:2 "Let us fix our eyes on Jesus, the author and perfecter of our faith, who for the joy set before Him, *endured the cross, scorning its shame, and sat down at the right hand of the throne of God."

*Definition of endure: To remain firm under anguish or misfortune, without yielding, with the hope of others being lifted up.

Jesus - who was intensely wealthy in the spiritual realm - was poor in spirit, and functioned as our Advocate, rating His own safety and comfort insignificant for our sake. In the beginning of this study, we included the definition of "advocate" as a basis for the theme that runs throughout these pages. To clarify what it means to be "poor in spirit," it will do us well to revisit what an "advocate" is.

The dictionary definition of "advocate" is "one that pleads the cause of another." Our mission is to be advocates for one another, maintaining a cause for each other in prayer at a minimum, and with our very lives as Jesus did, if necessary, through the power of the Holy Spirit.

We are to be advocates one for another, in support of Father God, and for the reputation of Jesus.

The New International Dictionary of the Bible defines "advocate" as "counselor, comforter, supporter, backer, helper." It says, "The Holy Spirit is the advocate of the Father with us, therefore our Comforter (KJV, John 14:16, 26; 15:26; 16:7; RSV, NIV translate, "Counselor"). As applied to the Holy Spirit, the Greek word is so rich in meaning that adequate translation by any one English word is impossible. The KJV "Comforter" is as satisfactory as any, if it is taken in the fullest sense of one who not only consoles but also strengthens, helps, and counsels, with such authority as a legal advocate has for his client."

Jesus functioned with an advocate heart in two ways -
toward His Father and toward us.
We are to do the same.

Jesus had a passion to empty Himself and live a life devoted to others. He would never lift Himself up or hold Himself in higher esteem than anyone else – even the lowliest leper. Even though He was God, He held everyone in His heart as more important than Himself; especially those who laughed at, tortured, and crucified Him. He could not be wounded by their sin; He could only see their desperate need.

In the true spirit of advocacy, Jesus also desires to see His Father put "first" and is constantly looking to have Him glorified. His delight is in having Father God as the object of esteem in the hearts of those He loves. All of His mortal life, and now all of His kingly life, undergirds and points to the Father. There is no "one-sidedness," however, as all of the Godhead - in unity of spirit, being one - point to each other's wealth.

Are you ever an honest advocate for anyone?

As the Author and Finisher of our faith, Jesus, who functions as our advocate, delights to see us accepted and perfected. He would gladly go to the cross again and again, if He had to, so that we could prosper and be complete in His Father's love; and so that His Father would continually have the pleasure of our company. (Praise God that everything was finished once and for all at Calvary!)

With Jesus as our example, and with the Father's love flowing through us, we are to walk as advocates for our Lord, each other as believers, and then on behalf of those who have need. Our adoption into the family of God, our sonship, gives each of us the heritage and ability to do so through the power of the Holy Spirit.

Characteristics of an Advocate

Those walking as advocates delight in seeing others become all that they can be in Christ. Seeing any less motivates them to respond for the good of those individuals, even at a loss to themselves.

When someone comes against the advocate heart, there is a godly desire to have the offender eventually walk in all of the wealth of the Lord, for the sake of the Lord. To respond in any form of retaliation would be unthinkable. Advocates will love deeper than any argument. In fact, any accusation or injustice only causes them to desire that the other is forgiven and restored before the Father, never from a position of loftiness, but from the heart of lowliness.

Recognizing their acceptance with God, their heritage, their rights, and their privileges (which come via the work on the cross,) but esteeming others more significantly than themselves or their own needs, people walking with the heart of an advocate are wonderfully free. Jealousy, loss of reputation, perceptions of others, fear, and pride have no hold on them.

They are the leaders who serve, the advocates of their accusers, the servants of those who wrong them; and the comforters of those who are against them. Because they are confident and comfortable in their position with God, there is no negative response when falsely accused, no need to be right when wronged; and no desire to be lifted up in any way.

As John the Baptist desired to decrease so that Jesus could increase, those living for the good of others ardently choose that others increase in their walk with the Lord. They are motivated to do something, anything, so that it might happen.

Any desire to see "more of Jesus" in someone else is the spirit of advocacy in action as it thrives and pours itself out to address the need. It is the catalyst to any form of outreach – the desire that the lost or hurting be brought back into fellowship with the Father, for His sake as well as for the sake of the individual. The rally cry, "Father, forgive them, for they know not what they do," transcends the corridors of time, and exists as if fresh from the lips of Jesus in the hearts of those who are poor in spirit, thriving in the spirit of advocacy.

How we live represents to others how powerful the work of the cross is.

In the same way, advocate hearts are the defenders of Jesus and all that He has done with His Father. We are to be advocates of the Godhead in defense of what they have done for all mankind, putting our lives on the line as their representative work.

Own this!!!

We are called to deny ourselves and all that we hold dear in this world, and through our lives defend the life of Jesus. Our purposeful insignificance brings significance to the Lord. (Read the previous line over as many times as it takes to get it into your "knower.")

Vertical Application of an Advocate Spirit

Those poor in spirit only desire to have "Abba Father" glorified. They are very comfortable in their acceptance whenever in God's presence. Because it pleases the Father, the proper posture in prayer is always as a defender of His perfect will, and also for the good of others.

Praise to Him is their ultimate fulfillment. Living a life that praises the Lord and longing to be in praise because it is a natural flow of lifting Him to His rightful position is their only purpose for existing. This is always from a posture of their own lowliness and complete acceptance. The desires of the Father are paramount; their own desires are deemed insignificant.

Horizontal Application of an Advocate Spirit

Wrong!!!

Fellowship with others provides the means for us to see when we are not functioning as their advocates. Instead of their "undoneness" motivating us to be advocates for them before the Father so that they might prosper, we tend to judge them, condemn them; and then eventually separate ourselves from them when it becomes uncomfortable.

An advocate is blind in his heart to the imperfections of those he encounters, other than to bear the weight of those imperfections before the Father on behalf of any given person. He strives to see others become all that they can be in Christ, either through prayer or by responding to their need.

Horizontal Application in Modern Marriage

Ideally, marriage partners are brought together because the Father desires to trust them with each other. His spirit of advocacy would hold no offenses, discard all wrongs, and esteem the spouse and his or her needs as most important.

Each would be safe in the care of the other and have fertile soil in which to grow, as they are both safe in the Father's Spirit and His love flowing through their spouse. They would be the best representative of each other no matter where they go or with whom they come in contact.

Poor in spirit, any imperfection in the other would only motivate the mate to strive, so that the other would be healed. He/She would gladly bear any consequence inflicted because of that imperfection. The honest, mature heart - one pumping with the nourishment of the spirit of advocacy - knows that the Father has chosen him/her as the single member of His spiritual family who could be trusted with the future wellness of his/her spouse. Any action done to elevate self rather than the spouse would hinder the desire of the Father for the spouse to be made whole, and also would not be the proper representation of the Father to him or her.

Application for Living Out Christ's Love (LOCL)

Everyone to whom you are told to present Jesus is very special to Father God. He is looking for those individuals to know who His Son Jesus is, so that they might embrace the love that He has displayed for them on the cross.

You are being called to exemplify that love. Your actions toward others - your prayer journal recipient, your church members, your mate, your children, those who have harmed you - will speak much more clearly than any words you might say about the One you say you serve.

If you approach everyone as one who has all the answers, or as one approaching a "poor sinner," the Father will never be able to trust you with their hearts. Any prayers you say for people, any actions you take, must originate from the heart of an advocate – one who is there on behalf of other people. They will see Jesus in your caring more for them and their needs than you care for yourself.

You will need to come back to this section on the characteristics of Jesus often, as the Lord teaches you lessons from your interaction with others.

My Father,

As I wait for the return of my Lord, and study who He is, I recognize that one of His characteristics is that He is poor in spirit. He willingly emptied Himself of all of His desires for the sake of His Father and others. He gave Himself away for the good of all.

I recognize that the sin of desiring to be lifted up and deemed significant is very evident in my life. I also need to be "right" and get my way in most situations. Forgive me and change me. I am helpless to change myself. I choose to no longer remain foolish and without the power needed to become like my Advocate and Lord because of my sin.

I fully understand that my selfishness must decrease, so that Your wealth might increase in me. I choose to empty myself for the sake of others.

Holy Spirit, please take full control over this area of my life, so that I will become more like my Lord Jesus. I pray that He will be pleased with my representation of Him when He returns.

Thank you,

Signed_____ Date_____

Questions about an Advocate Spirit
(Someone who is poor in spirit)

In your own words, what is an advocate?

Does being insignificant in your own eyes mean that you are worth nothing to God? Why?

How can you better practice this spirit in prayer?

Remember, we usually judge others by their actions.

We judge ourselves by our intentions.

Name anyone that you have harmed because you have strived to remain loftier than that person.

Is there anything you can do about it? Will you do it?

Mark the last occasion in which you did not function as an advocate toward your mate, another church member, or someone who does not know the love of Jesus. (We may all need several more pages.)

What steps do you know that you need to take to start functioning as an advocate toward others on behalf of the Lord?

How will this knowledge help you when you are Living Out Christ's Love (LOCL?)

A Spirit of Compassionate Insight
(Those who mourn)

Matt 5:4 NIV "Blessed are those who mourn for they shall be comforted."

Matt.5:4 Amp "Blessed and enviably happy [with a happiness produced by the experience of God's favor and especially conditioned by the revelation of His matchless grace] are those who mourn, for they shall be comforted!"

Matthew 5 The Message "You're blessed when you feel you've lost what is most dear to you. Only then can you be embraced by the one most dear to you."

A spirit of compassionate insight (mourning) is the spirit that "drove" Jesus from His kingly station in the heavens down to earth to take on the form of one of His own created beings. He placed Himself "in the shoes" of each one of us both in this life and for eternity.

Feeling our present and future pain of separation from the Father, there was nothing that He could do *but* spend His life for us. His focus was on our loss. He cared about what would happen to us if He didn't intervene on our behalf.

Having no separation between His heart and the heart of His Father, He also took as His own the loss that the Father had because of the sin of mankind, which caused separation. Father longed for all those He loved to cherish His glory for their well-being. Because the Father felt that way, so did Jesus - not in an elementary form of human caring, but with all of the compassions of the Father. When He moved in compassion, our needs and pains were taken on by Him as His own.

A spirit of compassionate insight "owns" the pain of another. Because of its nature, functioning in this spirit causes one to move on behalf of another.

"If anyone has material possessions and sees his brother in need but has no pity on him, how can the love of God be in him?" I John 3:17 NIV

A person walking in a spirit of compassion takes on the needs of others as if they were his own. There is no separation between a person's needs and his desires for those needs to be met in someone else's life. It is the spirit of God giving His kind of compassion for another.

He cared deeply and moved with His heart.

Material possessions are much more than money.

Jesus was the epitome of God's compassion (mourning) for those among whom He walked. The Father's heart pumped out loud before the worst sinners and vagrants. He experienced what the Father felt for them. In contrast, and in compassion for the heart of His Father, Jesus had little tolerance for the pompous, arrogant heart that wouldn't serve the Father.

The Heart of Jesus

Mt.9:36 NIV *"When he saw the crowds, he had compassion on them, because they were harassed and helpless, like sheep without a shepherd."*

Mt.14:14 NIV *"When Jesus landed and saw a large crowd, he had compassion on them and healed their sick."*

Mt.15:32 NIV *"Jesus called his disciples to him and said, 'I have compassion for these people; they have already been with me three days and have nothing to eat. I do not want to send them away hungry, or they may collapse on the way.'"*

Mt.20:34 NIV *"Jesus had compassion on them and touched their eyes. Immediately they received their sight and followed him."*

Mk.1:41 NIV *"Filled with compassion, Jesus reached out his hand and touched the man. 'I am willing,' he said. 'Be clean!'"*

Mk.6:30,31 NIV *"The apostles gathered around Jesus and reported to him all they had done and taught.*
31) Then, because so many people were coming and going that they did not even have a chance to eat, he said to them, 'Come with me by yourselves to a quiet place and get some rest.'"

Mk.8:2,3 NIV *"I have compassion for these people... some of them have come a long distance."*

Lk.15:20 NIV *"So he got up and went to his father. But while he was still a long way off, his father saw him and was filled with compassion for him..."*

God Labels His Compassion as Part of His Character

2 Cor.1:3 NIV "Praise be to the God and Father of our Lord Jesus Christ, the Father of compassion and the God of all comfort..."

Jas 5:11 NIV "... The Lord is full of compassion and mercy."

It Is Our Turn

Phil.2:1 NIV "If you have any encouragement from being united with Christ, if any comfort from his love, if any fellowship with the Spirit, if any tenderness and compassion,
2) then make my joy complete by being like-minded, having the same love, being one in spirit and purpose."

Col.3:12 NIV "Therefore, as God's chosen people, holy and dearly loved, clothe yourself with compassion..."

Characteristics of a Spirit of Compassionate Insight

A compassionate spirit only desires insights into the heart of God. It craves deeper intimacy with God to learn His heart as its only goal. It is a defender of the disadvantaged and the underdog. The compassionate heart takes on their burdens as if they were its own, just as Jesus does.

2 Cor. 12:15 Amp "But I will most gladly spend [myself] and be utterly spent for your souls..."

Gal. 4:19 NIV "My dear children, for whom I am again in the pains of childbirth until Christ is formed in you..."

Sensitivity toward the heart of God is the inward desire of the compassionate heart. This heart cannot be satisfied until God's heart is satisfied upon the completion of all things. It drives a person to whatever end will satisfy Father God's heart and allow others to see Him. Those with a compassionate spirit unconditionally surrender all control of their lives to the Lordship of Jesus and joyfully embrace a life of self-denial.

Vertical Application of a Compassionate Spirit

What are Your desires, Lord?

Those blessed to have compassionate insight enter the prayer closet on behalf of others and for the purposes of God. For others, they mourn because of the need being presented. More than simply "lifting up" someone, compassion drives them to remain "under" the need until something changes. It is their weight. Nothing but the solution will satisfy them.

When in prayer, all other needs are set aside to learn of Father God's desires. This heart waits until there is a sureness of His will. Upon knowing what His desires are, there is only one goal; it is for that purpose to be accomplished.

A wonderful example of the kind of compassion we are to have is the burdensome prayers in the Garden of Gethsemane just before Jesus was arrested. He was so moved that it is said He sweat drops of blood. Obviously, He was deeply involved in what the Father was doing at that moment. Driven to only fulfill the Father's plans and carrying the weight of our sins, compassion deeper than any of us could experience was manifested on our behalf.

Horizontal Application of a Compassionate Spirit

Compassion, which is stimulated by the spirit of mourning ever-present in the heart of Father God, is the conduit of the flow of power to heal infirmities and touch hearts. If it does not function in each of us, nothing eternal can be accomplished; only fleshly results will materialize. No wonder most of the church is powerless in so many situations.

We are finished only when God is finished.

Those who share the spirit of compassion with the Lord will not "weary in well–doing," and will work unflaggingly until the last soul has been brought into the Kingdom of God. As Paul said, *"I am again as if in birth pains until Christ is formed in you..."*

When the last soul has been brought in, when all of the intended work of the Father is finished, the compassion of the Father and those who have been made like Him will be satisfied. Only then will the compassionate be comforted and cease from laboring towards that end (mourning.)

The motivation of godly compassion is also to "cover" the sins of another, so that the person won't be exposed for who he/she really is. The mature heart of compassion finds no satisfaction in someone else hurting. In fact, it moves in the same Spirit of Father God for the hurting. It must see that sin covered even if it causes harm to the compassionate one. The person of compassion suffers on behalf of the hurting party and will enter into great loss (like Jesus) until the other person is in a place of safety, whether physically or spiritually.

Short Story

During most harvest seasons, Justus would normally have little time to take this kind of leisurely stroll to town. He had decided, however, that he owed it to himself to enjoy some precious moments in the warm sun that had hidden itself behind the foreboding clouds and the accompanying rain that had been present for the last several weeks. He had been fortunate to harvest his crop before the early rain had come. This had been a good year for him, not like the several years past when there was barely enough to feed his family due to falling crop prices and the droughts that had plagued the area.

His walk into town was a special blessing as he thought of how fortunate he was because of his father's inheritance. He wasn't rich, by any means; but he did have the liberty of not having to worry whether each year's crop would produce for him. (As evidenced in the lives of his neighbors, much hardship resulted from an insufficient harvest.) This freedom, plus the joy of the day, and the thoughts of his family and friends made his stroll quite enjoyable.

The joy of the day was diminished somewhat as the path he was on took him past the gates of his nearest neighbor. Set away from the path about forty feet, he saw the piece of paper hanging on the gate that signified trouble. Well acquainted with the unpleasant custom of posting your debts on the outermost part of your property, which signified your hardship, and in some instances revealed to others the embarrassment of improper stewardship of money, he turned off the path and walked toward the gate with a sense of apprehension.

Approaching the gate, his worst fears were confirmed. Abraham was in trouble. His crops had been washed away in the last torrent of rain, and he was about to lose everything because of the bills that he owed. The thought of his friend's misfortune broke Justus' heart.

Part of the custom of posting your bills on the front gate was a practice known as "the double." This meant that everyone who saw the posting had several choices they could make. A person could pass by and ignore the need; or he could fold the paper from bottom to top - in essence "doubling" it - meaning that he would take on the debt as if it were his own and pay it for the other person.

What would you do if you had the means?

Justus felt the pain and anguish that must have transpired in his long-time friend over the last months. He folded the paper and sealed it with his signet ring.

Horizontal Application in Modern Marriage

The truest and most satisfying application of the compassionate spirit is fulfilled when serving your mate. Most people do not understand that, in the truest sense of the word, (because the two of you are "one,") you are ministering from yourself, through God, to yourself, as you carry the burdens of the other.

All of the unity displayed in the Godhead and portrayed by Jesus to the church is exhibited in the marriage covenant. Any selfishness actually harms the one that is being selfish, because his/her foolishness hinders the flow of God's grace to the marriage.

Few realize the dynamic of living a life of godly compassion toward the other in marriage. Studying the needs of one's mate for the sake of serving him/her pleases the heart of God and displays the character of Christ to the world.

Application for Living Out Christ's Love (LOCL)

People instinctively know when someone really cares for them or when that person is simply going through the motions regarding compassion. They also see true compassion at work when someone is sincerely concerned for their needs. Jesus is only exhibited when honest caring is the motivation behind any action done in His Name.

When praying for someone, it is imperative that you find the heart of compassion in your private prayer closet before you represent Jesus to that person by committing to pray for his/her needs. Any action you may take once people correctly detect any hypocrisy in you is automatically nullified and of no effect in representing Jesus.

My Father,

I realize that my preoccupation with my own needs limits my insight into the needs of others. I find that I rarely carry the needs of others enough to present them honestly to You. I have little of Your kind of compassion for others. I never mourn for them. Please forgive me. Place in me your heart of compassion. Birth in me a heart of caring, first of all for Your desires; and then for the needs of others. I know that it is one of the character traits of Jesus in which I should be functioning to show the world His love. Help me. Thank You.

Signed _____ Date _____

Questions About a Spirit of Compassionate Insight

What is a spirit of compassion?

Have you ever had it for anyone - for God's reasons?

When have you seen it displayed in the church?

Where do you need to start to acquire a spirit of compassion?

Do you really desire to care for others, or is your own selfishness too strong at this point to even pursue it?

So what are you going to do?

How can Jesus be represented if you always serve yourself?

Is a "prune face" considered formal wear when acquiring a spirit of godly compassion? Why?

What is the utmost joy to the compassionate heart?

Prayers and thoughts

A Spirit of Meekness
(Humble Obedience to the Word of God)

Mt. 5:5 NIV "Blessed are the meek, for they will inherit the earth."

Mt.5:5 Amp "Blessed (happy, blithesome, joyous, spiritually prosperous - with life-joy and satisfaction in God's favor and salvation, regardless of their outward conditions) are the meek (the mild, patient, long-suffering), for they shall inherit the earth!"

Mt.5 The Message "You're blessed when you're content with just who you are - no more, no less. That's the moment you find yourselves proud owners of everything that can't be bought."

James 4:7-10 Amp "So be subject to God. Resist the devil [stand firm against him], and he will flee from you.

8) Come close to God and He will come close to you. [Recognize that you are] sinners, get your soiled hands clean; [realize that you have been disloyal] wavering individuals with divided interests, and purify your hearts [of your spiritual adultery].

9) [As you draw near to God] be deeply penitent and grieve, even weep [over your disloyalty]. Let your laughter be turned to grief and your mirth to dejection and heartfelt shame [for your sins].

10) Humble yourselves [feeling very insignificant] in the presence of the Lord, and He will exalt you [He will lift you up and make your lives significant]."

One dictionary definition for the word "meek" is that of enduring injury with patience and without resentment, being humble or gentle. It stresses a mildness or patient disposition, which is not easily stirred to anger.

"Humble" – reflecting, expressing, or offered in a spirit of deference or submission; having or showing a consciousness of one's defect; not proud; not self assertive.

"Obey" – to carry out the instructions or orders of; to be guided by; comply with. Obedient – submissive to the restraint or command of authority.

I Sam. 15:22,23a Amp "Samuel said, Has the Lord as great a delight in burnt offerings and sacrifices as in obeying the voice of the Lord? Behold, to <u>obey</u> is better than sacrifice, and to hearken than the fat of rams.

23) For rebellion is as the sin of witchcraft, and stubbornness is as idolatry…

Ps. 37:9 Amp *"For evildoers shall be cut off, but those who wait and hope and look for the Lord [in the end] will inherit the earth."*

Ps. 37:11 Amp *"But the meek [in the end] shall inherit the earth and shall delight themselves in the abundance of peace."*

Ps. 37:29 Amp *"[Then] the [consistently] righteous shall inherit the land and dwell upon it forever."*

For this study, it is increasingly clear that as the Lord was speaking, He was describing those who had a heart need to be obedient to the Word and plans of the Lord. Throughout the study of the Word of God, rebellion, disobedience, and self-service were the traits that described those who would not be part of anything that the Lord was doing. Their fate was separation from God.

Being meek is far from being weak!

In contrast, humble submission, loving obedience, and above all else, an ardent desire to serve the Lord alone describe the character traits of those destined for eternal fellowship with God. Therefore, it is our opinion that when the Lord was describing meekness, He was describing those who embraced the trait of *humble obedience* - to do only the will of God in all things - as those who could be trusted to inherit the earth.

The Obedient Servant

The man sat in the darkness, his legs aching from pacing a seemingly endless number of days in the cold six-by-six foot cell. "According to my calculations," he thought to himself, "either today or tomorrow should be my last day in this stinking place."

As he remembered why he had been given thirty days of solitary confinement, Dicky, "the Mask," Sullivan could feel the same intense hatred rise up within him that he had sensed at the time of the fight which had put him in "the hole."

"This time I'm going to finish the job," he swore to himself. "If it's the last thing I do, I'll kill him for what he did to me." The satisfying comfort of the thoughts of how he would make his latest enemy suffer, and the plotting of the ways in which he would get away with it again became his companions as they had many times this last month. Throughout the night - another hellish, endless night - he pondered his revenge. His anger festered with every moment, ending only as he fell into a fitful sleep.

"OK, Mask, time's up." The loud voice and the rattling of the keys against the cell door startled the sleeping man. "Have you learned anything yet?" the guard continued, as the burst of light that momentarily blinded Mask flooded the small cell.

244

"Is that you, Jensen?" Mask began, shielding his eyes from the unfamiliar brightness. "Of all people to see after thirty days, it had to be you, huh?"

Mask hated Jensen. He really hated everyone, but he hated Jensen more than the rest of them. Jensen represented everything that Mask had despised all of his life. Jensen was a Christian. Every time the tall, rugged-looking guard came near, Mask could feel the hair on the back of his neck stand up. Jensen never really did anything to Mask to make him hate him so - in fact, of all the guards he was the most fair - but that didn't matter, just being around him made his skin crawl.

"Are you going to preach at me again?" Mask started, spitting the words with disdain at the smiling guard, who stepped out of the narrow cell opening to allow room for him to pass. "You going to tell me again how I should give my life to this Jesus of yours, and be obedient to Him like you always are?"

Mask could feel the hatred rising up from within. "Well, I ain't gonna be obedient to no one - not you, not to the rules at this dump of a prison; and especially not to that Jesus of yours. Nobody ain't ever gonna tell me what to do - never," he continued. "You can keep me locked up in that stinkin' hole forever, but you won't get me to break. I ain't never gonna listen to no one but me," he cursed, as he walked down the corridor just in front of the smiling Jensen.

About twenty feet from the security door that led to the washrooms, Jensen stopped and told the cuffed man in front of him to stop also. Mask turned around to give the guard, who was signaling to another security guard on the other side of the door that everything was all right, another piece of his mind.

Before he could say anything, however, Jensen started speaking to him. "You know," he began, "I've seen a lot of men come through this prison, some real tough customers; but I haven't seen very many as stupid as you."

Mask was too startled by the statement that came from the normally courteous-no-matter-what guard to respond immediately. In fact, something inside of him told him to listen to what the man had to say.

Jensen continued. "You guys are all the same. You think that you're so smart and tough, but you don't know how ignorant and foolish you really are." The rage that Mask was beginning to feel because of the words spoken began to show visibly on his face. "Oh, stop it," Jensen continued, "all you really know how to do is get mad. Isn't it about time that you found some answers for your life? Just listen for a minute; then you can go and do whatever it is that you've been pondering all these days."

Mask just stood there. In all of the years he had been in prison, no one had ever had the guts to talk like this to him before, especially a guard. He was almost fascinated at the thought of what might come next.

"You keep spouting off about how tough you are, and that you won't ever serve anybody. Well, I have to tell you something,

245

my friend. You are one of the most obedient servants that has ever come through this place." Mask began to form some words with his mouth when Jensen cut him off. "Just shut up, and listen to some wisdom for a change. I'm going to tell you some truth. You can do with it whatever you want after I'm done; but it would be one of the wisest things you've ever done, if you listen real close. Now, here comes truth, whether you like it or not."

Jensen paused a split second to see that Mask was listening, then continued. "Truth is, everybody serves somebody; and you are one of the most foolish puppets of Satan that I have ever met. You don't even know how much he is laughing at you for serving him as faithfully as you do. He's a loser, and he has no hope; and he laughs at anyone that he can convince to be a loser as well. His rebellion got him thrown out of heaven and now he wants fools like you to be separated from God, too.

"You are one of his best pupils, a 'big time rebel,' and look at where it's gotten you. It makes him laugh even more because he knows that after you have been obedient to him all of your life - a loser like him - it will be too late for you to help yourself. You'll have been too busy serving him through anger, hate, and revenge to find out what the truth really is."

Jensen stopped for a moment, then continued unchallenged by the quieted man. "The fact is, there are only two masters of all people; and everyone, I mean everyone, is obedient to one or the other. They can serve God, through Jesus Christ, or they can serve Satan. The ones who are obedient to Jesus win forever, and those who serve Satan lose forever. I don't know if you've looked at your life lately; but it would seem to me that if this is the best your master can do for you, I'd think seriously about changing your allegiance."

Jensen gently took the man's arm, indicating that he was finished and it was time to go. Mask walked submissively ahead of the guard.

"Oh, one more thing," Jensen began again, while the two of them walked toward the door, one looking ahead, the other looking down at the floor. "The next time you start believing that you are in charge of your own life, and vow never to be obedient to or serve anyone, stop for a moment and listen quietly. The sound that you'll be hearing will be the laughter from the one that has conned you into being the big fool that you really are.

"He's laughing because he knows that in your rebellion and in your choice not to serve God, you are continuing to be one of his most obedient servants. He's got you and you don't even know it. That makes you a real fool."

The guard on the other side opened the door and Jensen transferred Mask to him. As the door closed, Jensen watched the two men through the small vertical window. Mask, who hadn't uttered a word the whole time, just kept walking with his head down. To Jensen, it looked as if the man's shoulders drooped slightly, and his steps were absent of the defiant gait normally exhibited for the benefit of those watching. It seemed as though Mask was thinking seriously about what had been said.

As Jensen retreated from the door to return to his station, he prayed to his Lord and Master that Mask would find his proper Master. He also said a prayer of gratefulness that he himself might become more obedient out of an ever-deepening love for Jesus.

Characteristics of a Spirit of Humble Obedience

To function in the Biblical definition of meekness requires as much strength of character as any other trait. The heart of humble obedience has determined long ago that the world and all of its influences rate a distant last place in comparison with the Word of God. Obedience in all things associated with God and His Word is the only desire of the truly meek.

The humbly obedient, or meek, understand that all of the economies of God are based on obedience to His Word. They are on a continual quest to willingly place themselves in full submission to God and His Word.

True obedience is simply the heart desire to do what God desires you to do. Meekness is the deep willingness to obey. Only true courage allows obedience to prevail.

A meek person under obedience to the Lord, although looked at by the world as weak, is the most courageous of all people. He will stand, empowered by the presence and unseen power of the Lord, when all others capitulate to the dictates of any given situation rather than the Word of God.

God's strength comes to those who are obedient. Jesus is our example of obedience. He did nothing on His own, but did only what His Father told Him to do, no matter what anyone else thought of His actions.

Pride or rebellion (the lifting up of one's self and personal desires) causes disobedience. It's the Burger King Syndrome - "Have it your way." Only repentance of our worldliness (the suffering and eventual death of our worldly desires) will bring true heart obedience or meekness.

Note: There is a vast difference between obedience and compliance. They look the same on the outside, but once again God looks on the heart. Obedience is willful submission to the Lord. Compliance is merely following the rules, rules which some people would quickly toss aside if they weren't required to follow them, due to the rebellion and control in their hearts.

Pride (self-importance)
or
loss of humility (submission to God,)
which leads to disobedience,
is
the root
of every sin
or evil.

A Spirit of Obedience (Meekness)

1 John 4:17-18 NIV "Love is made complete among us so that we will have confidence on the dayof judgment, because in this world we are like him.
18) There is no fear in love. But perfect love drives out fear, because fear has to do with punishment. The man who fears is not made perfect in love."

An ardent desire to obey overcomes every temptation of the flesh.

Jesus walked in perfect love, perfect obedience. Doing only the Father's will, no outside force, fear, or pressure could sway Him from that single, most important mission. His learned obedience set Him free from any common effect of His actions. Because all of His actions and causes were His Father's, whom He trusted completely, any potential harm that could come to Him because of them fell pale beside His ardent desire to obey.

So often in our walk with the Lord, our own desires and causes are the real motivation for what we do. We give lip service to good-sounding spiritual tasks; but the bottom line is still simple - selfish desires that will preserve our lives.

What is not understood during these times is that in our disobedience to the Lord, we have stepped into the realm of rebellion and are, in fact, obeying Satan. There are only two masters that can be served throughout the Bible. We can choose either God, our Father, or Satan, the father of lies. If we are serving one of them, we cannot and will not be serving the other. Our "harmless" sin of disobedience in any form is causing untold damage to our future ability to follow the Lord, because we have "elected" to again submit ourselves to the realm from which we have been freed by the blood of Jesus.

Suffering or Death to Our Own Desires Leads to Obedience

Heb.5:8 Amp "Although He was a Son, He learned [active, special] obedience through what He suffered."

Little is taught about the functions of the spirit realm because little is known. Our daily Christian walk is mostly devoted to attempting, in our own strength, to remove those things in our lives, which hinder our becoming like Jesus. We do it through our limited understanding of how things function in the spiritual realm and rely upon how things work in the physical world. We say that we are walking in the Spirit, but little more than fleshly results, derived from working in our own strength, are the "fruit" of our efforts.

Paul asks how we can complete in the flesh what has begun in the Spirit (Gal. 3:3.) We have all read it many times and never get it, because we know so little about God's spiritual ways.

In the spiritual realm, there is cause and effect, just as there is in the physical realm. We can understand that principle in our world, because we can see or feel most of the results of our actions as they play out. (If we do this, then that happens.)

In the spiritual realm, however, the results of our actions, good or bad, do not always have an immediate or visible presence, which causes us to be deceived about the effects of our actions. The result of our spiritual disobedience may be masked through circumstances, or explained away by natural means. We may never really comprehend the specific impact of our disobedience. Therefore we continue being disobedient because we see no apparent consequences resulting from our actions, even assuming that what we've been doing is actually OK.

A perfect example of this is our inability to obey because we will not submit ourselves to the tool that God has provided so that obedience can be formed in us - *the denial of self, or suffering.* (Read Romans 6:16-22.) We would rather "pray away" the tool God wants to use, and remain comfortable and unchanged, deluded in thinking that the Lord would not allow us to experience hardship because He loves us. In reality, it is because He loves us that the hardship comes. When we are finally forced to deny ourselves, we can begin to know God, how He works; and start submitting to Him and the changes He desires to make in us.

It is foreign to our thinking that if we embrace the concept of giving up something that we desire, then obedience will be formed in us because of it. That doesn't compute in our minds. Nevertheless, it is truth. However, because we can't, or won't get

How is your spiritual life working for you?

As a parent, have you ever wondered if your disobedience and rebellion have violated the covering over your children?

Have you ever wondered why they are in rebellion?

This could change your spiritual life!

249

it, our lives remain shallow, unproductive, and totally ineffective in presenting God's ways to the world through how we act.

Note: You would do well to meditate on the above paragraphs.

Acts 21 The Message Bible *"You're looking at this backwards. The issue in Jerusalem is not what they do to me, whether arrest or murder, but what the Master Jesus does through my obedience. Can't you see that?"*

A passionate life being lived before those who were still learning

Paul's suffering caused him to see how valueless it was to hold on to his mortal life and comfort. It caused him to sell out completely, which meant the death of his rights and comforts. He died to his need to survive. He laid down His life so that the Gospel of Jesus Christ would go forth.

Because of his growth, obedience was formed in him. He could do nothing but obey. God had given him the power to deny himself, so that change could be accomplished in him.

Vertical Application of a Humbly Obedient (Meek) Spirit

Approaching God in true meekness is a joy beyond description. When doing so, there can be no possible hindrances to the warmest fellowship. All is in order.

The humbly obedient heart desires only for the will of the Lord to prevail in all circumstances and it functions daily by submitting to the directions of the Holy Spirit. Any possible sin has been covered through repentance by the blood of Jesus.

Fellowship entered into by the meek one in order that he can do the will of God is complementary to the attitude of Father God, who desires what is best for His child. It is a perfect marriage of desires and is fulfilling beyond imagination.

Horizontal Application of a Humbly Obedient (Meek) Spirit

Those who are humbly obedient to the Word of God (the meek) are the true, most valiant warriors in the work of the Lord. They can be trusted with the things and purposes of God, because they have the same mind and heart as He does.

A person walking in this manner is distinguished in the world and in most church fellowships as somewhat unusual. He cannot be moved by the circumstances that move most individuals. He will not normally go along with the crowd.

What may seem like some form of rebellion, however, is quite the opposite. Being obedient to the Father in Heaven, he has only His best interests at heart. Programs, false motivations, dynamic coercion, and religious activities that replace fellowship with God as the catalyst for doing things cause the humbly obedient to appear to be non-conforming. They rarely attend these kinds of events.

The truth of the matter is that in their perfect conforming to the Word, they become non-conformists to foolish religion. They will humbly remove themselves from any resemblance of disobedience to God as they see it.

Horizontal Application in Modern Marriage

The marriage of two humbly obedient (meek) people is the flagship marriage for the body of Christ. Conforming only to the Word of God, both parties understand their position of submissiveness to the needs of the other and strive to serve the other.

The husband, obedient before his Father, crucifies his flesh in order to provide fertile soil for his bride to prosper. The bride, understanding that her marriage is the picture of the relationship of Jesus with the church, provides service to her husband, so that he can function in the will of the Lord. It is a union of two who combat anything that resembles a violation of the Word of God, joined in heart for the purposes of God and - knowing the heart motive of the other to be pure - for each other's best interests.

Application for Living Out Christ's Love (LOCL)

To those in the world, or to someone struggling with the life of Christianity, anyone who is immovable in his/her convictions - especially if that person is pure in motive and righteous before God - is a shining star. He/She would probably be considered the closest picture to what Jesus looks like. The concept of strength under obedient submission, combined with the other traits of the character of Christ, brings the Bible definition of who Jesus is to life in an everyday world.

A person who presents an immovable strength of conviction (which is founded on eternal truth and substantiated by a life of love and service) is magnetic and worth investigating to someone who needs foundational answers. The humbly obedient (meek) individual shows others Jesus.

You don't need to be perfect, but you do represent someone Who loves perfectly.

Note of caution: If the desire for obedience to the Word of God is not tempered by the other attributes of Jesus, it can easily become religious in nature and void of the heart of God. As an example, take a look at the Pharisees or modern day crusaders who shake their fist at the sinner, instead of hating the sin and loving the sinner as God does.

Questions About a Spirit of Obedience (Meekness)

Name someone you know who is absolutely obedient to the Word of God.

---.------------

What strikes you most about that person?

Do you want to be with him/her? Why or why not?

What areas is the Holy Spirit bringing to mind that need to be brought into obedience?

My Father,

I now realize that I have spent most of my life attempting to maintain my own comfort. I also now know that because that has been my main focus, I have not been able to grow in humble obedience to You. Please forgive me. I have been obedient to Satan, rather than to You. He has been the one to whom I have listened. I turn from that sin now, and submit to Your Lordship over my life.

I ask You to build in me the desire to no longer own my comfort zones and I release them to you. I now choose to embrace the crucified/resurrected life. Please give me the ability to deny myself. I realize that in doing so, I again submit myself to Your authority in this area of my life; and with it, to Your power which allows it to be accomplished in me.

I also realize that in submitting to You, I give up my right to remain who I am. Those habits or traits, which make me who I am, must go if You are to have Your way in me.

Accomplish obedience in me. Bring me to the place where I can say as Jesus said, "Not my will, but Your will be done" in all things, and have it be the truth. Bring me to the point where You can trust me with whatever You consider important. Forgive me, Father, and change me.

Thank You,

Signed _____ Date _____

Now, Doesn't That Feel Good?

Prayers and thoughts

A Spirit of Righteousness

Mt.5:6 NIV "Blessed are those who hunger and thirst for righteousness, for they will be filled."

Mt.5:6 Amp "Blessed and fortunate and happy and spiritually prosperous (in that state in which the born-again child of God enjoys His favor and salvation) are those who hunger and thirst for righteousness (uprightness and right standing with God), for they shall be completely satisfied!"

Mt.5 The Message "You're blessed when you've worked up a good appetite for God. He's food and drink in the best meal you'll ever eat."

Jesus Had the Heart to See Everyone the Way His Father Saw Them

As we, those who are as if brides waiting for Christ, choose to allow God to "build" the character of Jesus in us, we find that the spirit of righteousness is essential for proper construction. It is foundational to the rest of the work that the Lord will be doing in us. To see others as God does allows Him to move our hearts toward the rest of the things that please Him on our journey of becoming completely like Jesus.

The Word says that if we say we abide in Him (Jesus,) then we are to conduct ourselves as He did. Simply coming to Christ imparts His righteousness to us; and we, therefore, should act righteously in our world, treating others as He would.

To consciously begin to treat others the way Jesus would is the necessary, beginning step in following the ways of our Lord and walking in His steps. Remember that this can be accomplished only through the Holy Spirit, who gives you the power to allow Jesus to live His life through you. Jesus will honor this effort and bless it with Himself (His character, His presence) in order to truly change you. What may start out as an exercise with possibly less than pure heart motives can become real heart change when blessed by God and anointed through the Holy Spirit.

The righteous heart has the ability and desire to see one's neighbor as God sees him. It desires to think of everyone in the way we would want people to think of our own sons and daughters.

To have immoral thoughts about anyone is seeing him as Satan sees him. Anyone filled with a spirit of righteousness has the mind of Christ and brings every thought captive to Christ. Jesus stood in the courtyard with the naked woman caught in

In Christ, we have been made righteous and are being made holy.

We can now see the need to submit to the Lord, so that we can act as He would in our world.

adultery and saw her as His Father did. His compassion for her far outweighed any fleshly desires. He had no thoughts but His Father's thoughts.

Jesus was persecuted because He treated people as His Father did. His righteousness made the unrighteousness of those around Him all the more glaring.

Jesus endured people's reactions to His righteousness in order to see the light of life ignited in others. Righteousness never retaliates when it is wronged. Returning good for evil is a spirit of righteousness in action - the Spirit of Jesus. We must endure any harm or accusation thrust upon us for being righteous, so that others may see Jesus in us and be drawn to the Father.

We are to go so far as to actually respond to their evil by doing more good to them and for them, without any hope of notice for our actions. Through this discipline, we defer our immediate gratification in hopes of nurturing their eternal gratification, that of knowing the Father.

We nurture our ability to reveal Jesus by the right treatment of those around us. Righteousness treats everyone as Jesus would, for their good.

People will be reached by our righteous living in their midst. We are an extension of His plan to draw all people to Himself. If we are not holy (righteous) in their midst, no one will see God.

Righteousness (a heart that desires holiness) means to be set apart. Any ungodly person can return evil for evil, or good for good. Only a godly person can return good for evil.

Righteousness is a spirit of God. It is a quality of God. It can only develop as we submit to God. Righteousness is a heart desire, not just deeds done in the spirit of religion or only for external appearances.

Only in prayer can we develop the character of God. If we are being mistreated, we must take that person to God; first, to see him as God sees him, and then to deny ourselves the right to retaliate.

The Lord wants us to hunger and thirst, so that others are treated right. If the world is becoming worse, it is because we are living less righteously than Jesus would have lived before them. When we return evil for evil, even for right-sounding causes, the sin of those we oppose will always increase. In the end, evil will win because in fighting this way, we are using the world's approach.

Praying for those who oppose the things of God is returning good for evil. We are to rejoice when we are persecuted, because it gives us an opportunity to show them Jesus through our godly responses to their persecution. A spirit of righteousness is simply desiring to act as Jesus would toward everyone, to be like Jesus in every situation that we face.

Righteousness
is
the outward expression
of our inward
godliness.

A Spirit of Righteousness

1 John 4:17-18 NIV *"...Love is made complete among us so that we will have confidence on the dayof judgment, because in this world we are like him.*
18 There is no fear in love. But perfect *(righteous) love drives out fear, because fear has to do with punishment. The man who fears is not made perfect in love."

*Note: (righteous) is an editorial comment, not part of the Scripture.

When we function in the perfect love (true bridal love) of Jesus through a spirit of righteousness, our only desire will be to see each person with whom we come in contact blessed by God. Our only hope will be that others see Jesus simply because it will be good for them.

Remember foolish Tony? If he had seen Mr. Baxter through the eyes of righteousness, his only desire would have been to build the best house possible for him. Because he could not see past his hate and anger, his whole family lost out and he himself missed a true blessing. It is impossible to love people unless we can see them as our Lord sees them through a spirit of righteousness.

Most of us go through this walk with our God void of any of the fullness that was intended for us. Our days are filled with seemingly meaningless - but at the time urgent - tasks that fill our time until we are caught in an endless circle of lifeless days. There is reason for this: it is because we do not love others as God does. Listen to what His Word says.

We need to pursue God to learn to see others and love them as He does.

John 15: 9-14 NIV "As the Father has loved me, so have I loved you. Now remain in my love.

10) If you obey my commands, you will remain in my love, just as I have obeyed my Father's commands and remain in his love.

11) I have told you this so that my joy may be in you and that your joy may be complete.

12) My command is this: Love each other as I have loved you.

13) Greater love has no one than this, that one lay down his life for his friends.

14 You are my friends if you do what I command."

The Father saw Jesus through His kind of love and His joy was complete. Jesus saw us through His and His Father's kind of love, and His joy was complete. He told us of His Father's ways, so that our joy may be complete. He has us in mind in all that He does.

We see others through our imperfect, selfish kind of love and wonder why we have little or no joy. It doesn't take much reasoning to figure out the simplicity of God's equation.

Simple, huh?

It goes like this: Choose to love others with God's motives for loving someone, and then there will be great joy in every area of your life. If you choose not to love with God's kind of love, joy will not be found in you, at least not complete joy.

A spirit of righteousness sees others as God sees them. Someone functioning in a spirit of righteousness is always seeing and loving others as God does. Our Lord looked at everyone with one purpose in mind: He wanted them to be with Him for eternity. It didn't matter who they were, or what they had done, especially to Him. He could only see them in love.

In His heart, because He was righteous, it was impossible not to love. He even loved others deeply on His way to the cross, because He knew that some of those who were crucifying Him would be with Him in heaven because of what He was about to do for them.

If I repent of who I am not, He will make me who He is.

His righteous heart could not see their sin, only their need. While He hung there bleeding, He still was aware of the needs of those around Him. Looking left and right, He dealt with each person in His Father's love and willing acceptance, if they chose to accept them.

Looking to His mother, He could see her with spiritual eyes even then, and sensing her sorrow and loss, made provision for her needs. Looking to the mocking crowd in His righteous,

258

bridal love, He could only ache for their need of forgiveness and cry out on their behalf. Even now, in righteousness, He is praying for you and me, still looking past Himself to us. How can we not follow Him?

I am often in awe when I think of how Jesus could function righteously in all circumstances. It astounds me to think that part of His covenant promise and provision for us is to do likewise. It seems so remote, and at times even hopeless, as I see my sin. In those times, the only hope that I do have is His Word, and I can rely on that. He told me that if I repent of who I am not, He would make me who He is.

In Jesus' righteousness, you are freed from any fear of what others may do to you or think of you. Your only desire is to see them as God sees them, so that you can fill their needs. You have the opportunity to be able to show someone how Jesus would function, that they might come to Him - even if it means persecution to you - by observing your actions and responses.

If you could see those who have harmed you as Jesus does, you could forgive them and be healed of any scars that have been left.

You could actually pray that the Lord would heal them - for their good.

When I was young, probably just old enough to remember, I recall a specific instance when my father came home after what was probably a very hard day. I remember my mother looking concerned while she tended to his needs. While she got warm water for his feet and made him some soup, he was telling her about his day. I don't remember all that was said, but the gist of what my dad did for us that day lets me understand Jesus a little better.

My dad was working on the construction of what was then called the Treasure Island buildings. That morning, because of the extremely cold weather, which made working conditions very hazardous with its accompanying ice and snow, the foreman sent most workers home. He did say that those who wanted to stay could do so, although he did not recommend it. Most everyone went home. A very few stayed despite the dangers to themselves. My dad was obviously one of them.

While Mom and Dad talked, I remember going over to the window and looking at the raging storm that had developed sometime during the day. Later, possibly the next day, I recall my dad asking my mother if there would be enough at the end of the week. I'm sure he was questioning as to whether there was enough money to pay for the needed food or whatever else four kids required. As I reflect back, Mom and Dad were probably going through some very hard times; however, we kids never knew it.

He may never know how much his actions impacted me, after seeing how cold and worn out he was that day. He stayed, working in the cold for my sisters and brother and me, when he would have been more than justified to have gone home. I don't know if he knew the Lord during that time; but his cold and weary day, and his simple love toward us was the spirit of righteousness in action that even now - many years later - impacts my life.

King David,
despite his very visible failures,
maintained a thirst,
a hunt,
and an obsessive quest
for the presence
of the One who made him.

A spirit of righteousness in action would be, for example, dropping off some food on the doorstep of a needy family and leaving before they could find out who left it, having the heart that you would never be found out. In the event that you were found out, it would be unthinkable that the glory for the gift would be removed from Jesus and placed on you.

What fun to destroy the bondages that the world places on us!

It would be like actually trying to find a way to bless someone who has seriously hurt you, free from even the slightest desire for retaliation. You see that person as clearly as God sees him, understanding that his need to hurt you only exposes a need for the love of Jesus. You understand that God allowed you to receive the brunt of this person's sin, because He could trust you to respond to it as Jesus would. In righteousness, you become partners with Jesus in intercession and action for the other person. You love as He and the Father love.

Vertical Application of a Spirit of Righteousness

The righteous heart is always concerned for the best interests of everyone he takes to prayer. He only cares for the need of the one for whom he prays. The needs of Father God also mean more to the righteous heart than his own. Pleasing God and longing to see accomplished His desire that none should perish are foremost in every approach in prayer. Prayer is a loving interaction between a caring child and an adoring Father, each looking out for the other's best interests.

Horizontal Application of a Spirit of Righteousness

Jesus determined in His heart to leave heaven because it was good for those who were far from Him in heart. A righteous spirit longs for everyone to know God and for Father God to be blessed because of it. This heart knows that the relationship with Jesus is the best situation anyone could ever have, even its enemies, and longs that all enter into it.

Horizontal Application in Modern Marriage

The righteous heart is a "covering" heart, always looking out for the best interests of others. In a marriage situation, where selfishness tends to flourish, this heart functions in the opposite direction. It serves, even to its own detriment if necessary.

At times, a person functioning in righteousness may be seen as having no backbone; however, that is not the case. Laying personal needs down for the needs of the other, overcoming conflict through prayer rather than bringing harm to the relationship - even with words, meeting the other's needs at the expense of your own needs is the heart of Jesus, alive and functioning well.

Note: A righteous heart in action usually boils the potatoes of someone who wants conflict. It also exposes the sin of control and manipulation because that person thrives on being right at all costs. When a righteous heart will not fight or succumb to challenges against it, the other party has nowhere to go. When there is no fight, the fighter has no hold over the other person.

Conflict dies when it encounters a righteous heart.

Special note: <u>If you are in an abusive situation, it may be wise to separate yourself from that situation for your protection and exhibit the character of Christ from a place of safety.</u>

Matthew 26:53,54 NIV "Do you think I cannot call on my Father, and he will at once put at my disposal more than twelve legions of angels?
54) But how then would the Scriptures be fulfilled that say it must happen in this way?"

Luke 9:23-25 Amp "And He said to all, If any person wills to come after Me, let him deny himself [disown himself, forget, lose sight of himself and his own interests, refuse and give up himself] and take up his cross daily and follow Me [cleave steadfastly to Me, conform wholly to My example in living and, if need be, in dying also].
24) For whoever would preserve his life and save it will lose and destroy it, but whoever loses his life for My sake, he will preserve and save it [from the penalty of eternal death].
25) For what does it profit a man, if he gains the whole world and ruins or forfeits (loses) himself?"

261

Application for Living Out Christ's Love (LOCL)

Being an advocate in prayer for someone brings absolute freedom to you and to that person. You are free because you desire only the Father's will to be done in his/her life. You can then place no holds or restrictions on him/her. Even if you are rejected, your righteous heart understands that to be a sin or offense for you to hold before the Father. Your recourse is then to plead for mercy on behalf of that person.

The person you pray for is free because you can promise that there is no hidden agenda or ulterior motive attached to your gift of prayer, not even a demand that he/she desire anything of Christ. You are simply there for his/her good.

Prayers and thoughts

Do you know any truly righteous people? Who?

Have you ever functioned in a spirit of righteousness? Why or why not?

What are you going to ask the Lord to change?

My Father,

As I wait for the return of my Lord and study who He is, I realize how little I resemble Him in character and action. I understand that His desire would be for me to see everyone that He puts in my life the same way He does. Instead of simply seeing those who hurt and use me as in need of my love through Jesus, I so often have a desire for retaliation of some sort. In my heart of hearts, I really desire to gain something from every relationship or I leave it, instead of giving myself away as Jesus would.

This day, my Lord, I want to turn from my ways and begin to live my life as You would. I am sorry for the time and energy that I have wasted. I'm sorry for the sin of my unrighteous behavior and all of its effects. I'm sorry for the many people that You've sent my way, who have left without having had the opportunity to see You, because I have been too selfish and foolish. Please forgive me.

Change me and make me like You. Allow me to be obedient to Your command to love as You love, to see as You see, to live as You live. I choose to walk in Your ways; show me how.

Thank You,

Signed _____ Date_____

A Spirit of Mercy

Mt.5:7 NIV "Blessed are the merciful, for they will be shown mercy."

Mt.5:7 Amp "Blessed (happy, to be envied, and spiritually prosperous - with life-joy and satisfaction in God's favor and salvation, regardless of their outward conditions) are the merciful, for they shall obtain mercy!"

Mt.5 The Message "You're blessed when you care. At the moment of being 'care–full,' you find yourselves cared for."

A heart of mercy always wants to forgive, even when forgiveness is not asked for, nor deserved.

Mercy is our means to salvation. Without it, none of us would have the possibility of spending eternity with God. It was mercy that initiated Father God's sending His Son (Himself) for us.

To continue to receive mercy, we must give mercy. A heart of mercy will never focus on itself. As soon as it desires something for itself, it will lose the ability to be merciful.

The merciful heart always esteems others more valuable than itself. Those with mercy understand bankruptcy, and place themselves at the center of the need. Mercy drove Jesus to the cross.

Neglecting mercy cuts off the lifeline with God, because He always operates where mercy is demonstrated.

God's judgment, the separation of good from evil, is always an act of mercy. In His mercy, God reveals our sin for the single purpose of providing freedom for us.

Truth with mercy always brings life. Truth without mercy brings bondage, death, and a religious spirit. The heart of mercy always desires to treat others as God would treat them.

The kind of prayer that pleases God when praying for others, especially an enemy, is: *"Father, flood them with the same mercy that You have given me."*

1 John 4:17-18 NIV "...Love is made complete among us so that we will have confidence on the day of judgment, because in this world we are like him.

How blessed we are that God is merciful!

God's judgment is the precise separation of good from evil.

18) There is no fear in love. But perfect love casts out fear, because fear has to do with punishment. The man who fears is not made perfect in love."

When we function in the perfect love (a true bridal love) of Jesus through the spirit of mercy, our thoughts will never be on ourselves. The fear of any loss to us is eliminated by our desire to make sure that others, even those who hate us, are treated the way that God would treat them - the way that He has treated us.

Jesus is mercy. His leaving heaven, His walking among men, His dying for those who hated Him, and His pleading for mercy for those who were in the process of killing Him, all show the epitome of mercy. The whole purpose of His life was the expression of mercy toward those that deserved none – including us.

We need to understand that we need mercy, so that we treat others with mercy.

Most of us look at those who lived during Jesus' time and somehow detach ourselves from them, as if we would not have functioned as they did toward Jesus. Only after it is revealed to us that we, too, could have been in the jeering crowd, or one of the thieves, or possibly have even driven the nails in His hands, do we see our need for the same mercy that they needed.

When we hate, are we not murderers? When we esteem others less than ourselves, are we not thieves? When Jesus is not the Lord of everything in our lives, do we not crucify Him again? To walk as He did, we must understand our own need for mercy, or we will continue to treat others like the world does, not like Jesus did.

Some Random Thoughts on a Spirit of Mercy

The modern day church seems to be merciless. However harsh that statement may sound, it never the less is true when our actions are compared to the way Jesus told us to live. We tend to reject sinners and figuratively shoot those who are wounded.

God's judgment of our sin is an act of mercy toward us.

It allows us to have the opportunity to repent.

The result is that we have need of, and are experiencing, the judgments of God on our lives because of His great mercy toward us; and we don't even know it. We've become proud that we have been saved, rather than continually thankful for our salvation.

In doing so, our attitude toward those who have not accepted Jesus is far different than His. We see them from a lofty perspective, our being above needing His mercy, and somehow better than they are; whereas, He has only the heart of mercy towards everyone.

266

There is an old saying about a shepherd who is stationed as a watchman over his sheep: "The watchman has lost his perspective when he begins to enjoy killing wolves more than he enjoys protecting sheep."

In this saying, the merciful watchman has positioned himself to protect those that cannot protect themselves. He is showing mercy. Even if he should have to kill a wolf, his heart position is one of mercy toward the sheep.

In contrast, the other kind of watchman is simply a murderer. The true motives of his heart may be masked by the task that he is asked to perform - in this case, protecting sheep - but his joy is really fulfilled in the killing of wolves.

He is merciless, without any love, even for the sheep he is hired to protect. His job is only the covering for him to satisfy his murderous heart. Both watchmen look as if they are performing the same task, but the position of their respective heart motives separates them. There is no common ground for the two of them.

In the same way, we as Christians cannot say that we are following in the steps of Jesus simply because we are doing the "good" things that we think He might do. If our purpose for doing all that we do is not one of showing those who have not found the Lord who He really is; then, we have no common ground with Him.

In our religious activities, in all of our associations, in every act of kindness, if we don't have the desire that the recipients of our actions see Jesus in us that they might be saved; then our heart is no better than the shepherd who enjoys killing wolves. From a heavenly perspective, we really are like murderers. A person with a murderous heart cares little if anyone lives or dies, unless he somehow benefits from either prospect. We are merciless. Jesus, in contrast, willingly gave His own life, so that everyone would have the possibility of truly living. His heart was, and still is, full of mercy.

As our Lord prepares us for His coming, He is showing all of us how little we truly represent Him, even though we call ourselves by His Name and pretend to care as He does. He will not truly be joined with anyone who does not have the same heart attitudes that He does in every area.

In the book of Amos, it talks of two not being able to walk together unless they are agreed. How can we expect Jesus to overlook the filth of the world's attitudes that are still in us, when He died so that they might be eliminated? We are, in fact, saying that His suffering and death are of no consequence, if we refuse to allow lofty attitudes to be removed from our lives.

You can be doing many good things and still have murder in your heart.

It is time that we all acknowledge our need of God's mercy. It is also time that we understand that He is showing us our need; so that we, in turn, will function in His mercy towards everyone, as He has. He is being merciful at this very moment as we see who we are not.

To withhold mercy would, once again, show a wrong heart motive - one of consuming God's mercy while showing none. It is one of the most selfish of acts, most unlike the One whom we say we represent and for whom we are waiting, so that He might take us with Him because we are supposedly like Him.

The merciless heart is very much like that of the foolish virgins in Matthew 25. They came, not for the good of the master who was to arrive, but for their own good. They are also the ones pounding on the door after it had been closed and locked. Quite a sobering thought!

Vertical Application of a Spirit of Mercy

The merciless heart whines before God, challenges God, and complains before Him because its life is out of order. In contrast, the heart filled with mercy finds wonder in every moment of prayer. The interaction between Father God and a merciful heart is mercy meeting mercy. It is true "heart to Heart" communion.

The merciful person presents to God the sins they have seen on behalf of the sinner they hold before Him, desiring mercy to be given. He then intercedes on behalf of those who have no understanding of their need.

Horizontal Application of a Spirit of Mercy

A merciful heart challenges and even offends the worldly spirit. It is totally at odds with the self-serving, get-ahead attitude of those who need to excel above the ways of others, especially in the church.

Knowing its own need for mercy, it truly comprehends the inabilities of others to function any better than they do. It understands that everyone, whether they know the Lord or not, is doing the very best he/she can. This knowledge drives the merciful one to prayer for individuals the same way it drove Jesus to the cross for them.

Horizontal Application in Modern Marriage

Mercy for your mate is the heart that will sustain any marriage. Continual longing for your mate to receive mercy from the Lord, an awareness of your own need for mercy, and the willingness to give mercy are unbeatable combinations and astounding instruments for building a marriage God's way.

Once you eliminate mercy from your heart toward your mate, you ring a death knell for your marriage. You kill the marriage. Most people functioning in the spirit of control have little mercy toward the incapabilities of those to whom they are bonded. Their marriage is one-sided. The marriage becomes two people independently functioning in the same house, longing for things to be different; but usually on their own terms.

Application for Living Out Christ's Love (LOCL)

The person for whom you are praying has a right to the same mercy from God that you receive, no matter who he is or how badly he functions. An understanding that he is doing the best that he can compels you to have mercy on him rather than judgment on his actions.

Flood them with the same mercy that You have given me.

Your decision to commit to a person in prayer for one year is an act of mercy. God's desire to refine you through that commitment is an act of mercy to you. Sometimes, you will need God desperately during that commitment to deal with the issues involved. When you do, He will impart Himself to you and eliminate something in you that cannot love as Jesus loves. That is the ultimate act of mercy!

Is there anyone in your life to whom you are not extending mercy? Who and why not?

What are you going to do about it?

Why would you possibly think that he or she does not have the same right to mercy that you have been given by God?

Remember that you will not receive mercy until you give mercy. However, that is not the proper motivation for doing it. What do you think about that?

My Father,

It is evident, as I examine my heart, that I am without real, Christ-like mercy for those around me. Most of my thoughts and actions are self-motivated and void of true love and compassion.

I ask You to forgive me. I see who and what I really am, and am helpless to change myself. I realize that I don't even desire to change.

I want to go on serving myself, thinking only of myself. Please help me. Give me the heart of my Lord Jesus. As I am being changed, show me how to show mercy towards everyone, for I know I cannot exhibit Jesus without it.

Thank you for extending Your mercy to me,

Signed _____   Date _____

Prayers and thoughts

From Our Father's Heart

Purity has a purpose.
The pure in heart will be able to understand My heart.
You will be able to gain insight
into who I am and why I do what I do.
As you remove all of the clutter that darkens your reasoning
process, you will be able to move closer to Me.
We will move in concert.
I will be able to trust you with more of My plans,
for you will desire to implement them with honest motives.
Come to Me today to be cleansed from everything
that the world has to offer.
Come to gain My heart in everything you do.
If you see with My heart,
you will see Me and your world much differently.

Luke 12 The Message Bible "But Jesus' primary concern was His disciples. He said to them, 'Watch yourselves carefully so you don't get contaminated with Pharisee yeast, Pharisee phoniness...'"

Luke 21:1-4 The Message Bible "Just then he looked up and saw the rich people dropping offerings in the collection plate. Then he saw a poor widow put in two pennies. He said, 'The plain truth is that this widow has given by far the largest offering today. All these others made offerings that they'll never miss; she gave extravagantly what she couldn't afford - she gave her all!'"

A Spirit of Purity

Mt.5:8 NIV "Blessed are the pure in heart, for they will see God."

Mt.5:8 Amp "Blessed (happy, enviably fortunate, and spiritually prosperous - possessing the happiness produced by the experience of God's favor and especially conditioned by the revelation of His grace, regardless of their outward conditions) are the pure in heart, for they shall see God!"

Mt. 5 The Message "You're blessed when you get your inside world – your mind and heart – put right. Then you can see God in the outside world."

I John 4:17-18 NIV "...Love is made complete among us so that we will have confidence on the day of judgment, because in this world we are like him.

18 There is no fear in love. But perfect *(pure) love drives out fear, because fear has to do with punishment. The man who fears is not made perfect in love."

*Note: (pure) is an editorial comment, not part of the Scripture.

When we function in perfect love (true bridal love) through a spirit of purity, it is impossible to fear anyone or anything. The pure in heart always see every person and situation as God would see them.

Unpleasant circumstances are simply opportunities to wait for God to be Lord over that situation. The pure heart always trusts that the Lord knows best, regardless of how things appear; and it is not moved by anything but the will of God.

The Lord Jesus Functioned in a Spirit Of Purity – So Must We

To Jesus, everyone and all things were pure. As He walked through this world and saw everything through His Father's eyes, even the vilest action or the filthiest motive could not cause Him to remove Himself from His Father's plan - the salvation of souls.

The Oneness that He and His Father shared left no room for worldly ways to interfere with His purpose for being on earth in the first place. Because we do not determine to see everything from God's eternal perspective, our hearts will remain impure and our lives will remain unusable for the purposes of God. Only as we become a study of His motives and commit to trust Him at all times will He be able to fully use us.

When Purity is at Work

I think of Jesus as He was ministering to the woman caught in adultery, or as Mary was wiping His feet. His knowledge of their past only allowed Him to have more compassion on them, rather than lust after them.

If His Spirit had not been pure, there may have been the temptation to use them for His own satisfaction in some way. For that matter, anyone who had been helped by Jesus was potential material for a great portfolio in furthering His ministry. Instead, He continually lowered Himself, and allowed the Father's work to be accomplished.

A young child who is learning to speak may use words or phrases, in his innocence, that he will never say after he knows their proper usage. While he is in training, however, he sees only the purity of learning to speak. Even though the child may inadvertently use an incorrect or inappropriate word during the time of learning, his heart has no knowledge of the error. There is no wrong done.

The early Christians, when taken to the arena, had some real choices to make. Although it looked as if they were totally under the control of the government, their hearts were controlled only by whatever they allowed as an influence.

As with all of us to this present day, God was, in that time, mostly concerned that He be the only influence on their hearts. If He was Lord of their hearts, they could see His workings no matter how horrible things looked in their natural surroundings.

Those that were pure in heart understood that even their death was something that was in line with the plan of God. They may not have understood all of the reasons, but through their pure love they "saw" God in the midst of the violence.

Characteristics of a Spirit of Purity

The person who is pure in heart sees God in every encounter and every situation, because he has a pure heart for God. He also continually sees others as God sees them. The pure heart knows that God does everything out of love and understands that anything done in the flesh is opposed to God and embraces God's desire to remove it.

The pure heart willingly trades his legal rights for the higher calling of submission, repentance, and forgiveness; and will do whatever God asks, no matter what the cost, simply because God is pleased. The pure in heart no longer listens to any dictates of the flesh, so God is able to use him in any way that He chooses. He is subject to God's higher laws, and obeys only what God has determined to be true. He sees God's truths.

Pleasing God is the highest calling to the pure in heart.

Although the pure in heart obeys the laws of the land, there really is no need to make laws for this heart to follow. A person functioning in a spirit of purity always functions with integrity regardless of any external law. The impure heart will desire self-glorification. It sees no value in God's judgments, because it is in love with the old sin nature. It does not understand that mercy is available through Jesus Christ, so it gives no mercy.

Even as a Christian, the impure in heart has no understanding of the mercy he has been given, so he holds the same offenses toward others that he perceives are being held against him. He cannot give what he does not own.

Vertical Application of a Pure Heart

A pure heart is in complete union with the heart of God and therefore comes to God for God's reasons, and to facilitate only God's desires. There are no personal agendas, no hidden motives, and no quiet longings for independence of any kind.

Prayer is never a laundry list of needs, but a quiet waiting to hear the desires of the Lord and a zeal to implement whatever is required. A person functioning with a pure heart never second guesses or questions anything the Lord does. He is completely satisfied with all things, knowing that his very personal Lord is in control.

Horizontal Application of a Pure Heart

The lusts of the flesh have no hold over the person with a pure heart. Pornography is seen as an offense against God. Sin causes offense to the person with a pure heart, but only because it offends God.

Anyone functioning with a pure heart delights when others see things as God sees them. Witnessing about Jesus is not so much an action, but a life function done out of love for the Lord - so that Jesus delights when someone embraces Him and because salvation is the best situation in which anyone could ever find himself.

Horizontal Application in Modern Marriage

In a present day marriage situation, only the pure in heart can see God's plan. In difficult circumstances, the pure in heart sees the other's undoneness as an opportunity to pray for that person's needs. He/she "sees" God at every opportunity by laying down his/her own need to be fulfilled.

The impure heart will always look to the other to have its own needs met. When that does not happen, the heart becomes critical, hateful, and eventually "murders" any love, or potential love. The pure heart will always see the other person as God sees him/her, finding only the good; while the impure heart will eventually look outside of the relationship to be fulfilled.

God is in the business of creating pure hearts and marriage is one tool that He uses to do so. It is a representation of Christ and His relationship to us. Only as we become a study of His motives and commit to trust Him at all times will He be able to fully use us as a testimony to each other and to the world because of the visible appearance of God's ways in our marriage relationships.

If we look to be served by our mate, then all we have to look forward to is what is humanly possible in our lives. If we look to serve our mate, we can look forward to what the power of God will bring into our lives.

We honor our marriage because we honor our mate and we honor God.

Application for Living Out Christ's Love (LOCL)

The pure heart will only desire to see God's plan fulfilled in the life of the person for whom you commit to pray. Your attitude towards that person must be pure and free from any other desire except God's desire for him/her.

How does God see that person?

Prayers and thoughts

Questions About a Spirit of Purity

What is a spirit of purity as God sees it?

How can you function in it?

How would someone pure in heart treat another who spitefully misuses him/her?

What if that person continues to do so and never repents of his/her actions?

Dear Father,

I admit to You that I have done little or nothing from a pure heart. Please forgive me. Give me the ability to see things as You see them. Place in me the ability to see others as You see them.

I am sorry for how I have represented You in the past because of my clouded vision and faulty perspective of Your desires. Change my heart, Lord. Renew a right spirit in me.

Signed _____ Date _____

Prayers and thoughts

A Spirit of Completeness
(Peacemakers)

Mt.5:9 NIV *"Blessed are the peacemakers, for they will be called sons of God."*

Mt.5:9 Amp *"Blessed (enjoying enviable happiness, spiritually prosperous - with life-joy and satisfaction in God's favor and salvation, regardless of their outward conditions) are the makers and maintainers of peace, for they shall be called the sons of God!"*

Matthew 5 The Message *"You're blessed when you can show people how to cooperate instead of compete or fight. That's when you discover who you really are, and your place in God's family."*

A Spirit of Completeness

To function in all of the characteristics of Jesus

To have only the desire to emulate Jesus

To continually allow the character of God
to be in control of every aspect of our lives

To be at total peace in full surrender

To be a peacemaker, as God is a peacemaker

To allow no fleshly desires to remain

To reflect Jesus to everyone

To be the image of God to the world

To hate evil and love only God

To desire to see God's image restored in all people

To desire that only God be glorified in all things

It's all very simple to do, if we practice a life of allowing God to do it in us.

1 John 4:17-18 *"...Love is made complete among us so that we will have confidence on the day of judgment, because in the world we are like him.*
18) There is no fear in love. But perfect love drives out fear, because fear has to do with punishment. The man who fears is not made perfect in love."

Jesus walked in the fullness of the Spirit of His Father in heaven. There is no dissension, disagreement, or lack of unity in Their association, ever. Because the Spirit of Jesus was complete, (identical to His Father's and exactly the way His Father planned for creation to be from the beginning,) He was able to show us the relationship available to us through His death and resurrection.

He was our example of the freedom that we can have through complete submission to God's authority, mercy, and grace. He had to die, so that spiritual life would be available to all of us. We also die, (agree to the death of the old sin nature,) so that God's spiritual life can be ours. It is the completion of God's plan for created man on this earth.

Jesus walked with His Father in total unity of Spirit. It is the way that Adam and Eve were intended to walk, and the way that is intended for all who have entered into covenant with our Father.

In Christ Jesus, the creation circle is completed. Rebellious, fallen man has been redeemed from the curse through the life, death, and resurrection of the Lord. Peace was brought back into the relationship between God and man. In the process, Jesus demonstrated the kind of life that God's created man was privy to before his fall - a life that was complete in every way that God intended it to be.

Full of intimate interaction, perfect obedience, and wondrous love, Jesus and the Father lived completely for each other. There were no distractions for either of Them in Their love for each other. Jesus looked to His Father for all things, and Father God poured Himself completely into His Child.

John 8:28b Amp "... I do nothing of Myself (of My own accord or on My own authority), but I say [exactly] what My Father has taught Me."

In reality, the Adam (flesh, human) nature was crucified in the spirit long before Calvary. The old nature of man was destroyed by Jesus through the Holy Spirit while He lived on this earth, even though He was flesh and blood. His spirit was complete through the power of the Holy Spirit. In return for that total submission, and very much as planned, God's image poured through Him and then to everyone.

Heb. 5:8 NIV "Although he was a son, he learned obedience from what he suffered and, once made perfect, he became the source of eternal salvation for all who obey him...."

We are busy focusing on each and every sin, when God is desiring for us to repent of our whole lives. Most of us walk day after day in bondage without knowing it. We have fallen into Satan's trap of remaining hopeless, helpless, and perceiving ourselves still bound by our old sin nature. God has provided a way through Jesus Christ to literally put on His completed nature, to be like Him.

Rom. 13:14 NIV "...clothe yourselves with the Lord Jesus Christ, and do not think about how to gratify the desires of the sinful nature."

To do so, we must not simply confess our sins, but repent of (turn from, and no longer live in) our old life and all of its independent, rebellious, and ignorant ways. We must completely deny any resemblance to who we once were, and accept who He is in us.

We are destined to associate with everyone with whom we come in contact just as Jesus did. We are also privileged to associate with our Father God as Jesus did, through what He did on the cross.

We are to live our lives exactly as Jesus did because we are completely at peace with God. We have been empowered to do so through the completed work of God in each of us.

To choose to remain in the fallen state of man, while claiming to be in Christ, is a lie. It is a lie to which most of us have become accustomed, because we are attempting to do for God what He has already done for us - destroy the old sin nature.

In our own struggle to be good, we are, without knowing it, remaining alive to fight another day; when God is asking us to stay dead, and let His completed work through Jesus have its way in us. It is still that independent nature demanding its own way, to have some part even in its own death. We are attempting to have our own input, and assist the work of the cross. *It is pride in its purest and oldest form.*

It is Time to Accept a Spirit of Completeness

As stated in the beginning of this course, and as stated throughout God's Word, the real issue is the Lordship of Jesus Christ in our lives. As long as any part of our old nature is allowed to remain alive - even the part that is helping us to die, (or really, trying to help God complete His work in us,) - we will remain spiritually incomplete.

It's not just our sin; it's our lives that are out of order, if we are not fully surrendered to the life of Christ.

The Lordship of Jesus means total death to our old nature.

Then the pressures and policies of the world and its ways are no longer a factor in how we act or what we do.

It will only be as we assume our intended role of having no right to our own nature within us, that the fullness of the Nature of God, of Jesus, can work in us the spirit of completeness that is ours. His Lordship means our total death and total peace.

Our total death means that His completed life can flow through us. It is the way God has always meant it to be. It is the way that it will be for those who will surrender to be with Him, for Him, and of Him forever.

Vertical Application of a Completed Spirit

Approaching God with a heart that desires to be in order, for His honor, pleases Him. A peacemaker's heart desires that all of mankind be reconciled, so that that Lord's plans are functioning smoothly.

One functioning in the completed Spirit of Christ has full unity with God. There is no heart separation, no maverick desire, and no hidden agenda. Even petitions have been formed in unison with the Father and are presented with absolute confidence, because they are derived from the same heart and have the same goals.

How do you approach God?

What areas are not complete in you?

Horizontal Application of a Completed Spirit

Paul's desire to become all things to all people, so that all could come to Christ, flows in total unity with the Father's desire that none should perish. He could really be at peace with everyone, because he was finally at peace deep in his heart with God.

A completed spirit desires peace between everyone and God through Jesus, and peace among fellow believers. This is not a wimpy, milk-toast desire, but a powerful attitude that contends continuously for the honor of God. It is a war fought in the spiritual realm with powerful spiritual weapons.

How do you perceive others when they war in front of you or against you?

What do you do when this happens?

Are your actions the same as the actions Jesus would take? Why?

Horizontal Application in Modern Marriage

The peacemakers, those who function with a spirit of completeness, have the best interests of their mates in mind at all times and at all costs to them. Their highest joy is to provide fertile soil in which their mates can grow in the things of God, for His honor and their mate's benefit. Perfect unity - between God and the peacemaker, God and the peacemaker's mate, and the peacemaker and his/her mate - is at the very heart of all that the peacemaker does, simply because it is the heavenly order that pleases God.

How do you approach the sins of your mate?

Why do you suppose the Lord allows you to witness the spiritual incompletion of your mate?

What is out of order in your actions at present in dealing with your mate?

Phil.1:20-21 Amp "......*now as always heretofore, Christ (the Messiah) will be magnified and get glory and praise in this body of mine and be boldly exalted in my person, whether through (by) life or through (by) death.*
21) For me to live is Christ [His life in me], and to die is gain [the gain of the glory of eternity]."

Application of a Peacemaker for Living Out Christ's Love (LOCL)

Any contending views, any doctrinal differences or sinful actions on the part of the person for whom you are praying have little impact on the heart that only desires peace for and with that person. There is no place for arguments of any kind, no room for contention, because as you pray with a heart of completion (that of a peacemaker,) your opinions, your rights, and your needs have no audience in your relationship with the person for whom you pray. Your complete trust in the Father's hand allows you to remove any fleshly desire from your relationship.

My Father,

It is very clear to me how far I am from the life that You have planned for me, the life that glorifies You completely. It is also very clear to me that I am still trying to eliminate the sin in my life; instead of surrendering to the work of Your Son, and allowing that completed work to have its way in me.
I repent. I not only repent of my sins, but I repent of my life. The life that would not serve You at all is still trying to serve You - only partially and blind to Your ways.
I'm sorry that I want my own way and I surrender to the death that You require in me, so that Your life has complete dominion over me. Fulfill Your promised death and resurrection in me. I surrender fully to Your Lordship now.

Thank You,

Signed_____ Date_____

Prayers and thoughts

From Our Father's Heart

My children,
for a long time now,
I have called you to be like My Son, Jesus –
to be complete in Me –
but some of you have refused to listen.
You have chosen to remain in your sinful nature,
denying My power to change you.
You have a form of godliness,
but you do not let Me complete the work
that is necessary for you to show the world My Son, Jesus.
Soon,
the Holy Spirit will be moving in a direction
that is new to those who haven't chosen My ways.
He will execute My bold judgments
to make your rebellion bend to My ways,
instead of allowing you to continue in your ways.
There will no more be the kind of grace from Me
that has let you be less than I have determined for your life.
The kind of grace that I will send
will overpower your hardened heart.
I advise you to buy gold from Me that has been refined,
before I refine My gold in the fire of judgment
designed to change you.
Come to Me now. I am waiting.
Now is the time.
This season was My final call - My bridal call.
Do not turn from Me again,
or My eyes of judgment will turn toward your life,
for your good,
and the glory of My Son, Jesus.

Rev. 3:10-13 Amp "Because you have guarded and kept My word of patient endurance [have held fast the lesson of My patience with the expectant endurance that I give you], I also will keep you [safe] from the hour of trial (testing) which is coming on the whole world to try those who dwell upon the earth.

11) I am coming quickly; hold fast what you have, so that no one may rob you and deprive you of your crown.

12) He who overcomes (is victorious), I will make him a pillar in the sanctuary of My God; he shall never be put out of it or go out of it, and I will write on him the name of My God and the name of the city of My God, the new Jerusalem, which descends from My God out of heaven, and My own new name.

13) He who can hear, let him listen to and heed what the Spirit says to the assemblies (churches)."

One day those who are in the world and those Christians who have not chosen to submit to God's hand now will be immobilized with fear and out of answers. Will you understand the order and desires of God when things change so radically that you do not recognize your world? Will you not only be able to rise above the din that is so prevalent, but be able to prosper because you have taken on the life of Christ?

How are you going to get there from where you are at present?

Prayers and thoughts

A Spirit of Suffering

Mt.5:10 NIV "Blessed are those who are persecuted because of righteousness, for theirs is the kingdom of heaven."

Mt.5:10 Amp "Blessed and happy and enviably fortunate and spiritually prosperous (in the state in which the born-again child of God enjoys and finds satisfaction in God's favor and salvation, regardless of his outward conditions) are those who are persecuted for righteousness' sake (for being and doing right), for theirs is the kingdom of heaven!"

Matthew 5 The Message "You're blessed when your commitment to God provokes persecution. The persecution drives you even deeper into God's kingdom."

A Spirit Of Suffering

To willingly subject yourself to hardship or loss for the sake of others

To suffer any hardship rather than renounce Christ

To endure costly tribulations,
so that others can see Christ revealed through you

To go through anything, or become whatever is necessary,
so that others will see God - just as Jesus did

To joyfully embrace a life of self-denial

To deny all that you are,
so that you and others might see all that Jesus is

To unconditionally surrender
all control in your life to the Lordship of Jesus Christ

To accept affliction or poverty in your life,
if it is God's way to touch people through you

To take on the heart of God concerning the lost or needy

Jesus crucified is the suffering God.

*Easy to do when
your heart
is in
perfect alignment
with the
heart of
your "ABBA"*

A Spirit of Suffering

1 John 4:17-18 NIV *"...Love is made complete among us so that we will have confidence on the day of judgment, because in this world we are like him.*

18) There is no fear in love. But perfect love drives out fear, because fear has to do with punishment. The man who fears is not made perfect in love."

A spirit of suffering epitomizes the ability to love as our Lord loved. As Pilate was interrogating Jesus, and attempted to use the normal fear tactics against Him, he soon realized that they wouldn't work. The perfect love in which Jesus functioned - love that included the desire to deny Himself of His own comforts, even to His death - was foreign to the Roman mind.

In their opinion, the only thing that could be taken from Jesus was His life. In perfect love - love free from the fear of anything that Pilate or anyone else could do to Him - Jesus overcame. He knew that He and His Father were in perfect accord. Any power that Pilate had was given him by His Father, so even the threat of death meant nothing to Him. He was totally free from any threats or holds of mankind.

In fact, since Jesus embodied the spirit of suffering, which meant that He purposefully was there to give up His life, Pilate was only fulfilling Jesus' and His Father's desires by allowing for Him to be crucified. While functioning in perfect love through the spirit of suffering, nobody could rob Jesus of anything. He had already given everything away, even His life.

Today, Our Task is Little Different Than That of Jesus

Of course, we are not the Savior of the world, nor are we the Son of God or anything like that; but we are supposed to walk in the steps of Jesus. He showed us the way that we would be able to walk in this world - by His power. In covenant with Him, we have taken on His Name. We have chosen to represent Him above anyone else, and we have been given the commission to do so.

As ambassadors of His Kingdom, our task is to present to a lost world the elements of an abundant, truthful way to live. There is no room for a compromise of that mandate, if we truly desire to be in accord with His wishes. As we exhibit more of His character, the world will see more of Him.

Preaching alone won't do it. There is more preaching in this land, a land that has forgotten God, than in any other land in

What possible reason will we be able to give for not having walked as Jesus walked on this earth?

all of history. More churches with more programs are not the answer. "Good" programs and "righteous" meetings are counterfeited throughout the world, leading many who are confused or rebellious to a fate of eternal damnation. The only way to reach people and allow them to make the proper choices - God's choices for them - is to allow our lives to be the preaching and the programs for others to follow.

The life of Jesus stands alone, far higher than any other life; and it cannot be counterfeited when empowered by His Spirit. Anyone who attempts to do so, without the true Spirit of God, will eventually be exposed for his spiritual bankruptcy.

It is sad to say, but that is what is happening today. Those who have chosen not to fully take on the suffering character of Christ are being exposed by their inability to properly represent Him as things get darker. Powerless by God's standards, we are attempting to devise our own means to fulfill our commitments to God; rather than taking on the life of Jesus without measure, as is our heritage through His death and resurrection. The former is hollow religion; the latter is His representative life to others.

The continual denial of our own ways, (our putting them to death,) allows His continual resurrected life to flow through us to the world. A spirit of suffering (the willingness to deny our own ways through His power,) opens the door for God to work His ways in us, so that we might properly represent Him as the waiting bride of Christ.

What do you see as the answer to the poor presentation of today's church to the world?

From Our Father's Heart

I notice that at times you have a heavy heart.
I also notice that because you are My minister,
people consider your countenance to be a lack of faith.
It is expected by some that you must always remain joyful and
happy or there is something wrong with your walk.
You must not allow their immaturity concerning My Word
to bring you to a point of questioning
what I am doing in you during these times.
You, My ministers, are those whom I can trust.
I often place My burden for others and for this world
on you to hold them before Me.
It is My work being accomplished.
It is My birthing process.
During these times, you will feel some of the burden that I feel.
If you do not understand what is happening,
you will have a tendency to compare yourself
with those who are always happy
and think that there is something wrong with you.
That is not the case, so be encouraged.
Sometimes the burden will come unexpectedly and surprise you.
Do not be alarmed, and do not be confused.
You are at work for My kingdom.
Bring these unspoken burdens before Me,
even if you have little idea of what they are.
I know.
I have given them to you.
When My desire has been accomplished, the burden will be lifted.
During the time that you are carrying it for Me,
the weight of it might be very heavy.
It is not your lack of faith in Me; it is My great faith in you.
You are trustworthy.
Release everything to Me and I will support you
while you are at work.
I am with you.
I am proud of you.
Be encouraged; I love to trust you.

Gal. 4:19 NIV "My dear children, for whom I am again in the pains of childbirth until Christ is formed in you..."

2 Cor.1 The Message Bible "God of all healing counsel! He comes alongside us when we go through hard times, and before you know it, he brings us alongside someone else who is going through hard times so that we can be there for that person just as God was there for us.

...And he'll do it again, rescuing us as many times as we need rescuing. You and your prayers are part of the rescue operation – I don't want you in the dark about that either. I can see

your faces even now, lifted in praise for God's deliverance of us, a rescue in which your prayers played such a crucial part."

Colossians 1 The Message Bible   "Be assured that from the first day we heard of you, we haven't stopped praying for you, asking God to give you wise minds and spirits attuned to his will, and so acquire a thorough understanding of the ways in which God works. We pray that you'll live well for the Master, making him proud of you as you work hard in his orchard. As you learn more and more how God works, you will learn how to do your work. We pray that you'll have the strength to stick it out over the long haul - not the grim strength of gritting your teeth but the glory-strength God gives."

We need to be concerned for souls with Jesus.

As important as it is to suffer *for* Christ through the laying down of your own will so that the will of your Father can be accomplished, it is equally important that there are times when you are called upon to suffer *with* Christ. Few people in the church are willing to take on the burdens that Christ feels toward those who are not saved, or toward those who made a commitment, but are living far from Jesus. To care about what Jesus deems important, to hurt as He hurts for the lost, to be burdened with the things for which He is interceding is more than most of us delight in doing.

Not everyone accepts a suffering spirit when it is given. Some reject it because it is too difficult to carry. You simply do not fit in. It is for those of you who have felt the burden of God, and carry it with Him on behalf of another.

You may be at work and have little time to play when you are called to suffer with Jesus for a season.

However, leave the prune face at home.

Until you understand that some of what you feel is God working with you for the sake of others, you will believe that there is something wrong with you. You need to know that the Lord is asking you to suffer with Him in that specific area, to carry the weight that He is feeling for a specific situation. It will be an intense time and you may need to be alone with Him. There will be a myriad of people in the church who will be delighted to give their opinion, confirming that you have gone nuts. Don't listen to them. They cannot see and they do not understand intercession.

Other than in the movies, have you ever seen someone at war of any kind giggling while they fought? Of course not! They were intense until the battle was over. There is a vast difference between walking in fear and walking in an acute awareness of the danger, but standing to overcome in the Lord's strength.

If you constantly have no joy in the Lord, that is one thing. That is not of God. You need to get in the Word and understand who you are in Christ and what you have been promised because of what He has done for you. There is joy in your salvation.

If, however, you understand your heritage, but find yourself weighty at times, you may be an intercessor in the service of the Lord at that very moment. That sudden feeling that something's not right might be the Lord wanting you to lift something up on His behalf. No one will understand. Do not try to explain it. Just go to work with a spirit of gratefulness and peace in your heart. You sometimes can't listen to others when you are at work for your Daddy!

If you are a watchman, an intercessor, a prayer warrior, or in other services for the Lord, you are not to walk around prune-faced and morose as the Sadducees did to prove to others how spiritual they were. Walk in joy.

However, when in battle, don't pretend that everything is perfect. Fight the fight. The world is getting darker. Those of you who are able to see may be called upon often. It would be wise to avoid those who will not understand your situation during those times.

Are you a continual prune face with a wrinkled thumb when you are going through a trial? Why? (Take as much time and as many pieces of paper as needed)

What Suffering Does

Previous to this, all that has been written in this section has dealt with what a spirit of suffering *is*. Equally important would be for us to understand the impact of what a spirit of suffering *does*.

The underlying spirit in all that Jesus did, and the essence of all of the teachings of all of the books of the New Testament, have their foundation in the spirit of suffering.

Heb. 5:8 NIV "Although he was a son, he learned obedience from what he suffered and, once made perfect, he became the source of eternal salvation for all who obey him...."

Jesus Even Learned Through Suffering

Often, the message conveyed in Heb.5:8 drops to the ground before it impacts our lives. The plan of Satan is to see that we never really receive the truth that this Scripture imparts. If he can stop us from receiving, he can nullify our effectiveness, or completely destroy our relationship with the Lord because of our misunderstanding of His ways. Here's a real key:

Through suffering (denial,)
obedience
is
learned (Heb.5:8.)
Obedience leads to righteousness (Rom. 6:16,)
and
righteousness leads to holiness (Rom 6:19,)
which results
in
eternal life (Rom. 6:22.)

Most of us spend our lives avoiding suffering of any kind. Our comfort is of primary importance to us. Most of us also wonder why we have little power to obey God. The role that suffering plays never enters our rose-colored picture unless we allow the Holy Spirit to break through the fog that hinders our understanding. How can we progress, if we do not recognize the first step to holiness?

In our ignorance, we attempt to obey, always asking for God to help us do so; but we never hear the message that is woven throughout His Word. To be able to obey, we must actively pursue the denial of our own comforts - no matter what form it takes. Any discomfort comes against the flesh and self, and if embraced for reasons of becoming like Christ, produces obedience.

What does it mean to suffer *for* Christ?

What does it mean to suffer *with* Christ?

The Spirit of Suffering - First Century A.D.

A light layer of frost had formed on the stone ceiling. Michael sat quietly in prayer, holding someone's small child, trying to comfort the crying toddler from the pangs of hunger and ward off the cold ocean breezes that blew through the cracks in the frigid cell wall. People, many of them good friends, began to stir from their slumber and move out from pockets of people that had formed in an attempt to keep from freezing during the cold, fall night. Greetings of love and encouragement were heard everywhere as the new morning brought the reality of the day and its evils to each person, replacing the numbness of fitful sleep.

A young boy kicked aside a large rat with his swollen, bare foot in an attempt to again protect his small, sleeping sister from its sharp teeth. Michael smiled at the boy, remembering the promise the child had made to his parents to watch out for "little sister" if they went to be with Jesus first.

Thoughts of praise flowed from his heart as he saw the mercy of God even in the hungry rats that infested the crowded chamber. They gave the young boy a reason to be brave for his small sister; and by watching out for them, the time passed more quickly while waiting to be called into the arena.

Others, too, once fearful, were somehow calmed into acceptance of their fate by facing the smaller fear of the rats. It was as if their precious Lord had tempered their emotions by these unusual vessels of service. "Thank you, Lord," Michael said out loud, thinking of the goodness of his God and seeing His loving hand on His people even in times like these.

"We're really blessed, aren't we?" Epaphras spoke almost in a whisper. Still lying on his side and using his hands for a pillow, the man looked away from the same event that Michael had witnessed and spoke again. "Not only do we have the privilege to die for our Lord, but we have the additional blessing of knowing when we will see Him face to face. Just think," he continued, raising himself up and positioning himself next to Michael, both men having their backs against a large stone support pillar near the center of the vast chamber, "in about four hours, we will be with Jesus. It's almost too exciting to bear."

The two men sat silently for a moment, reflecting on the magnitude of the statement. Waves of peace and joy filled both their souls as the witness of that assurance was made real to them by the Holy Spirit.

"My only hope," Epaphras continued, "is that I can tell at least one more person about our Lord before my time on this earth is over."

This story brings things into perspective.

299

"You!" The sound of the guard's loud voice broke the quiet of the morning and cut short the words from Epaphras' mouth. Everyone looked in the direction of the guard and the small man he had pointed at when he spoke. "And you," he continued, grabbing a second man by the back of his garment and throwing him next to the first, "stand over here while I get some more."

The red-haired guard, known for his great cruelty especially with the women, swaggered deeper into the cell. "I need some special workers," he continued sadistically. "Some of you . . ." he emphasized his words by pulling men roughly to their feet and throwing them one-by-one to the other guard who pushed them with the "chosen" who had obediently lined themselves at the barred entrance.

"Some of you will have the privilege of seeing first-hand what is in store for the rest of you by cleaning up from yesterday. You are even going to have the greater honor of working all morning with me personally supervising you," he spat in mock humor, looking at his fellow guard who responded with a grin, knowing all too well what his superior meant.

About fifteen men and several of the younger women, who would be used as "entertainment" for the guards, had been selected before the man came near Michael and Epaphras. "You! Drop that kid and get over there!" the guard spewed at Michael, pulling the child from him and throwing it to the stone floor with a bone-cracking thud.

Judging by the force with which the small frame had hit the floor, and seeing no movement, Michael knew that what only moments ago had breathed the moist, dank air of this earth had already taken its first breath of heavenly atmosphere. The guard paused for a moment to look at the motionless frame, blood now flowing freely from its head, soaking the filthy straw that was strewn about the floor.

"One less piece of lion bait," he said jokingly, looking at the other guards who gave half-hearted, obedient laughter. "And you, slave," he said, pulling Epaphras to his feet, "you're used to doing slop work. Get over there with the rest. "

"Wait a minute!" he yelled as if some new thought for special torment had come to him. "Cassius," he started again, "make sure this big slave stays near me this morning. I've got some special tasks for him to do."

Epaphras was pushed by the guards into Michael, who had lined up near the entrance with the others. "So that's who the Lord wants me to talk to about Him," Epaphras whispered as they were led down the dark corridor to the arena floor. "Pray that I make proper use of this opportunity."

Just as he completed his statement, one of the rear guards grabbed the back of his garment and pulled him from the ranks, slamming him face-first into the corridor wall. "Wait here," the guard ordered as the others were kept moving toward their destination.

For the three years since Michael and his beloved Selena had given themselves to the Lord Jesus Christ, both knew that more than likely their portion would be as it had unfolded in the last few days. Even though persecution and hardship became their lot to prepare them for these present events, their love for their Lord and for each other made each day's peril easier to bear.

God's grace and mercy continually flowed to and from them as they worked side by side, fearlessly telling all whom they encountered about their Savior and His provision for their eternal happiness. Even the loss of their home, which they had to flee in the middle of the night, and the death of their infant daughter, Julia, who was not strong enough to endure the nomadic life that was theirs, could not quench their zeal for the lost souls who needed to hear.

Recently, as they were hiding in the orchards of the local magistrate, the soldiers had found them because of a "tip" from one of the gardeners whom Michael had shared Jesus with to no avail. "But it was all worth it," Michael said to himself as he entered the arena floor. "Even when they took my Selena yesterday, Lord," he said in quiet prayer, remembering the radiance on her face as they lined them at the cell entrance to be given to the lions. "Even then I knew that she had everything she needed because she had You."

Joy filled his heart as he thought of the bliss that his best friend on this earth must be enjoying at that very moment in the presence of her Lord. The morning sun warmed Michael's face, and at the same time, made his eyes squint before they adjusted to the contrast from dark corridor to stark brightness. Michael raised his hand to his forehead and shielded his eyes for a moment, while they adjusted to the light.

The movement of the guards herding yesterday's lions, which had been left on the arena floor overnight to "clean up," caught his attention. Now docile and too full to be aggressive, they moved to their pens as they were told. New lions, hungry because they hadn't eaten in several days, would be chosen for today's events.

Michael and the others were given the horrendous task of picking up the remains - some of them would be pieces of loved ones - and loading them on the carts provided. "Forgive them, Jesus," he said softly as the remains of men, women, and children lay before him.

It was clear that some met death very quickly, while others seemed to have suffered, even possibly remaining alive, long after the boisterous, jubilant crowds had gone to their homes. His thoughts went back to his good friend, Stephen, who saw the Lord before the first stone reached its mark.

"Please don't let me dishonor You today, my Lord," he said, as he mechanically put some bloody, torn clothing into one of the carts. As he walked to the next mound of once-living human beings, his heart seemed to stop for a moment. In the tangled, unrecognizable heap was a piece of the bright-colored scarf that he knew belonged to his beloved Selena.

For a few, brief moments he hesitated, immobilized by the gravity of the situation. Suddenly, with sharp pains across his back and the cursing voices of the guards goading him to do what only months before would have been unthinkable, he bent down under increasingly forceful, almost demon-inspired, blows.

As he began loading the precious remains onto the cart, he began to weep openly. His mind raced, remembering the cheers of the blood-thirsty crowd, the satanic guards, the beyond belief screams of pain from those who had gone before and now this; his tears flowed freely.

"I forgive them, Lord," he whispered, knowing that to do anything other than forgive would dishonor his Lord. As he forgave from the depth of his heart, a new strength, a power not his own, came upon him. Suddenly, he felt compassion, even love, for all those caught in the trap of such horrendous evil. Moments passed. Standing erect and turning toward the startled guard who was in mid-swing, about to strike another blow, Michael smiled at him and said, quietly, "And I forgive you, too!"

The guard, too startled to complete his intended task, dropped his arm to his side. For some time, the two men - one who was condemned to die, but was truly alive; and the other who would remain alive, but in fact was already dead - looked into each other's eyes. Finally, the guard defiantly braced his shoulders, cursed Michael and all those who "embraced such a stupid, weak religion," and turned and walked toward the arena wall, mumbling as he went.

By the time the workers had completed their task and had marched back to the cell, the enthusiastic spectators were already

302

filtering in, hoping to get a good seat for the day's festivities. The fiendish frivolity in the arena was in sharp contrast to the quiet joy and radiant beauty of the humble party of believers, who waited in the dank recesses below the stadium seating. Knowing they were moments away from seeing their Lord, each began to encourage the other with verbal blessings and words of praise to the Lord.

When the time came for them to be marched to the arena floor, loud songs of adoration were all that each could hear, even amidst satanic cheers of anticipation by the spectators. Michael and all who were with him *did* honor their Lord that day. The example of love and forgiveness that Jesus showed was the example that each presented to those who didn't have eyes to see.

It didn't matter that no one understood. They did what their Lord had asked them to do and had done Himself. Their heart attitude was of utmost importance. The rest was in the hands of their heavenly Father.

The Spirit of Suffering? - 21st Century A.D.

"Who was that at the door, dear?" Serena inquired of Mike, as she adjusted her left earring while walking toward him from the bedroom. "Mike, who was that?" she asked again, somewhat puzzled at her husband's slow response as he robotically closed the back door. Mike remained silent for what seemed like many moments, staring out the window of the door, his eyes following the lone, stoop-shouldered figure as he walked down the driveway.

"Huh? Oh, that was Terry from down the street," Mike responded somewhat dazedly as if waking from deep thought. "He ..." Mike stopped for a moment to reflect and fully comprehend what had just happened before he continued. "He just about ripped my face off because Julie left her bike in his driveway."

Mike became more animated, gaining momentum and becoming agitated as he related what had just occurred. "Man!" he continued, "who does he think he is? I mean, it's just a kid's bike."

Serena turned toward the bedroom to finish putting on her make-up. "Well, he probably didn't really mean to be so upset. He and Kathy have been having some problems in their marriage. They probably had a fight or something and he vented his anger on you," Serena commented, dismissing the situation. "Come on, we're going to be late for church. It's music night and I want to get a front row seat."

Mike followed her into the bedroom and sat down on the bed, still deep in thought about the recent confrontation. "It really was weird," he began, replaying the event in his mind as he spoke. "I mean . . .," he hesitated and stopped for a moment, holding his hand in the air in mid-gesture. "I answered the door all bright and cheery and out of nowhere he unloads on me. He didn't even give me a chance to say 'hi.' Wham! He just lets me have it!"

Mike got up from the bed, unbuttoning his shirt as he walked toward the closet. "Funny thing though . . ." he began again, stopping at the door, and silently hanging his shirt on the doorknob. "After he unloaded on me about the bike . . . " Mike turned toward Serena, who looked up from her mirror, still holding her eyeliner pencil, waiting for Mike to complete his sentence.

"After he finished yelling at me about my responsibility and how inconsiderate it was to leave the bike behind his car, he just stopped and looked at me. I mean . . ." Mike continued as he took a fresh shirt from the hanger, "for a couple of moments we just looked at each other. I was too dumbfounded to say anything and he didn't have any more to say, so we just looked at each other. That's when it got weird."

"What do you mean, weird?" Serena inquired, this time not looking up from the mirror.

"Well, we stood there and then . . ." Mike walked back over to the dressing table to look at Serena. "Then he started to cry." Mike held out his hands to indicate wonder and helplessness. "He just began to cry, dropped the bike, and then walked away. All I could do was watch him."

Mike and Serena continued dressing in silence. Both were thinking about the recent event and neither could think of anything more to say. Finally, Serena broke the silence. "Come on, we're late," she said, taking one last look in the mirror and removing a small amount of lipstick from the corner of her mouth with her little fingernail.

"You know," Mike started, as he followed Serena out the door, closing the door behind him. "I've been thinking about the hurt that they must be going through because of their problems. Maybe we should tell our evangelism team at the church to pay them a visit. They could tell them about programs that might help them through this hard time. Let's just hope they visit with him before he comes in my face again. I don't want to be a bad witness with what I might do."

Serena gave Mike a warm smile. She was proud of how much he had grown in the Lord and that he would care so much, especially about someone who had just offended him so deeply for no good reason.

What do you see as the main difference between the two stories?

How did the people of the first story get the kind of power they exhibited?

Vertical Application of a Spirit of Suffering

A suffering spirit comes upon someone who desires the will of the Lord, craves the heart of God, and moves as He directs. It willingly takes on the causes and cares of the Lord, carrying them as Jesus would until the heart of God is satisfied.

Horizontal Application of a Spirit of Suffering

The disobedience of others to the Word and to the desires of God make a suffering heart dive into the prayer closet, because he sees how the sin offends God and cares deeply for the offender. This heart desires reconciliation between any sinner and God. As Jesus was driven to the cross, offenses drive this heart to prayer.

Horizontal Application in Modern Marriage

A suffering heart is an interceding mate. It is also a mate who honors God's desire that he/she serve his/her mate as Jesus would. This heart lives to see the other enjoy the best possible standing before God, because it pleases Him, even to the point of a desire to see the other far surpass his/her own position with God. Any disorder is quickly worked to a godly conclusion to avoid possible footholds for sin that would grieve the Lord in any way.

Application for Living Out Christ's Love (LOCL)

Paul said: "... I am again in the pains of childbirth until Christ is formed in you..."

Caring deeply for someone brings the presence of God into that situation. Laying down your own time and moving toward the needs of others, instead of avoiding them or passing them off because of the inconvenience that would occur by getting involved, thrills the heart of God.

*We
should no longer
seek
presents
from God.*

*We
should do all that is within our power
to
seek
the presence
of God.*

My Father,

The longer I attempt to draw close to You, the more I realize how little I resemble You. I am acutely aware that You are asking me to lay my life down in every circumstance, so that others might see Your Son in me. As I understand a spirit of suffering, I again see my inability to do what You are asking me to do without Your power in me to do it. I need Your help.

Lord, I choose to live in a spirit of joyful suffering. I know that it will mean that I must be willing to no longer own the comforts in my life with which I have become so familiar, so that I can allow Your life to flow through me. I really don't know how to do that. Please do it in me. In Philippians, Paul desires to "... so share Your sufferings as to be continually transformed into Your likeness... ." Please do that in me. Help me to desire only Your ways, so that I may become like You. I submit to Your hand of change.

Thank You,

Signed_____ Date _____

306

Mt.5 The Message Bible "... count yourselves blessed every time people put you down or throw you out or speak lies about you to discredit me. What it means is that the truth is too close for comfort and they are uncomfortable. You can be glad when that happens - give a cheer even - for though they don't like it, I do! And all heaven applauds. And know that you are in good company. My prophets and witnesses have always gotten into this kind of trouble.

"Let me tell you why you are here. You're here to be salt-seasoning that brings out the God-flavors of this earth. If you lose your saltiness, how will people taste godliness? You've lost your usefulness and will end up in the garbage.

"Here's another way to put it: You're here to be light, bringing out the God-colors in the world. God is not a secret to be kept. We're going public with this, as public as a city on a hill. If I make you light-bearers, you don't think I'm going to hide you under a bucket, do you? I'm putting you on a light stand. Now that I've put you there on a hilltop, on a light stand – shine! Keep open house; be generous with your lives. By opening up to others, you'll prompt people to open up with God, this generous Father in heaven."

Prayers and thoughts

From Our Father's Heart

Choose Jesus!
In everything that you do, choose Jesus!
When temptation comes your way, choose Jesus!
When fear attempts to overpower you, choose Jesus!
Whisper it quietly, say it out loud, express it from your heart;
choose Jesus and watch the enemy flee.
Planted thoughts, wandering motives, and rampant temptations
have no power over your choice to surrender to Jesus
and all of His completed work in your life.
Choosing Him brings His resurrected life to you in full force to
overcome.
Cease from striving.
Call out to Jesus and invoke His covenant promises.
Choose Jesus over and over again
until your choice becomes an expression of praise
and a statement of rock solid commitment.
Choose Jesus!
He is Lord over all!

Summary

In completing this portion of this guidebook, you have just begun your journey. In the coming days and years, you will face many challenges that will bring to the forefront how you are doing in your walk with the Lord, especially when times become perilous. For the rest of your life, use these pages and your journal notes, so that you can remember and practice what you have learned while you were in this study whenever these challenges arise. Add the pages with new teachings and insights provided for you on our Web site, www.christspassionatelife.com. Continually update your working knowledge as you are led to closer intimacy with the Lord.

During times of challenge, it is vital to understand that the Lord is at work in your heart. Each "visit" with one of these challenges is causing you to go deeper with God. He is very much concerned with you becoming more like Jesus and has covenanted to take you there until you go home to Him. Use what you have learned to help you fulfill the Father's plan for your life.

As Merry and I have stated several times during these pages, the only way that any real change will be completed in you is to make communication and communion with your Father God a priority in your life. Your access to Him is the main reason Jesus lived and died and lives again. Use your privilege wisely. You are welcome into the throne room of the living God. It is where you will find the secrets of living Christ's passionate life as you quietly commune with Him.

If you are serious about allowing the Lord to be conformed in you, now is the time to implement some of the lessons you have learned. Put feet on what you've studied. That is why we have initiated Living Out Christ's Love. This opportunity - which uses the concepts presented in this guidebook combined with the challenges you will face because of your commitment to pray for another person for one complete year - will mature you in Christ as you lay your life down for someone else.

Your commitment to pray for at least one person for one year will also present an incredible example of Jesus to the person the Lord chooses for you, as you hold that individual close to the Lord. He/she will observe first-hand the heart of Jesus through your love. You, in turn, will allow the character of Christ to be developed in you, while you experience the joy the Lord has when He sees a life turn toward Him. Revisiting these pages often will help you to remain focused on the reason you are living your life for the good of someone else.

Start this day to live your life in Christ passionately for the good of others and for the glory of God. May the Lord continually bless you as you run hard after Him and bless others for Him. You are valuable! We love you!

Jim and Merry Corbett

Now seek intimacy with God.

Make your time with Him your priority.

He loves you and is waiting to impart Himself to you.

Now that you have completed the text on Living Christ's Passionate Life, your proper response is to do what is necessary to continue your quest to honorably represent the passionate life of Jesus to your world by living your life passionately for Him. Part of that process involves finding information that flows with the heart of your Lord. Visit our Web site, www.christspassionatelife.com, often to download free materials and audio teachings for you and your friends.

Tell others about what you have learned and the resources that are available to them. Help start someone else on his/her journey to the kind of life that honors Jesus by giving him/her a copy of A White Stone and telling that person of His love.

If you desire to contact either Jim or Merry Corbett, you can e-mail them at jim@awhitestone.com.

For copies of A White Stone, the Living Christ's Passionate Life guidebook and other ministry tools, visit our website: www.awhitestone.com or www.christspassionatelife.com.

A White Stone, the Living Christ's Passionate Life guidebook, Living Out Christ's Love, and the Christ's Passionate Life series and all of their components and concepts are owned by Jim and Merry Corbett.